How an
Unaccountable
Elite Is
Governing
America

The
Unelected

JAMES R. COPLAND

Encounter
BOOKS

New York • London

First American edition published in 2020 by Encounter Books,
an activity of Encounter for Culture and Education, Inc.,
a nonprofit, tax exempt corporation.
Encounter Books website address: www.encounterbooks.com

Manufactured in the United States and printed on
acid-free paper. The paper used in this publication meets
the minimum requirements of ANSI/NISO Z39.48–1992
(R 1997) (*Permanence of Paper*).

FIRST AMERICAN EDITION

LIBRARY OF CONGRESS CATALOGING-IN-PUBLICATION DATA IS AVAILABLE

LC record available at https://lccn.loc.gov/2020015909
LC ebook record available at https://lccn.loc.gov/2020015910

Interior design and typesetting by Bruce Leckie

In memory of Jim Dupree
and
in honor of Ben and Liz.

Contents

INTRODUCTION

As this book goes to press, America is facing a viral epidemic at least as large as any we've seen in a hundred years. The president has declared a national emergency and assumed broad authorities—invoking the Defense Production Act, typically reserved for wartime. Congress moved to action quickly—or at least quickly for Congress—passing emergency legislation unprecedented in size, spending more than $2 trillion in an effort to keep businesses solvent, citizens fed, and state governments functioning. Even the third branch of government, the judiciary, has been affected: the Supreme Court, for the first time in its history, is hearing its cases by telephone, simultaneously broadcasting them to the public. More than 100,000 Americans have died. And more Americans have lost their jobs more quickly than ever before; the current economic contraction far surpasses anything seen since the Great Depression.

Aside from the grim details of the public-health crisis, the questions about the science of a novel virus, and the fallout from a sharp drop in economic activity, much of the public attention has focused on our elected government actors. That's understandable. The president and many governors and local officials regularly hold televised conferences, sometimes daily. Congressional sessions are broadcast, too. We can see each bill, each executive order, in real time. We're unusually aware of these bills and executive orders, both because they're so consequential to our lives and because so many of us are at home—either working remotely or unemployed.

I

We've never been more connected to Washington—a place quite distant to the average American in the early years of the American republic. We have round-the-clock news on television and instant news on the Internet, giving us access to more information, more immediately, than ever before. Our plethora of information sources and our increased division have led many Americans to second-guess the elected officials on either side of the partisan political aisle.

To be sure, the actions of many elected officials warrant criticism (to put it mildly). That may be disheartening, but it's nothing new. And the actions of the president and Congress alike have in fact been consequential—emergency declarations and $2 trillion appropriations are quite extraordinary. But too much focus on the elected officials misses a lot of the picture. Behind the president and the Congress lie a host of *unelected* actors with government roles—and these actors, as much as the ones we vote on, are responsible for a great deal of the way our government influences our everyday lives, not to mention the response to the current viral pandemic.

Some of these actors, usually unseen, have emerged into public awareness in the crisis—such as Dr. Anthony Fauci, the director of the National Institute of Allergy and Infectious Diseases since 1984. Dr. Fauci has regularly appeared on national television alongside the president and other government officials in daily news conferences, winning the admiration of many (and the animosity of others who don't like his message). But Fauci is only one longtime player in a vast federal bureaucracy—which itself is but one piece of the unelected shadow government influencing our lives.

Consider the two federal agencies at the forefront of the American response to the coronavirus epidemic: the Centers for Disease Control and Prevention (CDC) and the Food and Drug Administration (FDA). After Chinese authorities uploaded the SARS-CoV-2 genome onto the Internet on January 10, scientists at the CDC developed a new testing protocol relatively quickly—by January 21, the same date that international scientists developed a different test, which was soon disseminated widely by the World Health Organization. But after that seemingly auspicious start, the unelected actors stumbled. Cumbersome regulations and the instinct of agency bureaucrats to prioritize perfection thwarted the creation of an efficient testing regime.

The problem wasn't with the laws enacted by Congress. The legislature had granted broad powers to the FDA—the federal government's arbiter of safety and efficacy in the development of drugs and medical devices—to permit the use of such products, whether previously approved or not, in a declared national emergency. The problem was that the officials staffing the federal bureaucracy did not exercise this authority with any haste.

On February 4, the FDA approved an emergency authorization for the CDC—and only the CDC—to conduct testing in the United States. The agency did not allow any private companies—or even state or local governments—to handle tests for the new virus until March 12, when it granted its first non-CDC testing authorization to the Roche company. In the interim, companies seeking emergency-use authorization were stymied by a maze of regulations—created by the agencies, not by Congress, but in any event not well suited to the urgency of the moment. Until the FDA eventually waived its own rule, companies were even required to mail in CD-ROMs for agency review, rather than submit online requests.

The federal agencies' decision to go it alone and reject private-sector involvement proved fatal to any hopes of an early, widespread American testing effort. The CDC test initially was beset by failures, and its rollout inhibited by critical shortages in the subcomponents necessary for the agency's test design. The same day that the CDC announced its testing protocol, January 21, saw the first documented American case of the novel coronavirus. South Korea also documented its first case that day. But by March 17, the United States had administered only 125 tests per 1 million people, while South Korea had administered more than 5,000 tests per 1 million over the same time span. By aggressive testing, South Korea was able to trace viral spread and substantially contain it. Without such a testing regime, the United States was left with little choice but the draconian measures that shut down much of American social and economic life.

I don't mean to cast undue blame on the federal agencies, which were dealing with a new virus, little understood, in a crisis setting. I sleep much better knowing that government experts like Anthony Fauci are on the job, backed by teams of other scientists who study viruses and epidemiology. Our specialized military has made a host of miscalculations and errors over the course of American history, at the cost of thousands of lives, but that certainly doesn't mean we don't need the armed forces, nor that we should fail to honor their service. It's worth noting that the governments of European nations also broadly failed in containing SARS-CoV-2, at least initially. And it's possible that no matter what the agencies had done, America would have struggled in its response to the viral pandemic.

The point is simply this: the story of modern American government is hardly one that begins and ends with our elections. Unelected actors—like agency officials at the CDC and the FDA—make countless decisions that have enormous impact on Americans' lives. The unelected players include not only agency officials who formulate policy but also those who enforce it. They include not only Dr. Fauci's 2 million federal-government colleagues but also some 1.3 million private American lawyers. And they stretch beyond the shores of the Potomac to fifty state capitals and more than 89,000 municipal governments.

Yes, Congress still passes legislation. Bills still become law with a president's signature. Yet legislation enacted by Congress is only a tiny part of how government works in the United States today. Many of the decisions through which government controls our lives are made by individuals with an attenuated relationship, if any, to the votes we cast in regular national elections. Considerable rulemaking power is wielded by unelected bureaucrats, prosecutors, and litigators—or by local officials aiming to set national policy. The modern regulatory state is a wide departure from the founding constitutional design, which was predicated on accountability to the voting public.

• • •

When America's Founding Fathers were gathered in Philadelphia to write a new constitution in 1787, a passerby approached the elderly Benjamin Franklin as he departed Independence Hall. The passerby asked what kind of government the leaders inside had fashioned for the new nation. Franklin quipped, "A republic—if you can keep it."

The design settled upon by Franklin and his fellow constitution drafters was remarkably adaptable and durable. The government they created has survived invasion, civil war, and foreign conflict; it has endured through national expansion, social transformation, and economic depression. From fewer than 4 million enumerated individuals in the first national census, the United States has grown almost two orders of magnitude in population. A largely rural nation with only five cities of more than 10,000—led by New York, with 33,000—became urbanized and suburbanized and modernized. The thirteen-state republic expanded to fill a continent and bestride the planet, with the largest economy and the strongest military the world had ever seen.

This doesn't mean, of course, that the new regime was without flaw. To the contrary. The most glaring defect of the original design was its implicit countenance of humans owning humans. The Massachusetts Supreme Judicial Court had ruled slavery unconstitutional in 1783, but slavery was legal in all other states at the time of the Constitutional Convention—and the Framers essentially punted the issue. (The only clear power the new constitution gave Congress to limit slavery was permitting it to outlaw the importation of enslaved people twenty years down the line. And the new rules of representation inflated the influence of states with more slavery, by apportioning partial representation in Congress for individuals who were legally treated as chattel.) It would take more than seventy years and a gruesome civil war before slaves would be emancipated nationwide. Full civil rights and voting rights—for women as well as for slaves' descendants—would be longer still in coming.

These and other central, tragic failings in the original constitutional design should not blind us to the novelty and overall genius of the republican structure that the Framers developed. The United States Constitution, formed through a process of political compromise, represented both a continuation of the social battles that Englishmen and American colonists had long fought with monarchs, and a new conception of government without a monarch at all. In the new view, the people were sovereign, but only through representation in a republican structure. The Constitution was designed to establish a government that was both energetic and accountable—capable of solving common problems, and responsive to public concerns. But the Framers also sought to limit the power of the government, to preserve individual liberty and to prevent one group of citizens from using the government's powers to other citizens' detriment. (Though yes, again, not all of the nation's people were citizens benefiting from this protection.)

In the more than 230 years since Franklin and the other Framers assembled at Independence Hall, the constitutional structure they developed has doubtless been improved in many ways—chiefly by ending human enslavement and expanding rights to the broader population. But something has also been lost. While the government has remained energetic—capable of acting, albeit not always correctly—the other core principles of the Framers' design have eroded.

It's obvious that today's American government far exceeds the original in size and scope—notwithstanding judicially led efforts to fence off protected zones where government may not tread, based on enumerated and unenumerated rights in the Constitution. In some ways, I believe the growth of American government is problematic—a theme many other books have chronicled. In other respects, a robust government makes sense today. For example, modern technology, in addition to extending lifespans and increasing human flourishing, gives nation-states and individuals alike the capability to unleash far-reaching forms of destruction unimaginable to Franklin and his peers. So however sensible the Framers' concerns about the dangers of standing armies, it's hard to see us going back to local citizen militias to protect ourselves against military threats. Other pressing threats may be even harder to confront, but do suggest a need for significant government action. In the current moment, it's become obvious that the rapid and wholesale global movement of people makes modern societies highly vulnerable to the rapid and wholesale global propagation of virulent infections. And the technological growth that has lifted billions worldwide out of absolute poverty also creates global risks, including environmental concerns that are not easily addressed by old-style legal remedies; one nation's pollution can affect its neighbor's air and water, and quite likely even its climate.

•   •   •

Serious, well-meaning people will disagree markedly in their proposed solutions, and on the proper scope of government action, even in the areas of national security and public health. Other policy divides may remain sharper still. Most debates about the size and scope of government are not easily resolved. There will continue to be a full spectrum of opinion, from libertarian to socialist, among those committed to some form of democratic republic. People will continue to debate *how big* government should be.

I have my views on this debate, which will doubtless shine through in this book. I'll admit my bias up front: I agree with the basic government philosophy of the American Founding Fathers—definitely not in every particular, but in the conception of self-government (publicly accountable), yet *bounded* government (limited in scope). I agree with more modern thinkers like Friedrich Hayek who believed that a government that grows too big is a government that cannot long endure as truly free; though I'll freely concede that polities can thrive even while government is much bigger than in the original American conception—as our own society and many more in the developed and developing world demonstrate.

But the growth in government's size is not my principal focus here, even if it interconnects with many portions of my analysis. Instead, this book focuses on the other founding principle that has been substantially lost: public accountability. Beyond the substantive debate over what government should do, the *processes* for deciding what government does have also changed radically from the original constitutional plan.

In one important sense, of course, modern American government is much *more* accountable to the public than it was in the late eighteenth century: we've dramatically increased the share of the population that has voting rights in the first place. Whereas the U.S. Constitution's original understanding of "the people" was implicitly limited to a white, male, propertied elite, voting rights in the modern United States extend to all adults born in the country or naturalized as citizens.

But in other ways, governmental accountability to the public has been substantially eroded. There is a new elite overseeing much of what we do— an *unelected* elite. That new elite, in general, is *unaccountable* to the rest of us. I classify this elite in four types: *rulemakers, enforcers, litigators,* and *new antifederalists.*

Congress has delegated huge chunks of its legislative powers to a gaggle of federal agencies staffed by permanent, professional government bureaucrats. Many of these agencies are independent of presidential control. Courts defer to their judgment. To a significant degree, the legislative powers today are exercised not in the chambers on Capitol Hill but in the back offices of the Food and Drug Administration, the Securities and Exchange Commission, the Federal Communications Commission, and all the rest. Among the estimated 300,000 federal crimes on the books, 98 percent were never voted on by Congress. I call the bureaucrats staffing the modern American regulatory state the *rulemakers.*

The broader rulemaking powers of the permanent regulatory government have grown in part from the expansion of the government's role, and from the difficulty of enacting new laws, which the Framers built into the Constitution. To enact a law, both houses of Congress have to concur—implicitly both a majority of the people and a majority of the states, the latter majority based on elections staggered over time. And the elected president has to concur, as well, unless there are congressional supermajorities. To be sure, the delegation of Congress's rulemaking authority to bureaucratic agencies is partly due to the need for expertise—the rationale often advanced for bureaucratic rulemaking in the Progressive Era of the early twentieth century. But there's no reason Congress couldn't direct agencies to advise it on new rules, while retaining the power to enact the rules itself. It's just harder to get Congress to agree and take action than for bureaucrats to act on their own.

As the volume of rules has grown, so has the scope for discretionary use of government power through enforcement—and the threat of enforcement. In contrast to rulemaking, enforcement is the core executive power under the three-branched government system we all learned about in grade school. The legislative branch makes the rules; the executive executes them. Policemen and prosecutors don't make the law; they enforce it. But when there are as many rules as there are today, and so many of the prohibitions in the rule-book go beyond intuitively bad conduct, it is impossible for individuals and small businesses to know how to comply. (Big businesses can at least pay for in-house legal teams.) Unknowingly violating a rule is not generally a legal defense, which means that enormous discretion is placed in the hands of prosecutors and civil-enforcement agents—whom I call the *enforcers*.

The enforcers also have power because the modern federal state is so expansive. Many businesses and nonprofit entities rely heavily on government funding. Some of these are obvious, like Defense Department contractors. In addition, both public and private universities receive sizable shares of their budgets from federal research grants, not to mention government-backed grants and loans covering student tuition. Pharmaceutical companies depend on getting reimbursed for their products through Medicare or Medicaid. And many industries not as clearly reliant on government funding still need government approval to operate (like financial institutions) or sell their products (like car manufacturers). Unlike individuals and small businesses, these big organizations can pull together large legal compliance teams. But "compliance" often means placating enforcers even in the absence of clear rules, because the stakes are too high to tell the government "no."

While government officials enforce civil as well as criminal rules in the United States, so do some private citizens: our next class of unelected actors, the *litigators*. They operate through the third branch of government, the judiciary, which is tasked with interpreting the law that the executive branch seeks to enforce, but also resolves disputes in which one private citizen takes another to court to remedy a wrong. Defenders of this regime sometimes characterize it as a "private" enforcement system, akin to the free market. But although it's not "top down," our litigation system is far removed from markets. Markets involve consensual transactions, in which each party to the transaction agrees to a deal. A lawsuit, in contrast, entails one party taking from another, unwilling party, who is engaged with the plaintiff only because the government forces the issue. In some cases, such after-the-fact lawsuits are preferable to one-size-fits-all, bright-line government rules. And in some cases, it's just the opposite. In either case, however, the end result is at least implicitly regulatory.

The American legal system is vastly more expensive than those of other advanced democracies as a percentage of the economy. Americans have always been litigious, yet the legal system we inherited from Britain has changed over time, becoming much more favorable to bringing a lawsuit. This has happened partly by accident and partly by design. And the design has often been made by individuals removed from public accountability. For example, the modern rule of civil procedure that allows the party suing to gain broad "discovery" from a defendant—demanding documents to be produced at the defendant's expense, in a lawsuit premised merely on "notice" to the party being sued, without any actual facts offered up in support of the complaint—was designed, with no precedent, by law professors from Yale and the University of Michigan. Similarly, the "class action" rule allowing lawyers to sue on behalf of a large group of people they've never met was developed by a Harvard law professor and his young protégé from Columbia, during a ferry crossing over to Martha's Vineyard.

Litigators are even less accountable to the public than rulemakers and enforcers. The latter are agents of the government and under the supervision of people appointed or confirmed by elected officials. Private attorneys, on the other hand, work for themselves and their clients, not for the public at large. Rulemakers and enforcers are often "true believers" in their mission—and thus willing to go further to advance it than would the people's elected representatives, who remain accountable to public sentiment. But most of the litigators who exert substantial power over private actions and national commerce through the courts are simply venal—helping their clients in most cases but also profiting handsomely off their unique access to government force.

Most of the regulatory work done by litigators is done in state courts. The constitutional framers divided power not just horizontally, among branches of the federal government—legislative, executive, and judicial—but also vertically, between the state and federal governments. This federalism makes it possible for people and firms to "vote with their feet." States with overreaching taxes and regulations—or those with poor infrastructure and services—will lose people and businesses to states with the "right" government balance. In the ordinary case, federalism thus tends to promote a "race to the top" among states. But federalism can also encourage a "race to the bottom," in which one state can dictate the terms of national commerce.

The litigation system shows both phenomena. A state that has overly loose laws permitting recovery for workplace accidents will see its companies at a disadvantage with competitors from other states, and some companies will relocate. A state that permits undue recoveries in medical malpractice claims will see doctors relocate, and its citizens will face higher health-care costs as tort awards are passed along to patients. But in other instances, the states have little incentive to pare back abusive lawsuits. Under federal rules that were developed by unelected judges, a company making a product in Nebraska can generally still be sued in California for alleged product defects, so relocating from the Golden State to the Cornhusker State makes little difference for the company. And in some cases, the California rule affects Nebraska citizens, as it raises their prices or drives products they would prefer out of the market.

This kind of situation, in which one state interferes with another's affairs, was a central concern at the Constitutional Convention in Philadelphia. In *The Federalist* no. 22, arguing for the new constitution, Alexander Hamilton decried the "interfering and unneighborly regulations of some States" that had "given just cause of umbrage and complaint to others" under the Articles of Confederation.

Those opposed to the constitutional design developed in Philadelphia were dubbed "Antifederalists" by its supporters. I call our final class of actors who unaccountably exert power over us the *new antifederalists*. They exert direct authority over national decisions from leadership perches in state and local government. They do it through lawsuits, sometimes farmed to private lawyers; through enforcement actions; and even through their management of public employees' pension portfolios. To be sure, these officials are not unelected, strictly speaking; they are ordinarily accountable to a local populace. But nobody in Nashville or Fargo or Phoenix voted for the mayor of New York City; and no one in Alabama or Montana or Indiana voted for the attorney general of California.

• • •

These four categories of unaccountable elites have extensive control over American government, with a broad impact on our lives. Independent agencies oversee most of the important sectors of the economy. A large percentage of the biggest companies operate under agreements with prosecutors that give the prosecutors substantial control over their affairs. Class action lawyers—and state prosecutors—reshape entire industries without ever taking their cases to court.

But it would be a mistake to think that unaccountable elites governing America affect only the biggest of big businesses. If anything, small businesses and individuals are affected more. Large companies have lobbyists to negotiate the thicket of agency rulemaking. They have in-house legal counsel to ward off government enforcers and private litigators alike. In some important respects, the complexities of modern unaccountable government work to their advantage, by making it harder for new competitors to emerge to challenge their industry dominance.

Ordinary people don't have these advantages. They get ensnared by the unelected, too. And this book will tell their stories.

Among these is a Maryland doctor who told fellow doctors about a new drug he'd successfully used with his own patients. He was paid a fee to speak to his colleagues, but his story was true, and the results he'd witnessed first-hand were backed up by empirical studies published in the leading medical journals. Yet he was criminally prosecuted for telling his story, under a rule drafted by bureaucrats and never voted on by Congress. He lost his medical license—sending his life on a heartbreaking downward spiral.

Another character we'll meet is a Michigan real estate developer who removed some tree stumps on his own land and backfilled the holes. He didn't have the proper permit. He too was criminally prosecuted, as well as civilly sued, by federal government officials for violating a "wetlands" regulation that Congress never approved. He fought the feds for almost twenty years, insisting that the dry embankment on his property couldn't possibly be what Congress meant when it passed a law about "the waters of the United States, including the territorial seas."

We'll also learn about a New Mexico auto-racing champion turned snow-mobile enthusiast who got lost in a wind-induced blizzard. He hiked some twenty miles in chest-high snow, through hypothermia, and was lucky to get back to civilization alive. But unbeknownst to him, he had driven into a protected federal area—protected under rules drafted by regulators, not Congress. In addition to being a three-time winner of the Indianapolis 500, he's now forevermore a federal criminal.

And we'll hear about a California entrepreneur who worked tirelessly to refurbish a historic hotel, only to see her efforts dashed when trial lawyers came to visit. As a favor to a friend, this aspiring hotelier underwrote a guest's stay while she was still fixing up the establishment. The guest brought her mother, who had a disability—and she had a lawyer, who filed a lawsuit claiming that the hotel bathroom and parking lot, then under renovation, were not disability-compliant. Though the entrepreneur ultimately won her legal battle, the lawyer tab from the effort was sufficiently hefty that she abandoned her project.

• • •

Most Americans learned about the three branches of government in grade school. We were told that the laws that govern our everyday lives were enacted by our elected representatives. Those of us who grew up in the 1970s, like I did—or a bit later, in the 80s or 90s—had this message reinforced when we watched Saturday-morning cartoons on network television. Between episodes of *Scooby Doo*, *Super Friends*, and the rest, children who tuned in to the ABC network's lineup also saw *Schoolhouse Rock!*, a series of animated musical shorts designed to educate young people. Among the most memorable *Schoolhouse Rock!* segments was one called "I'm Just a Bill," which first aired in September 1975.

"I'm Just a Bill" shows a talking piece of legislation explaining to a boy how a bill becomes a law:

> I'm just a bill,
> Yes, I'm only a bill,
> And if they vote for me on Capitol Hill,
> Well, then I'm off to the White House
> Where I'll wait in a line
> With a lot of other bills
> For the president to sign
> And if he signs me, then I'll be a law.
> How I hope and pray that he will,
> But today I am still just a bill.

These lyrics still explain the basics of how a bill becomes a law. But in modern America, the simplicity of "I'm Just a Bill" is increasingly quaint.

The modern reality was spoofed in November 2014 by *Saturday Night*

Live, the long-running NBC sketch-comedy show. *SNL* opened its program by lampooning a then-recent action taken by President Barack Obama. The president had been unable to secure congressional approval for his desired immigration reforms—including a path to legal status for individuals who had first entered the United States unlawfully but had long been living here without getting into any other criminal trouble. When Congress failed to act, the president announced unilateral *executive* action, which he called Deferred Action for Childhood Arrivals. Invoking "prosecutorial discretion," he said he would "defer" deportation for millions of undocumented aliens living in the United States—contrary to the laws passed by Congress—and would establish a process for many of these aliens to obtain formal work permits—without any congressional authorization whatsoever.

The comedy show's opening skit spoofed the "I'm Just a Bill" cartoon from *Schoolhouse Rock!* In the *SNL* version, the bill was replaced by a chain-smoking parchment that declared:

> I'm an executive order
> And I pretty much just happen.
> And that's it.

The *SNL* skit was funny because it captured a reality: a lot of what modern American government does isn't done the way we learned in grade school or on *Schoolhouse Rock!* It isn't done the way Ben Franklin and the Founding Fathers designed it.

President Obama's immigration order is a well-known example of government action that steps outside the *Schoolhouse Rock!* understanding of how decisions get made in our democratic republic. But Barack Obama was obviously an *elected* official, and his action was subject to legal challenge in court. (Federal courts reviewed various pieces of the president's executive actions, with different resolutions. Upon Donald Trump's election, the White House reversed course—and more lawsuits arose. As this book goes to press, the matter is before the U.S. Supreme Court, with an expected resolution soon.)

In contrast, many of the government actions we'll cover here are not subject to any judicial review or public accountability. Much of our national life is governed by people we never elected to national office, be they regulators, enforcers, litigators, or new antifederalists. This book will tell that story—the story of the unelected and their power over us.

Chapters 1 through 3 describe how we've come to concentrate so many of the powers of all three elected branches—legislative, executive, and judicial—in the administrative state. Unelected bureaucrats write the rules, often acting in ways that were unauthorized by Congress, are unaccountable to the president, and are essentially unreviewable by the courts.

Chapters 4 through 6 turn to unelected officials' enforcement powers, through which they effect policy not by rulemaking but by threat. Although the enforcement power is the core of the executive function, the modern variant is often even further removed from the elected government than the agency rulemaking. It is also in serious tension with the rule of law itself, as arbitrary and retroactive decisions are vested in unelected agents' discretion. Common citizens are at risk of unknowingly violating some obscure rule among hundreds of thousands, and institutions that depend on government sanction bend to government enforcers' will.

In the next several chapters, we look at the litigators, who have a regulatory role in the modern American system quite unlike what we see anywhere else. The law of torts—personal injury, product liability, and the like—was a legal backwater at the American founding but consumes an outsized portion of our modern economy, serving as a parallel regulatory system. This system is bottom-up—with the wrong decisions often driving out the right—and it can both exacerbate the errors of the administrative state and contradict the rulemakers and enforcers when they're on the right track.

The final chapters look at the new antifederalism that interferes with the vertical distribution of government power. We'll see how state and local officials have leveraged the upside-down regulatory system of tort law, as well as the unelected rulemaking of federal securities regulators, to drive national policy choices far beyond their borders.

This story might sound pessimistic, and indeed a reality-based accounting of where we stand and where we're going may necessarily be so, depending on one's political preferences. I have no illusions that we'll return to a government anything like that of 1787, either in size or scope or in the processes through which we make government decisions. In some regards, that's for the best—and not just in the obvious cases like emancipation and enfranchisement.

But I'm also convinced that there's a path forward—one that leads us back in the direction of a government that is more accountable, more consistent with rule-of-law principles, and more likely to reach decisions in the common good, rather than merely for the benefit of elites who know how to game the system. In the last chapter—before an epilogue reflecting on the unique moment, a viral pandemic—I will discuss various reforms that I think point us down that road.

CHAPTER 1

Legislating Without Congress

On Monday, February 7, 2011, Dr. Peter Gleason took his own life. A little more than a year earlier, he had been convicted of a crime in federal court. He had received only probation and a nominal fine. But his home state of Maryland, and several others, had yanked his medical license. The doctor could no longer practice medicine.

The events that precipitated Dr. Gleason's downward spiral began almost five years before his death. On March 5, 2006, Gleason had spoken at a lunch meeting in the Long Island office of Dr. Richard Blank, a neurologist. Among the subjects that Gleason discussed was his success in treating patients with the pharmaceutical product Xyrem.

The next day, Gleason was arrested by a gaggle of federal agents at a nearby train station. Initially he thought it was all a joke. It was anything but.

Gleason was charged with "engaging in interstate commerce of a misbranded drug." In addition to discussing Xyrem in Dr. Blank's office, Gleason had spoken about his patients' success with the drug at a variety of conferences and other settings.

Xyrem was a legal drug. It had been approved by the Food and Drug Administration (FDA), the federal agency charged with testing pharmaceuticals for safety and reviewing their labeling.

Gleason had prescribed Xyrem to patients suffering from insomnia, depression, and fibromyalgia. That was legal, too. When the FDA approved Xyrem, it did so only as a treatment for narcolepsy, but it is not illegal for doctors to prescribe drugs for uses other than those for which they received FDA approval. And studies published in peer-reviewed medical journals had in fact shown Xyrem to be effective for fibromyalgia and other uses in addition to narcolepsy.

So-called off-label drug prescriptions—for uses that go beyond those on the FDA-approved label—are commonplace. They're an important tool in medical practice. Peer-reviewed medical studies estimate that 21 percent of all drug prescriptions are for off-label applications. That's even more true for specialized uses—for drugs that treat rare disorders or uses that apply to narrow populations. Running FDA clinical trials can cost billions of dollars, and companies aren't going to spend money on trials for drug applications that won't pay that kind of money back. Some 79 percent of all pediatric prescriptions—generally not for long-term use—are off-label.

Although off-label drug prescriptions are legal, the FDA places significant limits on what the companies that manufacture pharmaceutical products can say about off-label uses. Of course, Gleason wasn't a pharmaceutical manufacturer. But federal prosecutors decided that he had broken the law because he had received payments from Xyrem's manufacturer, Jazz Pharmaceuticals. It didn't matter that the doctor's comments were based on his own experience. Nor that the off-label uses he was discussing were backed up by medical research. Nor that his comments were exclusively made to other practicing physicians, rather than to the general public.

In addition to Dr. Gleason, Jazz Pharmaceuticals also pleaded guilty to the government's charges. So did Al Caronia, the Jazz sales representative who had set up the talk in Dr. Blank's office.

But Mr. Caronia also challenged his conviction on free-speech grounds. And the U.S. Court of Appeals for the Second Circuit agreed with him. The court decided that the First Amendment to the U.S. Constitution protects truthful speech about pharmaceutical products. Alas, the court ruling came down in December 2012—too late for Dr. Gleason.

Peter Gleason's story is not just a tragic tale. Notwithstanding the Second Circuit decision in favor of Caronia, the federal government continues to pursue criminal actions targeting off-label drug promotion. Big pharmaceutical companies have paid out billions of dollars in fines for not following the FDA's rules. Trial lawyers regularly score millions of dollars in fees suing over off-label drug sales on behalf of state governments. (The state governments hire the private lawyers at the behest of state attorneys general who receive large campaign contributions from the very lawyers they hire.)

What's more, the rule that Gleason was accused of violating was written by the FDA, not by Congress. This kind of administrative rulemaking has become commonplace, too. The legislative branch regularly "delegates" broad authority to unelected officials in federal agencies, who are not accountable to the voters.

• • •

Legislators in America today typically pass open-ended laws and leave the details to the unelected "experts" in the executive branch. The rules that executive administrators develop never come back to Congress for approval, and these rules can have criminal teeth. Scholars estimate that more than 300,000 federal crimes are on the books, but 98 percent of these were never voted on by Congress.

As this estimate suggests, the volume of regulations and rules generated by the modern administrative state is vast. The government first started itemizing its new rules in 1976. Over the next forty-two years, the executive branch added 201,838 new rules to the *Federal Register*. A large flow of new additions to the *Register* has been generated almost inevitably, regardless of presidential administration—although Republican administrations typically have scaled back on rulemaking relative to Democratic predecessors.

Consider the Trump administration. It entered office with deregulatory zeal. In one of his first actions, President Trump issued Executive Order 13771, directing the government to eliminate two regulations for each new one created. At a December 2017 press conference in the White House's Roosevelt Room, the president boldly announced that his administration had begun "the most far-reaching regulatory reform in American history." With typical flair, he wielded a large pair of gold scissors and sliced through red tape connecting piles of paper that symbolized the growth of the regulatory state. The president proclaimed that "the never-ending growth of red tape in America has come to a sudden, screeching and beautiful halt."

The truth is somewhat more complex. In 2017, President Trump's first year in office, the executive branch added 61,308 pages to the *Federal Register*. But some of these—more than 7,500 pages—were added in the waning days of the Obama administration, before Mr. Trump's inauguration on January 20. And the number of pages added to the *Register* in President Trump's first year was actually *the lowest* since 1993, Bill Clinton's first year in office. The Obama administration had added 95,854 pages of new rules in 2016, its final calendar year.

In 2017 and likewise in 2018, fewer final rules were added to the *Federal Register* than in any previous year since counting began in the mid-1970s. Still, the total number of rules generated each year was strikingly high: 3,281 and 3,368, respectively. This isn't to slight the Trump administration's effort to lower regulatory burdens. *Deregulatory* efforts also require promulgating new rules. The Trump administration certainly slowed down, blocked, or reversed many costly Obama-era rules. And some of the administration's regulatory changes—such as the approval of the Keystone XL and Dakota Access pipelines—will have significant economic impact.

But the broader point is that even an executive branch focused on cutting regulations has been adding thousands of new federal rules annually, filling tens of thousands of pages. No one could hope to follow each and every one of these proliferating rules. And none of these rules were voted on by Congress, except in "enabling" legislation that vested rulemaking authority in executive-branch agencies in the first place.

• • •

For most of America's history, the notion that Congress could delegate the power to write laws to unelected officials in the executive branch was anathema. The Founding Fathers who wrote the federal constitution believed they were designing a system that prohibits the legislature from delegating its law-making authority. Anglo-American law at the time generally held to a maxim, *delegata potestas non potest delegari*—no delegated powers can be further delegated. This "nondelegation principle" was viewed as a central feature of the separation of powers among the three branches of the federal government.

The principle was expounded by two of the leading Enlightenment thinkers, John Locke and the Baron de Montesquieu. Locke argued that the legislative power existed "only to make laws, and not to make legislators." He viewed this principle as a linchpin of liberty. Joining the power to make law with the power to enforce it was the road to tyranny. As Montesquieu explained, there could be "no liberty" where the legislative and executive powers were "united."

The Founders viewed the English jurist William Blackstone's *Commentaries on the Laws of England*, published in 1765, as a definitive statement of the law at the time. Blackstone echoed Locke and Montesquieu. He observed that combining "the right both of making and of enforcing laws" in a "supreme magistracy" is a feature of "all tyrannical governments."

These scholars did not simply invent the nondelegation principle. The notion that the king of England could act only through laws enacted by Parliament was an idea the citizenry of Britain had fought and died for in the centuries preceding American independence.

To be sure, Parliament at times had granted the king broader swathe. In 1539, Parliament enacted the Statute of Proclamations, which essentially allowed Henry VIII, in many instances, to rule by decree. (The statute was a response to the king's frustration at limits placed by the courts on his assertion of authority.) But the Statute of Proclamations was the exception that proved the rule. Parliament repealed it just eight years later, after Henry's nine-year-old son Edward VI ascended the throne. Blackstone later characterized the Statute of Proclamations as "calculated to introduce the most despotic tyranny; and which must have proved fatal to the liberties of this kingdom, had it not been luckily repealed."

The abrogation of legislative authority is what led to the English Civil War. In 1628, during the early years of Charles I's reign, Sir Edward Coke led Parliament to pass the Petition of Right, to circumscribe royal power. Charles thereafter dissolved Parliament and ruled without it, in a period dubbed the Personal Rule (or, by later critics, the Eleven Years' Tyranny). Charles recalled the legislature in 1640 to authorize taxation, as he needed funds to suppress rebellion in Scotland. Parliament responded the next year with the Triennial Act, which required calling the legislature into session at least once every three years. A year later, civil war broke out. In 1649, King Charles was convicted of high treason and beheaded.

Against this backdrop, the Founding Fathers wrote prohibitions on the delegation of legislative authority into state constitutions. The Massachusetts Constitution of 1780, principally drafted by John Adams, declared: "The executive shall never exercise the legislative and judicial powers, or either of them ... to the end it may be a government of laws and not of men."

The first article of the U.S. Constitution, adopted in 1787, stated simply: "All legislative Powers herein granted shall be vested in a Congress of the United States." The use of the word "All" would seem to reflect an intent that Congress not be allowed to delegate its authority. But the nondelegation principle was not stated as expressly as it had been in some state constitutions, like that of Massachusetts. The Antifederalists who opposed the new constitution argued that the proposed founding document did not adequately maintain separate and distinct authority among the three branches of government.

James Madison, a principal author of the U.S. Constitution, defended it against this charge. In *Federalist* no. 47, Madison acknowledged that the "accumulation of all powers...in the same hands...may justly be pronounced the very definition of tyranny." His words echoed Blackstone; his argument cited Montesquieu with approval. Madison admitted that the new constitutional system would indeed warrant "a universal reprobation" were the Antifederalist critics' charges true.

The question of the extent to which Congress might delegate its powers under the U.S. Constitution emerged early in legislative debates. The Constitution gave Congress the power "To establish Post Offices and Post Roads." In 1791, the legislature was considering a list of roads to be built. Congressman Theodore Sedgwick—a future Speaker of the U.S. House of Representatives, president pro tempore of the U.S. Senate, and justice on the Massachusetts Supreme Judicial Court—proposed deleting the listed roads from the legislation and instead appropriating funds for roads "by such route as the President of the United States shall, from time to time, cause to be established." The amendment was defeated, after opposition from representatives who thought Sedgwick's proposal was an improper delegation of legislative authority. Among those opposed was none other than Representative James Madison, who argued that delegating the choice of roads to the president violated the Constitution's principles.

• • •

The extent to which Congress could delegate its authority was also a question the Supreme Court wrestled with in the early years of its existence. In 1813, the Court considered the case of *Cargo of the Brig Aurora v. United States*, which arose during the Napoleonic Wars. Britain and France had been interfering with American trade, and Congress responded in 1809 by imposing an embargo on imports from both countries and their colonies. But the embargo had an out: should either nation "cease to violate the neutral commerce of the United States," the embargo would be rescinded. Congress left it to the president to determine whether the nations had returned to good behavior.

The lawyer for the British vessel whose cargo was seized under the embargo argued that the statute was unconstitutional because "Congress could not transfer the legislative power to the President." Without further explanation, the Court declared that it could "see no sufficient reason, why the legislature should not exercise its discretion...either expressly or conditionally, as their judgment should direct." But determining that Congress could exercise its discretion "conditionally" as well as "expressly" is hardly the same thing as saying that it could delegate its exercise of discretion to the executive branch.

Unlike modern Congresses that delegate expansive rulemaking powers to the executive, the Congress that enacted an embargo in 1809 was establishing its own legislative rule, merely leaving it up to the president to determine the answer to a yes-or-no question. Such "conditional" exercise of discretion by the executive is inherent in almost any legal regime calling on executive enforcement. Indeed, it is intrinsic to all of statutory criminal law. If the legislature determines that certain conduct should be criminal, it passes a law proscribing it and laying out potential sanction. But it necessarily leaves to the executive the decision about whether a criminal law has been broken, and whether or not to prosecute an offense.

Answering the question may not be simple. But neither is many an exercise of prosecutorial discretion. And such a delegation makes particular sense in the context of foreign affairs: the Constitution expressly vests with the president the title of Commander in Chief of the military forces, as well as the power, with the advice and consent of the Senate, to make treaties and appoint ambassadors. It's hardly surprising that Congress, in an era when legislators were often far removed from the capital and had no rapid mode of travel or communication, would prefer to exercise its power to regulate foreign trade by enacting an embargo but allowing the president to suspend its terms if certain predetermined conditions were met.

If there were any doubt whether the Supreme Court believed that the Constitution forbade Congress from delegating its powers, it was answered twelve years after *Brig Aurora*, in the case of *Wayman v. Southard*. As in the earlier case, the Court upheld an act of Congress against a nondelegation challenge. But John Marshall, who towered over the Court as chief justice for most of the first thirty-five years of the nineteenth century, was clear and unequivocal: "It will not be contended that Congress can delegate to the courts or to any other tribunals powers which are strictly and exclusively legislative." *Wayman* involved the purported delegation of Congress's powers to adopt rules for federal courts, the *judicial* branch.

At issue was the constitutionality of one of the first acts of Congress, the Judiciary Act of 1789. This early act of legislation established the federal courts, consistent with a clearly enumerated legislative power. But rather than create new procedural rules, Congress declared that "rules of decision" in federal-court legal trials would track then-existing *state* court rules. In other words, the federal rule of procedure in each state would be the same as the rule in place under the state supreme court as of September 1789, when the statute was enacted.

Chief Justice Marshall's opinion noted that Congress had faced a "peculiar situation" in fashioning a federal judicial system thirty-six years before. There were already "distinct systems" of laws in the states, which varied across jurisdictions. Yes, Congress might itself draw up a single uniform set of rules for federal courts. But it need not. And courts had long routinely made "rules directing the returning of writs and processes, the filing of declarations and other pleadings."

Judicial language aside, *Wayman* was, on its facts, even easier than *Brig Aurora*. Congress was *not* delegating the actual writing of federal court rules to the judicial branch or to state legislative bodies. It was merely adopting a specific set of rules *already existing* in the various states. It was *choosing* a set of rules—saying that the rules of federal court in New York, South Carolina, and the rest would conform to those already existing in the respective state courts. (This decision, while sensible at the time, ultimately proved unwieldy. As state-law rules changed and federal-law rules were wedded to an earlier period, the federal rules were often little understood by current practitioners. Congress did not change the system until 1872.)

• • •

After the *Wayman* decision in 1825, the Supreme Court had little reason to reconsider the nondelegation doctrine for several decades. That's largely because Congress didn't delegate "powers which are strictly and exclusively legislative." Like the early Congress considering postal roads, nineteenth-century legislators decided not to delegate broad authority to the executive branch.

The general principle of nondelegation remained a central tenet of American constitutional law. It was "tacitly assumed...as a fundamental basis in the constitution of the United States," wrote Justice Joseph Story in his highly influential *Commentaries on the Constitution of the United States*, published in

1833. Justice Story served on the Supreme Court from 1812 to 1845, and alongside Chief Justice Marshall he was the most significant member of the Court in its first fifty years. When Story was writing, the legislature was clearly the dominant branch of government. In the great justice's view, the "entire safety" of the constitutional structure was demonstrated by "the experience of more than forty years," which had shown Congress to wield the "absorbing power" of the national government.

That would change—but only after the American economy began to be transformed in ways that led to demands for more regulation, which in turn would shift more decision-making power to the executive branch.

First steamships and then railroads would tie together national commerce. Mass-production industrial techniques emerged in Connecticut, led by arms manufacturers: Samuel Colt, who invented the revolver in 1836, and Horace Smith and Daniel Wesson, who developed the repeating rifle in the early 1850s. In 1856, an Englishman, Henry Bessemer, patented a process for steel manufacture that enabled large-scale industry and building. American business leaders quickly imported Bessemer's process, and American companies soon led world production. In 1859, Edwin Drake "struck oil" in Titusville in Western Pennsylvania. The substance would literally fuel American industrial development. At first, the most significant oil product was kerosene, which offered dramatically superior lighting relative to candle wax and whale oil. (Thomas Edison launched his Edison Electric Light Company in 1878, but it would be decades more until infrastructure transmitting electricity permitted widespread incandescent lighting in households.)

Populist political pressures in the wake of what economists now dub the Long Depression prompted the first large-scale federal regulatory efforts. In April 1873, Congress passed the Coinage Act, which put the United States on a pure gold standard. Previously, the country had followed a "bimetallic" standard, basing currency values on both gold and silver—as established in the Coinage Act of 1792, conceived by the first treasury secretary, Alexander Hamilton. Whatever the merits of ending bimetallism, the immediate practical effect of the 1873 Coinage Act, in modern economic terms, was to contract the U.S. money supply. Both prices and wages plummeted; the price of cotton halved. In May 1873, stock prices collapsed on the Vienna Stock Exchange. That fall, the financial contagion spread to the United States. On "Black Thursday," September 18, 1873, the Philadelphia financial firm Jay Cooke & Company, overextended on the Northern Pacific Railway, filed for bankruptcy.

A run on stocks—and banks—ensued. The New York Stock Exchange closed down for ten days. Thousands of businesses, including hundreds of railroads, went belly-up.

After the financial panic had passed, economic growth resumed. But only slowly. The National Bureau of Economic Research estimates that the economic contraction, beginning in October 1873, stretched to March 1879. Even with the contraction, industrial production soared: steel manufacture increased 2,000 percent from 1870 to 1890. But prices and wages continued to face downward pressure from monetary deflation throughout the two decades. The price of grain fell by two-thirds over that span. Such collapsing prices were a boon to *consumers*, even with falling wages. But they also created a class of economic losers—specifically farmers, who saw their livelihoods threatened.

And of course, the end of silver coinage was disastrous for western silver mines. The Coinage Act of 1873, which had established the gold standard, became a target of populist animus. Congress responded with the Bland-Allison Act of 1878 and the Sherman Silver Purchase Act of 1890, but these laws were more about propping up silver purchases to protect mining interests than actually reflating the currency. William Jennings Bryan would assail the Coinage Act as the "Crime of 1873" in his "Cross of Gold" speech at the 1896 Democratic National Convention—setting the stage for the first of his three unsuccessful runs for the presidency as the party's standard bearer.

Other targets of populist agitation were the railroads and the "trusts," the latter being the legal form initially used by John D. Rockefeller's Standard Oil Company as it consolidated oil-industry ownership through a series of acquisitions. The Interstate Commerce Act of 1887, enacted during the first presidential administration of Grover Cleveland, and the Sherman Antitrust Act of 1890, enacted during the administration of Benjamin Harrison, were direct responses to these concerns. The latter, while establishing new federal government powers, used traditional means: its enforcement mechanism was litigation in the courts. The former, however, established the Interstate Commerce Commission, often hailed as the progenitor of the administrative state in America.

But the new commission's powers were "meager." It lacked any independent enforcement power; if the commission found a railroad's rates to be "unjust and unreasonable," it had to refer the matter to the Department of Justice. "Just and reasonable" rates were terms defined by judicial precedents in the "common law"—the background of court decisions that evolved in England and long predated the American republic itself. The Commerce Act preserved these old common-law enforcement rights, and the Interstate Commerce Commission lacked any power to *set* railroad rates—a matter clarified by the Supreme Court in subsequent litigation.

• • •

The scope of the nondelegation doctrine reemerged as an issue in the late nineteenth century, in a dispute concerning the Tariff Act of 1890. This was the third major economic law passed that year, in addition to the aforementioned Silver Purchase and Antitrust acts, both bearing the name of Senator John Sherman of Ohio, the Civil War general's brother. In America's first 125 years, tariffs on imported goods were the principal means of raising revenues for the federal government—and the greatest source of political disputes, aside from slavery. (Income taxes first appeared during the Civil War but were repealed in 1872. A new income tax in 1894 was struck down as unconstitutional by the Supreme Court the next year. The Sixteenth Amendment to the Constitution, ratified in 1913, expressly allowed such taxation.)

Collecting tariffs required supervision of rather complex schemes to determine charges, depending on counts or weights. These had to be administered at far-flung customs houses. The Tariff Act of 1890 was no exception. To administer the series of textile and apparel tariffs under the law, Congress set up a Board of General Appraisers. Its decisions could be appealed to federal court.

To promote "reciprocal trade," the Tariff Act created exemptions for certain countries' products. But it allowed the president to suspend such exemptions were he to find other countries' tariffs or trade regulations "reciprocally unequal and unreasonable." The retailer Marshall Field challenged the law. In 1892, the Supreme Court upheld it in *Field v. Clark*. Unsurprisingly so, since the Court had upheld the delegation of a very similar yes-or-no trade decision to the president seventy-nine years earlier in *Brig Aurora*.

In his opinion for the Court majority, Justice John Marshall Harlan viewed the delegation as very similar to that upheld in earlier tariff acts. Two justices disagreed and thought the new law's delegation went too far. But the Court unanimously embraced the nondelegation doctrine overall. Justice Harlan's majority opinion for the Court declared: "That Congress cannot delegate legislative power to the President is a principle universally recognized as vital to the integrity and maintenance of the system of government ordained by the Constitution."

The Court would face a similar case in 1928, *J. W. Hampton, Jr. & Co. v. United States.* This time, the justices were considering the Tariff Act of 1922. That law contained a "flexible tariff provision," which permitted the president to adjust tariff rates based on international price differentials. The president was required to give thirty days' notice. And the tariff rate imposed could increase by no more than 50 percent above what the statute prescribed.

J. W. Hampton imported barium peroxide. Under the Tariff Act of 1922, he would have paid four cents per pound on his imported product, but a presidential finding under the flexible tariff provision of the statute increased the assessed tariff to six cents. Hampton challenged that assessment in court.

The Supreme Court upheld the flexible tariff rule. Writing for a unanimous Court, Chief Justice William Howard Taft observed that the "well-known maxim *delegata potestas non potest delegari*" not only applied to "the law of agency in the general and common law" but also had a "wider application in the construction of our federal and state Constitutions." But, he noted, "Congress has found it frequently necessary to use officers of the executive branch within defined limits, to secure the exact effect intended by its acts of legislation." What was critical, in the Court's view, was that Congress lay out an "intelligible principle" with which the executive branch could conform.

The Court determined that the principle laid out for the president in the Tariff Act of 1922 was "perfectly clear and perfectly intelligible." Congress's statutory plan was obviously to "secure revenue." But the legislature also wanted to "enable domestic producers to compete on terms of equality with foreign producers in the markets of the United States." And "changing conditions" might necessitate "readjustments" over time "to give effect to the principle on which the statute proceeds."

With such clear principles at play—and such circumscribed authority granted—the president's discretion to increase tariffs with defined limits under prescribed conditions "was merely in execution of the act of Congress. It was not the making of law." As was the case thirty-six years before in *Field v. Clark*, which the Court cited with approval, the president was "the mere agent of the lawmaking department to ascertain and declare the event upon which its expressed will was to take effect."

Thus, 140 years into the American constitutional experiment, the nondelegation doctrine that the Supreme Court called "vital" in *Field v. Clark* had never been invoked to declare a federal statute unconstitutional. Essentially, that's because Congress refrained from violating it. Congress sometimes conditioned a policy on executive fact finding—and the Supreme Court said fine, while affirming the nondelegation principle itself.

But all that was about to change, soon after the stock market crash of October 1929 had ushered in the Great Depression.

• • •

Like the Long Depression that began in 1873, the Great Depression of the 1930s was politically consequential. In the election of 1932, the Democratic candidate for president, Franklin D. Roosevelt, swamped the Republican incumbent, Herbert Hoover, in a landslide—carrying forty-two of forty-eight states and winning the national popular vote by almost 18 percentage points. Roosevelt had promised "a new deal for the American people" when he was nominated for the presidency. Scarcely three months after his inauguration, Congress passed the National Industrial Recovery Act, the heart of Roosevelt's New Deal agenda, and it would push the Supreme Court to invoke the nondelegation doctrine for the first time in its history.

There had been earlier steps toward empowered executive-branch administration. In 1906, Congress beefed up the powers of the Interstate Commerce Commission in the Hepburn Act, giving the commission the authority to set the maximum rates that railroads could charge. The same year, Congress enacted the first broad federal consumer-protection statute, the Pure Food and Drug Act—the antecedent to legislation empowering the regulatory regime that ensnared Dr. Gleason. Later, during Woodrow Wilson's administration, Congress enacted legislation that delegated substantial authority regulating banks (the Federal Reserve Act of 1913) and administering antitrust enforcement (the Federal Trade Commission Act of 1914).

What was different about the National Industrial Recovery Act of 1933 was its sweeping scope. It established two new administrative agencies, the National Recovery Administration and the Public Works Administration. The latter spent money on infrastructure and other projects designed to create jobs in the era of high unemployment. The former was tasked with setting up various "industrial codes" through which the federal government would regulate business. This regulatory effort came under legal challenge. And in a pair of 1935 cases, the Supreme Court struck down portions of Roosevelt's signature act as unconstitutional delegations of legislative power to the executive branch.

The first case, *Panama Refining Company v. Ryan*, involved a challenge by petroleum companies to a section of the act that gave the president authority to regulate the oil industry. The delegation of power to the president was far broader than what was authorized in earlier legislation upheld by the Court:

> The President is authorized to prohibit the transportation in interstate and foreign commerce of petroleum...in excess of the amount permitted to be produced or withdrawn from storage by any State law or valid regulation or order prescribed thereunder, by any board, commission, officer, or other duly authorized agency of a State.

As in the Judiciary Act of 1789, Congress had allowed another branch of the federal government to look to state law for rules. But it merely *authorized* the president to act, without offering any standard for deciding when or when not to do so. In the view of the Court, that was a step too far.

Was the Court overreaching in *Panama Refining*? Perhaps. The powers vested in the president to regulate oil shipments were indeed substantial, but the *legislative* choices were essentially left up to the state governments. Because there were a panoply of varying state-law rules that might come into play, the rule established by Congress left businesses with little clarity—and the executive branch with broad discretion whether to act. Still, the executive role could probably best be characterized as the power to enforce state-law mandates. It would not have been a stretch for the Supreme Court to invoke *Wayman v. Southard* and say that it was fine for Congress to choose to adopt state-law rules on oil regulation as a federal standard and to empower the federal executive to enforce them—subject, as in all cases, to prosecutorial discretion.

But whether or not *Panama Refining* might fit into the *Wayman* precedent, another case soon arose under a different section of the National Industrial Recovery Act, in which Congress's delegation of lawmaking authority to the executive branch had gone much further. Some five months after *Panama Refining*, the Supreme Court considered *A. L. A. Schechter Poultry Corp. v. United States*, involving Congress's decision in the Recovery Act to give the president broad power "to approve 'codes of fair competition'" across whole swathes of industry. Congress offered no guidance clarifying what that meant. Nor did the statute explicitly or implicitly reference an underlying common-law legal standard, as in the Sherman Antitrust Act of 1890. Essentially, what "fair competition" meant was left up to the executive branch. The New Deal Congress, rather like the sixteenth-century Parliament that enacted the Statute of Proclamations, had authorized rule by executive decree.

Under this extensive delegation of authority, the Roosevelt administration started drafting regulatory codes with gusto. Among the industries affected was poultry production. On April 13, 1934, the president approved by executive order a Live Poultry Code. The code applied in the New York metropolitan area, extending into parts of New Jersey and Connecticut. It set standards for wages, hours, and other labor conditions. It established an "industry advisory committee" composed of trade associations and poultry businesses. It required poultry businesses to supply weekly reports to the government. And it proscribed various "unfair methods of competition." Perhaps unsurprisingly, the code had been substantially drafted by some poultry producers in the New York metropolitan region, who had every reason to craft rules to buttress their market position and interfere with competitors.

The A. L. A. Schechter Poultry Corporation, a Jewish kosher butcher, was indicted for eighteen counts of violating various provisions of the Live Poultry Code. Among these were alleged violations of the code's wage and hour rules, as well as ten separate counts alleging illegal "killing" of chickens. Many of these violations stemmed from the owners' interpretation of Jewish kosher food laws.

A unanimous Supreme Court sided with the Schechters' challenge to the law under which the code had been issued, declaring the "fair competition" provision of the Recovery Act unconstitutional. In his opinion for the Court, Chief Justice Charles Evan Hughes reiterated the nondelegation principle that had long been fundamental in American constitutional law: "The Congress is not permitted to abdicate or to transfer to others the essential legislative functions with which it is thus vested." His opinion observed that the delegation in question went much further than *Panama Refining*, in which "the subject of the statutory prohibition was defined," and the Court's decision hinged on the degree of discretion left to the president. In contrast, the portion of the act at issue in *Schechter Poultry* left "fair competition" undefined—and the Roosevelt administration's interpretation had stretched it far beyond the common-law meaning. Justice Benjamin Cardozo, the leader of the Court's progressive wing and the lone dissenter in *Panama Refining*, wrote separately to emphasize that this provision of the Recovery Act was "delegation running riot."

Although the Court's decision in *Schechter Poultry* was unanimous, it provoked a furious backlash. New Deal advocates decried the Supreme Court as an "economic dictatorship." On February 5, 1937, President Roosevelt introduced the Judicial Procedures Reform Bill of 1937, which would have packed the Court with more justices amenable to his New Deal legislation.

The highly controversial bill—the first effort to change the size of the Supreme Court since the immediate aftermath of the Civil War—stalled in Congress. But the Court soon backed away from any efforts to constrain New Deal overreach. Later that summer, Roosevelt named a loyalist, Hugo Black, to the Court, replacing the retiring conservative stalwart Willis Van Devanter. By 1943, Roosevelt had successfully nominated all but one of the sitting justices. The Court quickly reversed course and rubber-stamped the rest of the New Deal. Today, *Panama Refining* and *Schechter Poultry* are judicial anomalies: never since has the Supreme Court stricken a congressional enactment on nondelegation grounds. And the sort of congressional delegations of lawmaking powers to the executive branch that Justice Cardozo viewed as "delegation running riot" are now the norm.

· · ·

The Supreme Court rejected an opportunity to revive the nondelegation doctrine in 1989, when it considered Congress's delegating to the United States Sentencing Commission the power to set legally binding "sentencing guidelines" that affect all federal criminal defendants. But it has used parallel rationales to rein in at least some of the administrative state's most aggressive forays into lawmaking under broad congressional delegations of authority. In the *Wayman* decision in 1825, Chief Justice Marshall wrote that Congress might give the executive branch the power to "fill in the details" of a "general provision," but took pains to emphasize that "important subjects...must be entirely regulated by the legislature itself." The Court's modern application of this principle is what it calls the "major questions doctrine." Under this doctrine, administrative agencies *cannot* fill in "statutory gaps" when those gaps center on "a question of deep 'economic and political significance.'" Applying this doctrine, the Supreme Court in recent decades has stepped in to block executive-branch efforts to regulate cigarettes or greenhouse gas emissions without clear congressional guidance.

More recently, the Court has signaled that it might soon start taking nondelegation principles seriously again. In June 2019, in *Gundy v. United States*, Justice Neil Gorsuch dissented from a decision upholding a criminal conviction. Gundy had been convicted of violating the terms of the national sex-offender registry developed by the U.S. attorney general under the authority of the 2006 Adam Walsh Child Protection and Safety Act. Gundy's conviction predated the enactment of the law. And in crafting the law, Congress had not clearly stated that prior offenders should be included in the new registry—instead vesting with the attorney general "the authority to specify the applicability of the requirements…to sex offenders convicted before" the Walsh Act's enactment.

To Justice Gorsuch, the question of whether the law's new registry requirements should apply retroactively to those previously convicted was precisely the sort of question that should be resolved by the legislative branch, not the executive. In his thirty-three-page opinion in *Gundy*, Gorsuch openly called on the Court to consider reviving the nondelegation doctrine. Joining him were Chief Justice John Roberts and Justice Clarence Thomas. Justice Samuel Alito did not join his fellow right-of-center justices, but instead concurred with the Court majority upholding the criminal conviction being challenged. But Alito wrote separately to emphasize his discomfiture with Congress empowering "agencies to adopt important rules pursuant to extraordinarily capacious standards." Alito noted, however, that the Court had long acquiesced in these broad delegations. Still, he "would support" reconsidering this acquiescence—but only along with a majority of the justices. A fifth justice who might create such a majority, Brett Kavanaugh, had not taken part in the *Gundy* decision, having joined the Court after the case had been argued. But he had been a major proponent of the major-questions doctrine on the D.C. Circuit Court of Appeals—leading some Court watchers to speculate that he might be sympathetic to Justice Gorsuch's invitation.

Unlike *Schechter Poultry*, however, such a court decision would be sharply divided, not unanimous. Defenders of the modern administrative state would doubtless howl.

Those who support broad, open-ended laws enabling agency rulemaking do have a point: it's harder to "get things done" when Congress cannot punt all the hard questions to the executive. But for those who value democratic accountability and the limited-government principles embedded in our Constitution, that's a feature, not a bug.

Unless and until the Supreme Court steps in and starts pushing back on a Congress that continues to punt the hard work of lawmaking to the executive branch, we can expect thousands more rules and tens of thousands more pages to be added to the *Federal Register* each year, without any affirmative congressional vote on the specifics. And tens of thousands of citizens will be more at risk of falling into the administrative state's crosshairs.

CHAPTER 2

Administering Without the Executive

I t was like a scene out of an old Hollywood screwball comedy. On the Monday morning after Thanksgiving 2017, two people showed up at the Washington headquarters of the Consumer Financial Protection Bureau (CFPB), each reporting for the same high-level executive-branch job.

Mike Mulvaney, who had previously served as director of the White House Office of Management and Budget, showed up to the CFPB offices at 1700 G Street carrying a bag of doughnuts for the staff. At 7:56 a.m., he tweeted a picture of himself "hard at work" as acting director of the agency—a role to which President Donald Trump had appointed him.

Exactly one minute later, Leandra English sent an email to staffers, signed by herself as "acting director" of the CFPB. Three days earlier, she had been named the agency's deputy director by Richard Cordray, the departing CFPB director. Cordray, who had been appointed by President Barack Obama, would be leaving the post mere hours later.

Ms. English immediately filed suit asking the courts to install her, not Mr. Mulvaney, as agency head. Her claim rested on a provision of the 2011 Dodd-Frank Wall Street Reform and Consumer Protection Act, the statute that created the CFPB. The statute prescribed that "in the absence or unavailability of the Director" of the agency, "the Deputy Director...shall serve as acting Director."

Mulvaney and the Trump legal team's lawyers, however, pointed to a different federal statute, the 1998 Federal Vacancies Reform Act. That law empowers the president to fill temporarily vacant executive officer positions with other executive officers already confirmed by the Senate—like Mulvaney.

The Dodd-Frank law contained no express language stating that it overrides the earlier, broad grant of authority to the president to fill an executive-branch position. Thus, the Office of Legal Counsel for the federal Justice Department and the general counsel of the CFPB opined that Mulvaney's appointment was valid. A federal judge refused to grant English an injunction blocking Mulvaney's ascension to the role of acting director. In June 2018, English dropped her suit, as President Trump nominated a new director, Kathy Kraninger, who would ultimately be confirmed to the position by a party-line vote in the Senate.

The dueling tweets and emails of two claimants to the CFPB crown was a remarkable spectacle. But so was the general line of argument advanced by Ms. English and the proponents of her claim. In her legal memorandum supporting her effort to get the federal judge to unseat Mulvaney, she argued that "Congress determined that [the CFPB] needed to be an independent regulator—insulated from direct presidential management and control." As English noted, the Dodd-Frank statute made the agency fundable through the Federal Reserve System (thus outside congressional appropriation authority) and its director removable only for "good cause" (thus outside presidential oversight).

In other words, the agency *by design* was insulated from both Congress's power of the purse and the president's control over the executive branch.

•   •   •

An agency design like that of the Consumer Financial Protection Bureau is in significant tension with the U.S. Constitution. Article II of the Constitution begins simply, "The executive Power shall be vested in a President of the United States of America." The Constitution specifies further that the president himself "shall take Care that the Laws be faithfully executed."

To be sure, the president's constitutional power over the executive branch is not absolute. He can appoint executive-branch officials, but only with the advice and consent of the Senate. The Constitution is silent as to whether the president can *remove* such officials at his discretion. And the issue became a topic of heated debate in the very first Congress. The Constitution's principal drafter, James Madison, argued that the vesting of executive power with the president and the constitutional obligation upon the president to "take care" that the laws be executed *required* that the president be able to remove officers as a "species of power which is necessary to accomplish that end." Congress ultimately agreed and acknowledged the president's constitutional removal power in the "Decision of 1789."

In the Second Congress, in March 1793, Madison further expounded his view that the executive power vested exclusively in the president. On the floor of the House, Madison accused Alexander Hamilton, the treasury secretary and by then his chief political rival, of inappropriately acting at odds with the orders of President George Washington. Congress had appropriated two separate sums to pay down debts, one for foreign and one for domestic debt. The president had ordered, pursuant to these statutes, that the first sum go to pay down "the Foreign Debt." But Hamilton instead proclaimed, "I destine a part of the money only to that purpose, and a part to be brought to the United States for other purposes." Madison assailed Hamilton's action as "singular and remarkable." Not only had Hamilton's proclamation contravened the spirit of Congress's appropriations, but it seemed to override the president's own judgment: "The subordinate Officer appeared in direct opposition to the Chief Magistrate. The agent was seen as overruling, by his own orders, the orders of his principal."

Hamilton defended himself by claiming that his decision comported with the president's intentions. And the president backed up his treasury secretary. But Washington generally defended the idea that the president retained full authority over executive-branch departments—else "perplexity and confusion will inevitably ensue."

Washington's successor, John Adams, maintained that "a divided executive" was the "worst evil that can happen in any government...and incompatible with liberty." And when the Democratic-Republicans won control from the Federalists, President Thomas Jefferson reaffirmed the principle that there should be a "unity of object and action" in the executive branch. The idea that the president would have full authority over the executive branch—what scholars, echoing Jefferson, call the "unitary executive"—would continue to be one that governed the Republic's early years.

• • •

Through the first few decades of United States history, the president's removal power, while acknowledged, was rarely used. In part that owed to a lack of partisanship. Notwithstanding political disagreements among various national factions, Jefferson's Democratic-Republican Party maintained its grip on the presidency for twenty-four years. The White House was inhabited throughout this period by Jefferson, Madison, and James Monroe—three close friends who all hailed from a small area around Charlottesville, Virginia.

The partisan unity ended in 1824. John Quincy Adams won a minority of electors and popular votes but was elected president in the House, through what the leading vote-getter, Andrew Jackson, assailed as a "corrupt bargain." Jefferson's Democratic-Republican Party broke apart. Four years later, Jackson's election ushered in what historians call the Second Party System.

Jackson adopted a "spoils system" in which he used the president's removal power much more aggressively to reward political allies with patronage jobs in the administration. Unsurprisingly, he met with congressional resistance.

Jackson's fellow Democrat and former vice president, John C. Calhoun, inveighed against his patronage practice. In Calhoun's view, the presidential use of patronage:

> tended to sap the foundation of our institutions, to throw a cloud of uncertainty over the future, to degrade and corrupt the public morals, and to substitute devotion and subserviency to power in the place of that disinterested and noble attachment to principles and country which are essential to the preservation of free institutions.

This strong rhetoric notwithstanding, Calhoun's proposed remedy for patronage was fairly modest: he sought an annual report by the president to Congress on all government officers removed and the reasons for their removal. Congress enacted Calhoun's transparency legislation in 1835.

Members of the National Republicans opposed to Jackson—and their successors in the Second Party System, the Whigs—pushed back against the Democrat Jackson even more forcefully. Calhoun's fellow senator Daniel Webster, a Whig, argued against the constitutional case for presidential removal itself—a striking argument from perhaps the leading constitutional litigator of the era. Webster acknowledged that the "early decision" in 1789 adopted the construction that the president could remove officers "at will," and that subsequent laws had "uniformly sanctioned it." But he maintained that "the original decision was wrong" and that "those who denied the power, in 1789, had the best of the argument."

Not all Webster's fellow Whigs agreed; Charles Francis Adams called Webster's ideas "ominous to the stability of our institutions" and inconsistent with the Framers' vision. But the Whigs broadly supported checks on the president's removal power and ultimately embraced the position that presidents could remove officers only with Senate approval. Yet they never enacted this position into law. And when a Whig, William Henry Harrison, won the presidency in 1840, he used the removal power *more aggressively* than his Democratic predecessors, filling offices with Whig replacements. As explained by Joseph Postell, a legal historian and one of the leading modern chroniclers of the period, "the Whigs and their ideological successors, the Republicans, eventually acquiesced to the [patronage] practice, eventually becoming more adept at it than the Democrats."

• • •

In addition to asserting the presidential removal power more aggressively than had his predecessors, President Jackson more boldly asserted authority over the executive branch. In particular, he applied presidential power to undercut the Second Bank of the United States. This in turn prompted a Whig backlash.

The chartering of a national bank was a significant source of political conflict not only in the Jackson administration but throughout the early years of the Republic. The First Bank of the United States had been chartered for a term of twenty years in 1791, at the urging of Alexander Hamilton, the treasury secretary. Thomas Jefferson, James Madison, and Washington's attorney general, Edmund Randolph, opposed the bank's charter and argued that it was unconstitutional. In 1811, Congress failed to renew the charter and it expired. The bank's facilities and most of its stock were acquired by Stephen Girard, one of early America's wealthiest men. Girard Bank was a leading financial institution until well into the twentieth century; it merged with Mellon Bank in 1983.

Girard Bank served as the principal creditor for the United States during the War of 1812. After the war ended in 1815, political demand grew for chartering another federal bank. The Second Bank of the United States was chartered for a twenty-year term in 1816. In 1832, the bank's president, Nicholas Biddle, worked to secure in advance an extension of its charter. He was aided by Henry Clay, the National Republican who was challenging Jackson for the presidency and who viewed the opportunity as a winning campaign issue. Clay and Daniel Webster secured the bank's charter renewal in Congress, but President Jackson vetoed the legislation—characterizing the bank as representing the "monied interest" opposed to "the planters, the farmers, the mechanic and the laborer." Jackson decisively defeated Clay to win reelection.

Jackson then ordered U.S. deposits withdrawn from the national bank. His treasury secretary, Louis McLane, refused. Rather than sacking McLane, Jackson appointed him secretary of state and named a new treasury secretary, William Duane. But Duane also refused to yank the deposits. And Congress had specified by statute that the treasury secretary, not the president, had discretion over whether to remove federal deposits from the Bank of the United States. Jackson bristled, arguing that "the entire executive power is vested in the President of the United States," and that officers such as the secretary of the treasury were "subject to the supervision and control of the President." Jackson removed Duane and named his attorney general, Roger Taney, treasury secretary in a "recess appointment" while Congress was away. Taney ordered that by October 1833, all U.S. funds be withdrawn from the national bank and redeposited in state-chartered financial institutions.

The Whigs were furious. Clay argued that the treasury secretary was for these purposes an "agent or representative of Congress," which had vested authority in the lesser officer, not the president. He introduced a resolution assailing the president's action as unconstitutional. Jackson responded with a "protest" reasserting the unitary executive power, vested in the president alone. Jackson ultimately won the fight. The bank was not rechartered, it struggled in the financial Panic of 1837, and in 1841 it dissolved. And the unitary-executive principle was strengthened.

• • •

The president's removal power came under a renewed challenge in the wake of the Civil War. In 1864, President Abraham Lincoln had run for reelection on a "National Union" ticket. His running mate, Andrew Johnson, was a Democrat from Tennessee. Johnson had been the only senator from a state joining the Confederacy not to resign his seat but to remain in Congress, supporting the Union. Lincoln was assassinated scarcely six weeks after being inaugurated for a second term, and six days after the Confederate forces had surrendered to the Union at Appomattox.

Assuming the presidency, Johnson supported quick readmission for the former Confederate states, with few reprisals—and few protections for the newly freed slaves. Johnson opposed the Fourteenth Amendment, which would enshrine civil rights for freedmen into the Constitution. On March 2, 1867, he vetoed the First Reconstruction Act, which congressional Republicans had crafted to order the readmission of Southern states into the Union.

Republicans were incensed. Congress overrode Johnson's veto of the Reconstruction Act on the same day. Also on the same day, they overrode the president's earlier veto of the Tenure of Office Act. That law was a direct attack on the president's removal power, which had existed since the Decision of 1789. It gave the Senate direct authority to reject or ratify removal of officers. If the Senate disagreed with the president's decision to remove an officer, the president had to reinstate him.

Johnson decided to challenge the Tenure of Office Act. In August, while the Senate was in recess, he suspended his secretary of war, Edwin Stanton, a supporter of congressional Reconstruction efforts who had been undermining the Johnson administration's policies from within. Johnson named Ulysses S. Grant, the war hero, as Stanton's acting successor.

When Congress reconvened in January 1868, the Senate rejected Johnson's decision. Johnson defied the Senate vote. On February 21, he notified Congress that he was again suspending Stanton and naming Lorenzo Thomas, adjutant general of the army, as interim war secretary. The same day, the Senate passed a resolution declaring Johnson's act illegal. Three days later, the House voted to impeach the president. Johnson survived the impeachment trial in the Senate—escaping removal by a single vote—after which Stanton tendered his resignation.

The back-and-forth between Johnson and the Senate was in no small part a tussle over the president's executive power itself. But after Reconstruction went forward and Johnson left office, things returned more or less to normal. One month after Grant was inaugurated as president, Congress amended the Tenure of Office Act, eliminating the Senate's purported power to reinstate officers dismissed by the president. In 1887, the act was repealed altogether.

Almost forty years later, in 1926, the Supreme Court opined that President Johnson had been correct and that the Tenure of Office Act had been unconstitutional.

In *Myers v. United States*, the Court considered the case of Frank S. Myers, a postmaster in Portland, Oregon, appointed and confirmed by the Senate to a four-year term in 1917. President Woodrow Wilson demanded Myers's resignation in 1920. Myers refused. The postmaster general then dismissed him from his position, on the president's order. The president filled Myers's post with a recess appointment. Myers sued for back pay.

The 1876 statute that created Myers's position supported his case. It provided: "Postmasters of the first, second, and third classes shall be appointed and may be removed by the President with the advice and consent of the Senate." The Senate had not acquiesced in Myers's removal.

But the Supreme Court affirmed the basic understanding of presidential removal power that had been established in the Decision of 1789. The Court declared: "The power to remove inferior executive officers, like that to remove superior executive officers, is an incident of the power to appoint them, and is in its nature an executive power." In an extensive discussion of the Tenure of Office Act of 1867, the Court opined that it was an unconstitutional "attempt to redistribute the powers, and minimize those of the President":

> It exhibited in a clear degree the paralysis to which a partisan Senate and Congress could subject the executive arm and destroy the principle of executive responsibility and separation of the powers, sought for by the framers of our Government, if the President had no power of removal save by consent of the Senate.

The Court held that "the provision of the law of 1876, by which the unrestricted power of removal of first class postmasters is denied to the President, is in violation of the Constitution, and invalid." Myers lost his case.

• • •

Aside from Andrew Johnson, the Republican Party controlled the office of the presidency from 1860 through 1884. But intraparty factions vied for power. One faction, led by Senator Roscoe Conkling of New York, supported the party's use of traditional patronage powers. Against Conkling's "Stalwarts" stood reformists who wanted to establish civil service rules insulating federal workers from party-machine politics and the electoral spoils system. The Stalwarts gave such reformists the derisive label "Half-Breeds," deeming them only half Republican. It was essentially a nineteenth-century version of the "RINO" epithet ("Republicans In Name Only") recently attached to moderate Republicans by more purist diehards.

Ulysses S. Grant became the first U.S. president to support civil service reforms. In 1871, Congress created the United States Civil Service Commission. Upon the commission's recommendation, and Grant's order, the federal government developed hiring and promotion practices, including civil service examinations. But Conkling and other congressional leaders who relied on patronage to build their political power base objected to the reforms. Congress did not reauthorize the commission, and it ended at the close of 1874.

Even as President Grant supported civil service reform, he gave Conkling a gift. In 1871, the president appointed a Conkling ally, Chester A. Arthur, as collector of the Port of New York. In that role, Arthur would oversee the New York Customs House, which meted out duties and tariffs on 70 percent of imported goods coming into the United States. It paid out millions of dollars in annual salaries to hundreds of employees. Under Arthur, the Customs House became Senator Conkling's patronage base.

Grant's successor, Rutherford B. Hayes, took up the reform mantle. Hayes sought to make merit appointments with examinations to screen out unfit candidates for federal posts. Hayes appointed reform-minded cabinet members. And they soon crossed Conkling. Hayes's treasury secretary, John Sherman—the general's brother who would later lend his name to the Antitrust and Silver Purchase acts—ordered an investigation of the New York Customs House. A report prepared by John Jay—grandson of the Founding Father and first chief justice—found gross mismanagement and abuse.

U.S. law at the time rewarded customs officials with a share of the proceeds when they discovered frauds. By gaming this system—against importing businesses that essentially had to pay off agents—Customs House employees were bringing in multiples of their official salaries amounting to nearly $1 million annually in individual earnings, in today's dollars. A portion of this bounty was kicked up to the Conkling machine. Workers were regularly redeployed at campaign time to assist in electoral efforts. Turnover was extreme, bribes were commonplace, and actual work tended to be minimal.

Hayes was unable to get traction for reform in a Congress that Conkling dominated. So he issued an executive order protecting federal workers from being required to perform electoral duties or make campaign contributions. Arthur and his deputies refused to follow his order—and refused the president's demand to resign. Hayes nominated replacements but was rebuffed in the Senate Commerce Committee, which Conkling chaired. Finally, in the summer of 1878, Hayes sacked Arthur during a congressional recess. His named successor, Edwin Merritt, was confirmed by the Senate, over Conkling's opposition, when Congress reconvened the next winter.

Hayes declined to seek a second term in 1880, and Republicans split over the preferred successor. Conkling and the Stalwarts sought to renominate Grant for a third term. Reformists rallied around Senator James Blaine of Maine. Others supported John Sherman. With no one able to secure the nomination, after two full days of voting, Blaine and Sherman threw their support behind the "dark horse" candidate James A. Garfield, the senator-elect from Ohio, who won the nomination on the thirty-sixth ballot. Garfield being in Blaine's reformist camp, the party added Conkling's old ally Chester Arthur to the ticket as vice president to appease the Stalwarts.

Garfield was elected, but mere months after his inauguration he was assassinated. His killer, Charles J. Guiteau, was a campaign supporter disappointed that he had not secured a plum appointment in Garfield's new administration. The assassination prompted a public outcry. Arthur ascended to the presidency, and became an unlikely champion of civil service reform. In 1883, he signed the Pendleton Act—named for Senator George H. Pendleton, a Democrat from Ohio—which reestablished the U.S. Civil Service Commission. The new legislation required exams for hiring, outlawed firing federal employees for political reasons, and outlawed requirements that civil servants pay fees back to party machines. Initially applying only to about one-tenth of federal employees, the Pendleton Act and its successors reach most federal civil servants today.

• • •

As this history suggests, the civil service reformers of the nineteenth century were "good government" advocates. They took important steps to weed out corruption and the overt politicization of executive-branch administration. In the Progressive Era, however, a new class of reformers emerged and sought to remove the growing federal administrative state from the political process altogether, preferring the rule of unelected administrators driven by scientific calculation.

Two years after passage of the Pendleton Act, a twenty-nine-year-old graduate student at Johns Hopkins University, Woodrow Wilson, published *Congressional Government: A Study in American Politics*, which started laying the foundation for what became the Progressive political movement. Wilson did not regard the Constitution's separation of powers and its system of checks and balances as essential guarantors of liberty, but rather as a "radical defect" in the founding document. In his view, effective government required vesting political authority in a single locus, so that a single decision maker could "decide at once and with conclusive authority what shall be done."

Two years later, in 1887, Congress passed the Interstate Commerce Act, establishing the Interstate Commerce Commission as the first "independent" federal agency, tasked with railroad regulation. As discussed in the previous chapter, the commission at first had limited powers; it certainly lacked the broad rulemaking authority that would later be given to such agencies. But young Professor Wilson—then a newly minted PhD teaching at Bryn Mawr—envisioned more. In an influential article published that year in *Political Science Quarterly*, "The Study of Administration," Wilson argued that policymakers needed to engage in "administrative study" to fix the "problem" of "meddlesome" public opinion. "The field of administration is a field of business," he wrote. "It is removed from the hurry and strife of politics."

On one level, Wilson's view was doubtless correct. There was great risk in permitting political operatives to seize patronage jobs—for example, as customs agents collecting import duties—and essentially extract public wealth to entrench their political positions. But in trying to draw a line between popular sovereignty and efficient administration, Wilson seemed to veer toward an administrative state altogether immune from political control. He argued that it was "harder for democracy to organize administration than for monarchy," and saw this as the central problem for the modern state.

Wilson may well have been right about the relative inefficacy of administration under democracy, but his preferred solution was in essence to turn the constitutional design on its head. On the one hand, there was an echo of the Founding Fathers' worries about mob rule in Wilson's lament about the "unphilosophical bulk of mankind." And when he asserted that the purpose of modern government was "to prevent" the excesses of "popular sovereignty," his argument paralleled James Madison's concern that "democracies have ever been spectacles of turbulence and contention." But whereas Madison thought the remedy for democratic excess lay in limited government that divided and checked power, Wilson called for the inverse. In Wilson's worldview, "large powers and unhampered discretion" were "the indispensable conditions of responsibility."

Notwithstanding this assertive view of concentrated federal government power, when Wilson sought the presidency as the Democratic Party's nominee in 1912—after serving as president of Princeton and governor of New Jersey— he staked out a position as the moderate reformer in the race. To his right was the conservative Republican incumbent, William Howard Taft, who had used new antitrust authority to break up monopoly businesses during his term but who was viewed as too cozy with business for Progressive reformers. Staking out the more radical position to Wilson's left was Theodore Roosevelt, the former president now running on a third-party Progressive line.

The young Roosevelt had emerged on the national scene as chairman of the U.S. Civil Service Commission, serving under both Republican and Democratic administrations. He ascended to the presidency (in parallel fashion to Andrew Johnson and Chester Arthur) when William McKinley was felled by an assassin's bullet. In his nearly two full terms in the White House, he focused on civil service reform, busting up monopolistic trusts, establishing consumer protections under laws like the Pure Food and Drug Act, and creating new national parks out of the vast natural resources in the West.

But by 1912, Roosevelt had abandoned his earlier "trust buster" strategy and was arguing instead that "combination in business should be, not prohibited, but supervised and controlled." His new view was that the national government should "assume powers of supervision and regulation over all corporations doing an interstate business." The bombastic Roosevelt lampooned Wilson's "New Freedom" agenda—and its aggressive call to break up monopolies—as a hapless throwback to a bygone era of Jeffersonian individualism. Roosevelt had come to view the "dissolution" of monopolies as a "purely negative" remedy "of little permanent avail." He now preferred "administrative action" through a "Federal Commission" that would "furnish a steady expert control...adapted to the problem."

Wilson won the election. But Roosevelt's new vision carried the day.

In the first year of his administration, Wilson signed into law the Federal Reserve Act—the first major federal entry into the banking space since the charter for the Second Bank of the United States expired in 1836. Many leaders in both parties had rallied behind a perceived need for a central bank after the Panic of 1907, a financial crisis in the latter half of Roosevelt's second term in which a 50 percent drop in the stock market precipitated a series of bank runs. A broader crisis had been averted only after J. P. Morgan stepped in to shore up banking reserves.

The new Federal Reserve Act established a series of twelve regional Federal Reserve Banks that together could make loans to other banks and collectively serve as a lender of last resort. A seven-member Federal Reserve Board—appointed by the president but with staggered terms, and independent of presidential authority—would oversee the operations of the twelve regional banks. (The Federal Open Market Committee, which has the vast powers associated with the modern Fed, was created in an expansion of the original act in 1933, during the early days of the New Deal.)

Less than a year later, Wilson signed into law the Federal Trade Commission Act, which at least partially realized Roosevelt's big-government vision for dealing with monopolies. In place of the old Bureau of Corporations, a division of the Department of Commerce and Labor, the new Federal Trade Commission (FTC) was a five-member bipartisan board independent of presidential control. The commission had direct regulatory authority that sidestepped the slow method of enforcing antitrust actions through the courts, although it lacked formal rulemaking authority until 1975. The commission was empowered to police "unfair methods of competition" and a host of new areas outlined in the Clayton Antitrust Act, which was signed into law by Wilson the following month.

• • •

The Federal Trade Commission would come under constitutional challenge in the first term of Teddy Roosevelt's cousin, Franklin. FDR was upset with William Humphrey, a holdover appointed to the commission by Roosevelt's predecessor, Herbert Hoover. Roosevelt viewed Humphrey as unsympathetic to his New Deal agenda and asked for his resignation. Humphrey refused. Roosevelt then made his request a demand: "Effective as of this date, you are hereby removed from the office of Commissioner of the Federal Trade Commission." But Humphrey kept coming to work.

The Federal Trade Commission Act allowed Senate-confirmed commissioners to be removed by the president only for "inefficiency, neglect of duty, or malfeasance in office." Roosevelt made no such claim against Humphrey. But was the act's rule constitutional—or an abrogation of the president's executive-branch removal power?

Humphrey died before the Supreme Court heard his case, *Humphrey's Executor v. United States*. A unanimous Supreme Court handed down its decision in favor of Humphrey's estate.

Humphrey's Executor was decided in 1935, only nine years after the Court had reached a differing decision in *Myers*, where it ruled that an 1876 law limiting the president's authority to remove postmasters without Senate approval unconstitutionally impinged on presidential power. How did the Court distinguish these two similar cases? The Court emphasized that the holding in *Myers* applied to "purely executive officers." In contrast, the *Humphrey's Executor* opinion emphasized, the Federal Trade Commission was a "*quasi*-legislative" and "*quasi*-judicial" body. In the Court's view, the purpose of the Federal Trade Commission Act was "to create a body of experts who shall gain experience by length of service—a body which shall be independent of executive authority except in its selection, and free to exercise its judgment without the leave or hindrance of any other official or any department of the government." Without citation or any real analysis, the Court asserted that the "authority of Congress, in creating *quasi*-legislative or *quasi*-judicial agencies, to require them to act in discharge of their duties independently of executive control cannot well be doubted."

President Roosevelt was upset by the decision, which he viewed as a result of spite. The Court's unanimous decision in *Humphrey's Executor* came down the same day as *Schechter Poultry*—May 27, 1935. While each is predicated upon the separation of powers, the two decisions do seem in some tension on their faces. In *Schechter Poultry*, the Court decided that the sweeping legislative powers delegated by Congress to the executive branch in the National Industrial Recovery Act were an unconstitutional delegation of Congress's legislative authority. But in *Humphrey's Executor*, the Court permitted Congress to delegate quasi-legislative powers to an agency insulated from the control of the elected president. Somewhere, Woodrow Wilson must have been smiling at the latter decision.

• • •

Although Roosevelt lost the battle in *Humphrey's Executor*, he effectively won the war. Al Smith, the Democratic Party's nominee for president in 1928, had lamented that the government was "submerged in a bowl of alphabet soup," an allusion to the acronyms popularly used to denote the independent agencies and other government offices springing up at the time. But after Roosevelt's election in 1932, the alphabet agencies multiplied. His administration created more than a hundred agencies during his time in office, through statute as well as through executive order. Many of the independent agencies created during the early New Deal—the FCC, the FDIC, the NLRB, the SEC—are still among the most significant federal regulatory authorities in the modern era.

Humphrey's Executor remains the law of the land, but the Supreme Court may limit further incursions by Congress on presidential control over the administrative state—such as the unique structure of the Consumer Financial Protection Bureau (CFPB) highlighted in the dispute over the identity of its interim director.

In 2010, in *Free Enterprise Fund v. Public Company Accounting Oversight Board*, the Supreme Court considered the constitutionality of the Public Company Accounting Oversight Board. The PCAOB was an independent agency created by the Public Company Accounting Reform and Investor Protection Act of 2002, popularly known as the Sarbanes-Oxley Act. Unlike other independent agencies, the PCAOB was appointed not by the president with the advice and consent of the Senate, but by another independent agency, the Securities and Exchange Commission (SEC).

Like FTC commissioners, SEC commissioners cannot be removed from office by the president except for cause, i.e., "inefficiency, neglect of duty, or malfeasance in office." And under Sarbanes-Oxley's terms, the PCAOB board members could be removed only "for good cause shown" by the SEC. The Court determined that this "dual layer" of insulation from the elected president unconstitutionally infringed on the president's constitutional powers. The Court thus struck down the law's provision that PCAOB board members could not be removed by the president.

The CFPB's idiosyncratic structure—insulating not a commission but a single administrator from presidential removal, and insulating the agency's budget from congressional oversight—is also being challenged in the courts. The Ninth Circuit and the D.C. Circuit federal courts of appeals upheld the agency's structure as constitutional. But at the D.C. Circuit, Judge Brett Kavanaugh (now a Supreme Court justice) dissented from the broader court's holding. He argued that in vesting authority with a single director rather than a commission, the Dodd-Frank Wall Street Reform and Consumer Protection Act went beyond *Humphrey's Executor* and unconstitutionally infringed on the president's removal power—a position the Trump administration's Justice Department, and now the CFPB itself, have argued in parallel litigation.

On September 6, 2019, in *Collins v. Mnuchin*, the full Fifth Circuit Court of Appeals ruled that the structure of the Federal Housing Finance Agency (FHFA) was unconstitutional. The FHFA was established during the 2008 financial crisis to oversee the assets of the insolvent Federal National Mortgage Association and Federal Home Loan Mortgage Corporation, the government-sponsored enterprises popularly known as Fannie Mae and Freddie Mac. Like the CFPB, the FHFA vests full authority in a single director not removable by the president. The court found that the "for-cause removal protection" of the FHFA director "infringes Article II" by limiting the presidential removal power. The court emphasized that *Humphrey's Executor* applied "only to multi-member bodies of experts" and that a "single agency director lacks the checks inherent in multilateral decision making and is more difficult for the President to influence."

The courts of appeals are thus split on the question of whether Congress can insulate a single director from removal by the president. The Supreme Court is currently considering the question, in *Seila Law LLC v. Consumer Financial Protection Bureau*—which is likely to be decided in June 2020, after this book has gone to print. But even if the Court agrees with the Fifth Circuit and strikes down this structure, it is much less likely to be willing to reverse course and overturn the broader independent-agency structure upheld in *Humphrey's Executor* almost eighty-five years ago. Which means that Congress can keep creating unelected commissions that act as quasi-legislatures promulgating rules and as quasi-judiciaries interpreting them. And individuals and organizations will have to navigate a thicker alphabet soup.

CHAPTER 3

Judging Without the Judiciary

John Rapanos, a real estate developer in Midland, Michigan, settled a legal dispute with the federal government in December 2008. He'd been battling the feds for almost twenty years.

The son of Greek immigrants, Rapanos had pulled up some trees from a fifty-four-acre parcel of land, back in April 1989. He used sand to backfill the holes left by the removed tree stumps.

Rapanos owned the land. But he didn't have a permit for his work. Federal regulators accused him of violating the Clean Water Act. They filed civil and criminal charges. The potential penalties were steep: more than five years in prison and millions of dollars in civil and criminal fines.

The Clean Water Act was enacted by Congress in 1972. It forbids the "discharge of a pollutant" into "navigable waters." It goes on to define "navigable waters" as "the waters of the United States, including the territorial seas."

Mr. Rapanos's land was eleven miles away from the nearest body of navigable water. But it was sometimes water-saturated.

That soil saturation mattered, because the Army Corps of Engineers had promulgated regulations interpreting "navigable waters" to include "interstate wetlands," including those that "are or would be used as habitat" by migratory birds. Subsequent regulations held that "the waters of the United States" extended to "ephemeral streams" and "drainage ditches," or any area of soil in which rainwater or drainage might leave "the presence of litter and debris."

Under what authority had a federal agency derived such a broad reading of "the waters of the United States"? The agency interpretation was certainly not clearly implied by the statute's actual text. And for more than a century up to the passage of the Clean Water Act, the Supreme Court had interpreted "navigable waters of the United States" to mean "navigable in fact"—i.e., waters that "are used or are susceptible of being used in their ordinary condition as highways for commerce over which trade and travel are or may be conducted in the customary modes of trade and travel on water." In other words, "navigable waters" means, quite sensibly, boating throughways. That's a far cry from soil that sometimes is saturated and capable of gathering litter in a rainstorm, or that might on occasion drain into a waterway eleven miles away.

The Army Corps had originally interpreted "waters of the United States" in the Clean Water Act consistent with the way the Supreme Court had traditionally defined it for the last hundred years—applying only to waters that were "navigable in fact." But that interpretation was challenged in a lawsuit filed by the Natural Resources Defense Council. In 1975, the government settled that lawsuit and accepted a shockingly expansive redefinition. Under the government's new reading, the Clean Water Act "asserted federal jurisdiction over the nation's waters to the maximum extent permissible under the Commerce Clause of the Constitution."

Such moves have been enabled by the rise of the modern administrative state. The courts have abdicated the interpretation of laws—the core function of the judicial branch—to unelected agency officials. Unsurprisingly, those officials have acquired more power by stretching the plain meaning of the laws enacted by Congress beyond recognition.

This judicial abdication meant trouble for Mr. Rapanos. In a 1985 decision, *United States v. Riverside Bayview*, the Supreme Court had upheld the Army Corps' "wetlands" interpretation of the Clean Water Act's very different text.

Rapanos's initial criminal prosecution ended in a mistrial. The government prosecuted him again. A jury convicted him this time on two felony counts—but the federal district judge trying the case overturned his conviction. A federal appellate court reversed that judge's decision. The case went up and down in the courts two more times. Ultimately, Rapanos was fined $5,000 and given three years' probation.

But resolving the criminal case didn't end things for Rapanos. He still faced potentially millions of dollars in civil fines, which can be levied on top of criminal penalties. He continued to dispute the civil case, which also went before the U.S. Supreme Court. The Court vacated the initial judgment against Rapanos in June 2006. That didn't end things; it just sent the case back down to the trial court, again, to start over, again. Two years later, Rapanos finally gave up fighting. He settled with the government for almost $1 million, without admitting any wrongdoing.

• • •

In the early American republic, the federal courts reviewed executive-branch actions for compliance with congressional statutes *de novo*—that is, "anew," without any deference to the executive's interpretation. From a rebuke of the president exceeding congressionally delegated embargo powers in the early nineteenth century, to reviews of the new Interstate Commerce Commission exercising authority to regulate railroads in the early twentieth century, the Supreme Court made clear that it was tasked with determining the degree to which the executive branch was following the language of the laws passed by Congress. The executive branch was afforded no special "deference" in interpreting the laws that granted and circumscribed its authority.

This approach is illustrated in a Supreme Court case decided in 1804, against the backdrop of the Napoleonic Wars. Congress passed a law in 1799 empowering the government to seize any U.S. vessel sailing to any French port. But President John Adams issued a broader order, transmitted to the secretary of the navy. Under that presidential directive, a *Danish* vessel sailing *away* from a French port was captured on the high seas. In *Little v. Barreme*, the Supreme Court determined that this seizure was illegitimate, since Congress's statute only authorized grabbing *American* boats that were sailing *to* a port in France.

In time, however, executive-branch agencies assumed their own form of adjudicatory power. An early example concerns the distribution of federal lands. At first the Treasury Department, and later the Land Department (beginning in 1812) and the Department of the Interior (beginning in 1849) were given administrative responsibility to resolve disputed claims to government land grants. Matters resolved administratively would be appealable to federal courts. The courts broadly followed a standard of review similar to what was applied in trial courts overseeing ordinary disputes. Disputed questions of law—such as challenges to jurisdiction—were reviewed *de novo*. In factual disputes, on the other hand, courts deferred to the determinations of the trier of fact—in this case, the Land Department or other agency. Courts thus focused their review on what judges are trained to do—assess legal claims—while deferring to decision makers closest to the dispute to make judgment calls on the facts.

These disputes were far simpler to adjudicate than later claims made by the more extensive administrative state. But the early courts regularly handled legal challenges to administrative decision making long before passage of the Interstate Commerce Act of 1887.

The 1906 Hepburn Act, as noted earlier, vested the Interstate Commerce Commission with new rate-setting and adjudicatory powers. Before its enactment, the law stalled in the Senate because of concerns about constitutional constraints on agency powers and the scope of judicial review over the commission's decisions. Legislators eventually compromised on ambiguous language that left the scope of judicial review unclear.

In a series of cases at the turn of the century, before the Hepburn Act came into force, the Supreme Court had taken to scrutinizing the *substantive* basis of ICC decisions, which angered government leaders in Theodore Roosevelt's administration. The Court subsequently reversed course and returned to its more traditional practice. In *Interstate Commerce Commission v. Illinois Central Railroad* (1910), the Court reserved the right to review *de novo* "all pertinent questions as to whether [an] administrative order is within the scope of the delegated authority" under the statute, but it would not review "whether the administrative power has been wisely exercised." Instead, it would grant discretion to the agency's factual determinations.

· · ·

Progressives eventually attacked the fact/law distinction upon which the traditional standards of judicial review were predicated. In 1927, a Harvard lecturer named John Dickinson published an influential book, *Administrative Justice and the Supremacy of Law in the United States*, which argued that questions of fact and law "are not two mutually exclusive kinds of questions." As the Roosevelt administration launched the New Deal, it seized upon Dickinson's analysis to reconceptualize as factual questions issues that had previously been deemed questions of law—and to begin a new push for full-throated administrative discretion. As described by James M. Landis, a Harvard law professor and the second chairman of President Roosevelt's Securities and Exchange Commission, the administration's regulatory goals "could not be achieved" without forestalling the "intermittent intervention of the judicial process."

As FDR filled the Supreme Court with justices predisposed to support his administrative-state vision, the Court began embracing the new deference to agency decision making, even when those decisions involved legal interpretations. Three decisions in the early 1940s charted a new course. They considered how the administrative state characterized (1) a railroad that produced coal for its own use, (2) "newsboys" who delivered papers for a large publishing company, and (3) employees who stayed on site at a packing plant after hours to serve as fire marshals.

In 1941, in *Gray v. Powell*, the Supreme Court considered a case arising under the Bituminous Coal Act of 1937. The Seaboard Air Line Railway Company sought to avoid a 19.5 percent tax under the act, based on a statutory provision that exempted companies that were both "producers" and "consumers" of coal. Seaboard clearly consumed coal in its railroad operations. Seaboard also leased lands and equipment and hired a contractor that delivered coal, for its own exclusive use. Nevertheless, the Roosevelt Department of Labor determined that the company was not a coal "producer" and thus was not exempt from the tax.

Gray v. Powell is less notable for its holding against Seaboard than for the breadth of its logic. The Court's majority opined:

> Where as here a determination has been left to an administrative body, this delegation will be respected and the administrative conclusion left untouched.... Although we have here no dispute as to the evidentiary facts, that does not permit a court to substitute its judgment for that of the Director.

Three justices dissented: "There are limits to which administrative officers and courts may appropriately go in reconstructing a statute so as to accomplish aims which the legislature might have had but which the statute itself, and its legislative history, do not disclose."

The author of the *Gray* dissent, Justice Owen Roberts, would find himself dissenting again three years later in *National Labor Relations Board v. Hearst*. This case too hinged on a rather straightforward legal question. The Hearst Corporation contracted with newsboys who delivered its papers. But were these newsboys "employees" under the National Labor Relations Act of 1935, subject to the authority of the National Labor Relations Board (NLRB)—or were they independent contractors?

Rather than answering this question directly, the Court deferred to the NLRB's interpretation sweeping the newsboys under its authority. The Court acknowledged that "questions of statutory interpretation...are for the courts to resolve." But the Court decided that "where the question is one of specific application of a broad statutory term in a proceeding in which the agency administering the statute must determine it initially, the reviewing court's function is limited." Justice Roberts objected: "The question of who is an employee...is a question of the meaning of the Act and, therefore, is a judicial and not an administrative question."

A little more than seven months after *Hearst*, the Supreme Court decided another labor-law case arising under a different New Deal–era statute, the Fair Labor Standards Act of 1938. *Skidmore v. Swift* involved the interpretation of the new law's overtime rules.

Swift & Company maintained a packing plant in Fort Worth, Texas. Some employees who were part of the plant's fire-response team alternately stayed on the company premises for about half the nights of the week, in addition to their forty-hour workweek, in case of a fire alarm. Unless an alarm rang, these employees were permitted to sleep or spend their time in leisure. In addition to their weekly pay, the employees received fixed wages any time they had to respond to an alarm. Such alarms were rare; no fire occurred during the period over which seven employees sued their employer for back overtime pay, seeking extra compensation for the time they were on premises under this arrangement.

The text of the Fair Labor Standards Act required that employers pay an employee "at a rate not less than one and one-half times the regular rate at which he is employed" for "his employment in excess" of the maximum hours prescribed under the law. Neither packing-plant work nor fire-marshal duties were exempted from the act's maximum-hour and overtime-pay requirements. The statute defined "employ" simply as "to suffer or permit to work." Did the sleep and lounging around while on site, in case of an alarm, fit under this definition?

In his short decision for the Court in *Skidmore*, Justice Robert Jackson did not attempt to parse the statutory language and apply it to the facts of the case, which at least arguably seemed to lie outside the situations contemplated in the act itself. Instead, the Court's decision proclaimed that there was "no principle of law found either in the statute or in Court decisions [that] *precludes* waiting time from also being working time." And rather than interpret the statute on its own, the Court relied on the determination of the administrator of the Wage and Hour Division of the Department of Labor—a position established under the act to administer Congress's fair-wage-and-hour program.

The Court's opinion observed that Congress had not asked the courts to defer to the administrator's judgment in the statute itself. And it acknowledged that "rulings of this Administrator are not reached as a result of hearing adversary proceedings in which he finds facts from evidence and reaches conclusions of law from findings of fact." Nevertheless, the Court decided that the administrator's interpretation, while not "conclusive," was "entitled to respect." The administrator had reached the conclusion that hours spent asleep or eating were not entitled to overtime pay under the act, but that all other hours "on call" were entitled to overtime. Without any real textual or logical analysis, the Court agreed to "respect" the administrator's interpretation.

• • •

Deference to agency interpretations of Congress's statutory language was ascendant in the Roosevelt administration and winning the day at the Supreme Court, but it faced fierce criticism from some quarters. Among the early critics was Roscoe Pound, the longtime dean of the Harvard Law School.

A Nebraska native, Pound had been an intellectual leader in the Progressive movement since its early days. But he had also long been skeptical about granting the executive branch the authority to act without being subject to legal challenge and judicial review. In a 1907 article in the *American Law Register*, "Executive Justice," Pound concluded: "Nothing is so characteristic of American public law of the nineteenth century as the completeness with which executive action is tied down by legal liability and judicial review." Even at that early date, Pound worried about the "recrudescence of executive justice." He argued that "powers which fifty years ago would have been held purely judicial and jealously guarded from executive exercise are now decided to be administrative only and are cheerfully conceded to boards and commissions."

In 1938, Pound authored, on behalf of the American Bar Association, a "Report of the Special Committee on Administrative Law." Pound argued that the bar should press back against the constant pressure of "administrative bureaus and agencies" to expand their jurisdiction, exempt from judicial review. The ABA report warned against the new "administrative absolutism" that it compared to "Soviet Russia," in which "there are no laws—only administrative ordinances and orders."

Notwithstanding this pointed language in the 1938 ABA report, Pound had been brought in to chair the special committee largely to *tone down* its rhetoric. The previous chairman, "Colonel" Ollie Roscoe McGuire of Kentucky, had emerged as a "one-man committee" in the view of the new ABA president, Arthur T. Vanderbilt. Having collaborated with James Montgomery Beck, former U.S. solicitor general, on an anti-agency polemic entitled *Our Wonderland of Bureaucracy* (1932), McGuire had written "a flood of wildly bombastic articles and speeches attacking administrative agencies" while serving as a member and then chairman of the special committee from 1933 through 1937. Sensitive to the political controversies swirling around the federal judiciary in the wake of President Roosevelt's court-packing plan, Vanderbilt hoped that the august Pound—who had recently stepped down as Harvard Law School's dean after twenty years in the job—would lend gravitas to the special committee's endeavors.

And in that role, Pound was largely successful. Beyond its criticisms of "administrative absolutism," the report of the ABA special committee also suggested reforms to rein in administrative abuse. First, it called for formal rulemaking, with publication of all rules and regulations—as opposed to the Roosevelt administration's practice up to that time, which involved ad hoc adjudications. Second, Pound's ABA report argued that such rules should only follow public notice, with the opportunity for comment from affected stakeholders and other interested parties. Finally, the report called for appropriately reasserting judicial authority over executive action.

Pound's ideas helped frame Congress's postwar effort to rein in the new administrative state. The first serious reform effort, the Walter-Logan Act of 1939, passed both houses of Congress but was vetoed by President Roosevelt. Named in part for McGuire's fellow Kentuckian, Senator Marvel Mills Logan, the bill would have created formal trial-type mechanisms for both rulemaking and adjudication in administrative agencies, appealable to "internal review boards." The bill also envisioned a robust role for the judiciary in overseeing administrative action and decision making, including in the realm of fact finding.

But even as Walter-Logan was being crafted in Congress, Pound was laying the foundation for a different approach—one that harked back to the old understanding of reviewing the administrative state's legal interpretations *de novo* but avoiding undue second-guessing of actual fact finding. In May 1938, Pound testified before a Senate subcommittee and emphasized that judicial review was essential for any administrative agency decision or action. But the principal purpose of that review was to make sure that the agency "kept within the limits prescribed by law with respect to power, and that its proceedings are in accordance with processes of law." In Pound's view, the "judicial tribunal" should not substitute for the "administrative tribunal" when it comes to "reviewing facts." Administrative fact finding should generally be upheld if reasonably supported by "substantial evidence."

Following the president's rejection of Walter-Logan, congressional critics of the new administrative law returned to the drawing board. The compromise proposal they eventually settled on was the Administrative Procedure Act (APA), enacted in 1946, some five years after *Gray v. Powell* and just two years after *Hearst* and *Skidmore*. The APA continues to frame the formal administrative law.

In keeping with Pound's 1938 ABA report, the APA established new procedures for administrative rulemaking, following formal public notice and comment. The APA also broadly adopted Pound's suggestion that the courts follow the old standards of legal review, reserving *de novo* review for legal questions while being far more deferential on questions of fact. Section 706 of the law specified that federal courts reviewing challenges to agency actions "shall decide all relevant questions of law, interpret constitutional and statutory provisions, and determine the meaning or applicability of the terms of an agency action." But as long as agency actions, "findings," or "conclusions" were "in accordance with law," courts were ordered not to overturn them unless they were "arbitrary," "capricious," or "an abuse of discretion."

•   •   •

The modern judicial approach to reviewing agency actions essentially inverts the longstanding schema, reestablished by statute in the Administrative Procedure Act. Under the pretense of "arbitrary and capricious" review, courts regularly engage in a "hard look" at administrative fact finding— though such "looks" are generally "harder" when administrative agencies deregulate than when they create a new regulation. But in interpreting the law—as specified by congressionally enacted statutes—the courts "defer" to agencies' interpretations, at least if statutory language is "ambiguous" to the lawyerly mind.

A twin pair of Supreme Court decisions handed down in successive terms in June 1983 and June 1984 established these new, inverted mechanisms for administrative agencies' judicial review: *Motor Vehicle Manufacturers Association v. State Farm* and *Chevron v. Natural Resources Defense Council.*

State Farm involved safety standards developed by the National Highway Traffic Safety Administration under the National Traffic and Motor Vehicle Safety Act of 1966. In drafting that statute, Congress gave the agency limited guidance. The law merely stated that safety regulations "shall be practicable, shall meet the need for motor vehicle safety, and shall be stated in objective terms." In putting together safety standards under such a broad mandate, the agency undertook about sixty early administrative rulemakings—and multiple policy reversals.

In the first year after the Safety Act's passage, the Department of Transportation mandated that all new cars include seat belts. Usage rates remained low, so regulators looked for new alternatives. For a two-year period in the early 1970s, the department mandated an "ignition interlock" device that prevented new cars from being started unless seat belts were fastened. But the starter-device mandate proved so unpopular that Congress overruled it in the Motor Vehicle and School Bus Safety Amendments of 1974.

Two other safety mandates became the focus of administrative efforts: installed airbags and automatic seat belts, each deemed "passive restraints" because they did not depend on driver or passenger action. In 1969, the Department of Transportation proposed passive-restraint systems, and then in 1972, after a series of revisions and amendments, mandated "full passive protection for all front seat occupants of vehicles manufactured after August 15, 1975." But when 1975 rolled around, the Department of Transportation put off the date of that requirement by a year. In 1976, the secretary of transportation, William T. Coleman, announced a new rulemaking process—and indefinitely suspended the passive-restraint requirement.

After Jimmy Carter, the Democratic presidential candidate, defeated the Republican incumbent Gerald Ford in 1976 and assumed the presidency, the new transportation secretary, Brock Adams, reversed course again. Adams issued a new rule, once again requiring passive-restraint safety mechanisms—this time, by 1982 for large cars and by 1984 for all new cars. Manufacturers would have the choice to use either airbags or automatic seat belts. A reviewing appellate court approved the regulation—finding it not to be "arbitrary and capricious"—just as a different court had approved the original 1972 mandate.

Following Ronald Reagan's defeat of Jimmy Carter in 1980, the Department of Transportation again switched its position. Near the beginning of President Reagan's term, in February 1981, his new secretary of transportation, Andrew Lewis, reopened the department's passive-restraint rulemaking. Two months later, Secretary Lewis extended the deadline for the large-car mandate by a year. After a notice-and-comment period, the secretary rescinded the mandate altogether.

Undoubtedly, the Reagan administration's shift in direction was initially prompted by economic factors. The country had entered an economic recession; the U.S. auto industry was struggling in the wake of oil-price shocks, and Congress had approved an emergency loan to Chrysler in 1979 to stave off the company's bankruptcy. The Transportation Department estimated that the regulatory requirement would cost the industry $1 billion to implement.

But Secretary Lewis also pointed to new facts not in evidence when Secretary Adams had issued his passive-restraint mandate in 1977. That mandate was predicated upon an assumption that airbags would be installed in 60 percent of new cars, and automatic seat belts in 40 percent. But by 1981, carmakers had announced plans to install automatic seat belts in 99 percent of all new vehicles—which meant that the "lifesaving potential of airbags would not be realized." Further complicating the issue:

> [T]he overwhelming majority of passive belts planned to be installed by manufacturers could be detached easily and left that way permanently. Passive belts, once detached, then required "the same type of affirmative action that is the stumbling block to obtaining high usage levels of manual belts." For this reason, the agency concluded that there was no longer a basis for reliably predicting that the Standard would lead to any significant increased usage of restraints at all.

The administrative agency also argued that "the high expense and limited benefits of detachable belts" might induce consumers to "regard the Standard as an instance of ineffective regulation" and thereby poison "popular sentiment toward efforts to improve occupant restraint systems in the future." Such concerns were at least somewhat understandable in light of Congress's 1974 action to overrule the Transportation Department's earlier ignition-device requirement.

This time, the Court stepped in to overrule the administration's action as arbitrary and capricious. The agency had erred, in the Court's view, in not assessing whether it would be feasible to mandate airbags, regardless of the seat-belt feature—or to disallow detachable seat belts.

But in fact there was substantial additional evidence, undiscussed by the Supreme Court, that mitigated against the view that the 1977 mandate would improve customer safety, on net. For one, the significant cost of complying with the mandate would increase the cost of new cars, which would reduce new-car purchases. A slowdown in new-car sales would affect not only industry revenues but also safety, as a higher percentage of consumers continued to drive older cars that were not subject to the government mandate, and lacked the automatic seat belts being installed in virtually all new vehicles. In addition, the evidence that airbags would deploy correctly was then still sketchy, at best—not to mention that they could create additional safety hazards for some passengers, especially infants.

The point is not that the Reagan administration was clearly correct in deciding to rescind the Carter administration's rule. It's that there was undeniably "substantial evidence" to support its decision. And the Supreme Court was interjecting itself as the finder of fact assessing the agency's interpretation of that evidence—rejecting any pretense of deference to agency expertise in the field.

Over time, the courts' "hard look" has increasingly turned "arbitrary and capricious" review of administrative-agency fact finding on its head. Not always, but usually so when judges look at administrative decisions to *rescind* regulatory rules once deemed appropriate, as in the *State Farm* case.

In 1985, the young lawyer who had successfully argued the *State Farm* case at the Supreme Court published an article in the *Harvard Law Review*, "Deregulation and Judicial Review," assessing the courts' new "quasi-procedural 'hard look' doctrine" which envisions a "substantive review" for "deregulation." The young lawyer, Merrick Garland, argued that courts *should* apply a stricter factual review to deregulatory administrative decisions than to agency decisions not to regulate in the first place or to promulgate a new regulatory mandate. Garland went on to serve as chief judge of the U.S. Court of Appeals for the D.C. Circuit, which hears most appeals of federal regulatory actions. And as political junkies and court watchers are well aware, President Barack Obama unsuccessfully nominated Garland to the Supreme Court in 2016, following the death of Antonin Scalia.

. . .

If modern judicial practice is to insert itself into administrative fact finding by giving "hard looks" to deregulatory decisions, it follows the opposite path when it comes to agencies' views of their own statutory authority. The 1984 *Chevron* decision undergirds the federal courts' acquiescence in agencies' aggrandizement of their own statutory authority.

Chevron, like *State Farm*, stemmed from an early Reagan administration effort to roll back Carter administration regulations deemed imprudent. The agency head leading this deregulatory charge, the new Environmental Protection Agency (EPA) administrator Anne Gorsuch, was a hard-charging former Colorado legislator with a predilection for wearing fur coats and smoking Marlboro Red cigarettes. (Her son, Neil, would eventually become a federal judge and later a Supreme Court justice, nominated by President Trump to fill the late Justice Scalia's seat—the one previously offered by President Obama to Merrick Garland.)

Among the Carter-era regulations that Gorsuch sought to roll back was a rule implementing part of the 1963 Clean Air Act, as amended in 1977. By that time, some but not all states had met EPA national air-quality standards. Congress had determined that states falling short of the agency standard had to develop a permit program for "new or modified major stationary sources" of air pollution, such as smokestacks.

The underlying dispute over how to implement this statutory mandate between the Carter and Reagan administrations was, as in *State Farm*, one centered on policy. But in court, the dispute centered on the definition of the term "stationary source."

Toward the end of the Carter administration, in August 1980, the EPA had reversed its earlier judgment that "stationary source" could be interpreted to apply to an entire manufacturing plant, not merely to a single smokestack. Under the prior EPA rule, a company emitting air pollutants was allowed to make changes to plant design—including adding new smokestacks—so long as overall emissions did not increase.

Such a "bubble concept" regulatory approach has the salutary effect of allowing companies to make efficiency improvements—boosting capacity—while not increasing overall air pollution. But environmental groups at the time objected. They preferred a system in which any new smokestack added to a manufacturing facility needed a government permit. The Carter administration's August 1980 interpretation implemented this policy preference, by reading "source" narrowly to apply to smokestacks rather than plants.

Five months after Anne Gorsuch was confirmed by the Senate as EPA administrator, the agency promulgated a new regulation returning the reading of "source" to its earlier definition as an entire plant. The Natural Resources Defense Council sued. And the Supreme Court, in a unanimous decision authored by Justice John Paul Stevens, essentially threw up its hands and said it would defer to the agency's interpretation of what "source" was supposed to mean.

In setting out its approach, the Court adopted a "two step" review process. If "the intent of Congress is clear," then an administrative agency "must give effect to the unambiguously expressed intent of Congress." But if a statute is "silent" on a "specific issue," or "ambiguous," then an agency has the discretion to interpret a statutory mandate by any "permissible construction." The Court decided that the definition of "stationary source" in the statute—"any building, structure, facility, or installation which emits or may emit any air pollutant"—did not evince a clear congressional intent as to whether the single-smokestack or whole-plant regulatory view was required. In the Court's view, the statutory language "simply does not compel any given interpretation of the term 'source.'" Because the Gorsuch EPA's interpretation was a "permissible construction," it was upheld.

The *Chevron* opinion itself makes clear that the justices hoped to avoid interjecting themselves into the assessment of complicated policy tradeoffs more appropriately decided by the elected branches. The opinion emphasizes that the dispute over statutory interpretation in the case "really centers on the wisdom of the agency's policy," and that "federal judges—who have no constituency—have a duty to respect legitimate policy choices made by those who do." For an administrative agency to "rely upon the incumbent administration's views of wise policy to inform its judgments" was wholly appropriate, in the Court's view. At least if the judicial branch is willing to allow Congress to punt hard policy questions to the executive, that view makes sense. There's little reason why *judges* would be better suited to figure out the best way to regulate pollution.

But because *Chevron* was framed as a question of statutory interpretation rather than policy assessment, it placed judges in the strange position of deferring the interpretation of legal language, in laws passed by Congress, to the executive branch. And this deferential posture was in serious tension with the hard-look review adopted just one year earlier in *State Farm*, as applied to deregulatory policy decisions. The *policy judgments* of administrative agencies are given tough scrutiny, at least when agencies are scaling back the regulatory state. But the *legal interpretations* of administrative agencies are given broad deference—notwithstanding that interpreting statutory language, rather than forming policy judgments, is what legally trained judges are best equipped to do.

• • •

The *Chevron* decision, of course, grants deference to administrative agencies only when a statute's terms are "ambiguous." But lawyerly types can often find ambiguity when there is none; Bill Clinton famously claimed to find uncertainty in the meaning of the word "is" during the deposition testimony that led up to his impeachment. And real ambiguity in statutes is unfortunately the norm rather than the exception. Congress regularly writes open-ended statutes without clear definitions, largely because punting the hard questions is much easier than deciding them. Rather than debating whether a regulatory scheme ought to apply to a smokestack or a factory—and having to make compromises to resolve disagreements—it's far simpler for legislators to "do something" to address a problem and leave the details up to the agencies to decide.

In one sense, leaving the questions of governance up to "the experts" rather than "the people" is the Wilsonian ideal—if one in tension with democratic and republican norms. But in practice, different presidential administrations with different policy worldviews seize on *Chevron* deference to shoehorn their policy preferences into action without having to go to Congress for approval, as was the case in the *Chevron* decision itself. As long as a policy shift can be couched in statutory linguistics, the executive branch can effect radical about-faces in policy on its own, inverting the legislative lawmaking in the constitutional design.

Consider telecommunications. In 1996, Congress amended the Communications Act of 1934 in light of the nascent Internet, clarifying that although providers of "telecommunications services" remained subject to a host of regulations under the Federal Communications Commission, "information service" providers were not. The Telecommunications Act of 1996 defined information service providers as those "making available information via telecommunications," such as electronic publishers—but it expressly clarified that its definition of information service provider "does not include any use of any such capability for the management, control, or operation of a telecommunications system or the management of a telecommunications service."

One might think that's rather clear—not ambiguous. And the FCC initially decided that cable companies were telecommunications service providers, and not exempt from FCC regulation as information service providers. After all, a cable company, like a traditional telephone company, is principally in the business of running a wire into consumers' homes. But that was the Clinton administration. In the first year of the George W. Bush administration—just five years after Congress had spoken—the FCC changed leadership, and changed course. Hoping to spur competition for broadband Internet capability, the FCC now decided that cable companies offering broadband were information service providers, after all.

The Bush team may or may not have been correct on the policy merits of deregulating cable companies' provision of broadband services, but the statute enacted by Congress had not changed. And in 2000, the U.S. Court of Appeals for the Ninth Circuit ruled that cable companies offering broadband services constituted a telecommunications service, not an information service. Nevertheless, when the inevitable litigation over the matter reached the Supreme Court in 2005, in *National Cable & Telecommunications Association v. Brand X Internet Services*, the Supreme Court rubber-stamped the FCC's revised view—albeit over a scathing dissent by Justice Antonin Scalia. Justice Clarence Thomas's decision for the Court majority invoked *Chevron* and deferred to the "expert policy judgment" of the FCC. The Court noted that the agency "is in a far better position to address these questions than we are."

In the wake of *Brand X*, the FCC continued to yo-yo its policy judgments from administration to administration. In 2015, under President Obama, the FCC reclassified all broadband service providers as "common carriers." As the Interstate Commerce Commission had required of the railroads—and like many a public-utility regulatory scheme—providers of Internet access were required to offer their services to all comers at a common price, rather than price-discriminating (i.e., charging discount rates to heavy users, like Netflix and other high-bandwidth streaming services). Just two years later, under an FCC now controlled by President Trump's chosen commissioner, Ajit Pai, the agency reversed course and repealed its "net neutrality" rule. Protesters howled—and actually surrounded the FCC leader's residence—claiming that the Internet itself was in serious jeopardy from the agency's choice. Yet whether the Obama or Trump appointees were correct on the merits of the policy dispute is somewhat beside the point, which is that the statute as passed by Congress had not changed.

Similarly, the executive-branch interpretations of the "waters of the United States" that ensnared John Rapanos have vacillated wildly from administration to administration, without any change in the language of the law enacted by Congress. As discussed at the beginning of this chapter, the Supreme Court vacated the civil judgment against Mr. Rapanos in 2006. But in doing so, the Court failed to reach any consensus on whether to accept or reject the government bureaucracy's interpretation of the underlying statute. Four justices followed a decision by Antonin Scalia that would have limited "waters of the United States" as defined in the Clean Water Act to "only those wetlands with a continuous surface connection" to bodies of water that are actually navigable. That's broader than the meaning of the statutory language as it had long been interpreted—i.e., waters that were actually navigable themselves—but it's at least reasonably circumscribed. Four other justices, however, joined a dissenting opinion by John Paul Stevens that would have affirmed the government's even broader wetlands definition. They relied on the Court's 1985 *Riverside Bayview* legal precedent. And Justice Anthony Kennedy, writing only for himself, suggested that a wetland could fall under the Clean Water Act if it had a "significant nexus" to an actual waterway—and that such decisions had to be made on "a case-by-case basis." Justice Kennedy's case-by-case standard would offer landowners like Rapanos no guidance at all.

In the wake of the Supreme Court's incoherent standard in *Rapanos*, succeeding executive-branch administrations unsurprisingly flip-flopped in interpreting "wetlands." Also unsurprisingly, this led to yet more litigation.

In June 2015, the Obama administration's Environmental Protection Agency promulgated a seventy-five-page "clean water" rule that further expanded the definition of "navigable waters." The district and appellate courts blocked its implementation.

Before the new rule could be fully litigated, the Trump administration came into power, with a differing view. In February 2017, President Trump ordered the EPA to review the Obama administration's new clean-water rule. The agency subsequently announced its intention to rescind the prior administration's interpretation. On September 12, 2019, the Trump administration announced that the Obama-era rule on the "waters of the United States" had been formally repealed.

Throughout this period of litigation and rulemaking, the operative language in the statute enacted by Congress in 1972 had not changed.

• • •

Although *Chevron* has served as a bedrock of modern administrative law, its rationale has been questioned by several justices, and the Court may reexamine its core reasoning in the not-too-distant future. Chief Justice Roberts and Justices Alito and Thomas have questioned *Chevron* to various degrees. Justice Neil Gorsuch—the son of the EPA administrator involved in the *Chevron* dispute—openly challenged *Chevron* when serving as a lower-court judge. He suggested that the Supreme Court's deferential doctrine allows "executive bureaucracies to swallow huge amounts of core judicial and legislative power and concentrate federal power in a way that seems more than a little difficult to square with the Constitution of the framers' design."

In 2020, dissenting from the Supreme Court's decision not to review a lower-court decision, Justice Thomas signaled his willingness to reconsider the *Brand X* decision, in which he had authored the majority Court opinion fifteen years before. Thomas wrote: "Although I authored *Brand X*, it is never too late to surrender former views to a better considered position." He opined that it was "regrettably" the case that the Court's prior position had led to "administrative absolutism" in which "agencies are free to invent new (purported) interpretations of statutes and then require courts to reject their own prior interpretations." And Thomas questioned whether the Court's position in *Brand X* was "inconsistent with the Constitution, the Administrative Procedure Act (APA), and traditional tools of statutory interpretation."

Even if the Supreme Court rethinks its approach in *Chevron* and *Brand X*, however, administrative agencies will still have significant freedom to draw their own conclusions—at least as long as Congress continues to give the executive branch a virtual blank check to develop substantive regulations. And unless and until the Court revisits *State Farm*, judges will still be able to subject deregulatory policies to a "hard look" review while turning a blind eye to most new regulatory efforts under a deferential standard more consistent with the Administrative Procedure Act's "arbitrary and capricious" standard—an approach that enshrines a one-way regulatory ratchet.

Moreover, in assessing administrative agencies' powers to regulate, it is important not to focus too much on formal rulemaking processes themselves. The formal process under the Administrative Procedure Act—with open notice-and-comment periods and extensive agency analyses—is onerous, albeit a much lower hurdle than passing actual legislation through a bicameral Congress and presenting it to the president. But the executive branch has a significant degree of freedom to force its will upon citizens and businesses without any formal rulemaking at all.

In recent years, presidents of both parties have regularly issued "executive orders" that reshape federal government policy from the White House. The most prominent example is President Obama's directive (and President Trump's reversal) on the treatment of millions of undocumented aliens, the Deferred Action for Childhood Arrivals, discussed in the introduction.

Courts have also generally deferred to executive agencies' interpretations of their own rules and regulations, though that deference has recently been narrowed. Administrative agencies thus write rules, enforce them, and interpret them—collapsing all government authority into a single nexus. In essence, unelected regulators often serve as lawmaker, policeman, judge, and jury.

The executive branch is thus able to effect broad policies through "guidance" and "opinion" letters spelling out its interpretations of underlying legal and regulatory regimes that often bear little if any relationship to the government's current position. And that's often enough, as most people will not follow Mr. Rapanos's example and fight a twenty-year battle against the federal government. A litany of harsh sanctions—including potential criminal penalties—spur many an ordinary business or citizen into compliance. This is the story of the next few chapters.

CHAPTER 4

Regulating Without Rulemaking

Matt Boermeester kicked a 46-yard field goal with 27 seconds left in the 103rd Rose Bowl, on January 2, 2017. His kick sealed an improbable comeback win for the University of Southern California Trojans over the Penn State Nittany Lions. Although Boermeester had college eligibility remaining, he was unable to return to school the next fall. Not long after his star turn in the Rose Bowl, the star kicker fell victim to the university's "Title IX" sexual-regulatory apparatus.

Title IX refers to a provision of the Higher Education Amendments of 1972. It prohibits sex discrimination in educational institutions that receive federal dollars. The actual law enacted by Congress contains a rather simple statement: "No person in the United States shall, on the basis of sex, be excluded from participation in, be denied the benefits of, or be subjected to discrimination under any education program or activity receiving Federal financial assistance." From that broad command, the executive branch has developed an extensive system of enforcement rules, including those providing for women's sports teams, which were created by a "policy interpretation" in 1979.

The scope of Title IX has continued to expand, without any changes to the underlying statute, and sometimes without any formal regulatory rulemaking either. That's what ensnared Boermeester.

The assistant secretary for human rights in the Obama administration's Department of Education, Russlynn Ali, sent a nineteen-page "dear colleague" letter to universities on April 4, 2011. It stated that the government now took the view that sexual harassment and sexual violence alleged by students were forms of discrimination under Title IX. The letter offered "guidance," setting forth the government's view of exactly how universities needed to revamp their disciplinary processes for handling any alleged offenses of this type. University administrators, heavily dependent on federal grants and student aid, immediately scrambled to reboot their systems to comply with Ali's letter.

In Boermeester's case, the Title IX process developed by his university can only be described as Kafkaesque. Not long after the Rose Bowl, Boermeester was accused of sexual violence. Such allegations can often devolve into "he said, she said" disputes, particularly among acquaintances in workplace or collegiate settings. But in this case, he and she said the same thing. The accusation had been made by a third party, reporting what his roommate said he thought he had seen, through his window, at night.

The alleged "victim" of Boermeester's assault, Zoe Katz—captain of the USC women's tennis team, and his girlfriend of more than a year—emphatically denied the charge. She tweeted in February 2017, "I am the one involved in the investigation with Matt Boermeester. The report is false." In July of that year, she issued a longer statement that was similarly unequivocal: "I want to be very clear that I have never been abused, assaulted or otherwise mistreated by Matt. I understand that domestic violence is a terrible problem, but in no way does that apply to Matt and me."

The university, however, would not take Ms. Katz's "no" for an answer. USC had been placed under investigation for its Title IX compliance by the Obama Education Department in 2013. In the university administration's view, informed by Ali's "dear colleague" letter, it had an obligation under Title IX to follow up on the complaint, however tenuous it was.

When Katz told university administrators that she hadn't been abused, the response was: "I'm sorry that you feel that way." After Katz sent her tweet calling the allegation false, the university's Title IX officer gave her a threatening warning: "You're jeopardizing and interfering with an ongoing investigation. You do that again, there could be consequences for you. Don't ever tweet anything like that again." So much for empowering sexual-violence survivors.

Boermeester was ultimately expelled.

The Obama administration's "dear colleague" letter did not go through any agency rulemaking procedures. But in that respect, it is hardly unique. Given that the judicial branch has traditionally given the executive branch broad discretion to interpret its own operative rules and regulations—and has made it hard to challenge informal "interpretations" that do not rise to the level of final rules—agencies regularly find it convenient *not* to go through formal rulemaking that might be subject to legal challenge. Merely pronouncing a viewpoint is often sufficient to induce the subjects of regulation to act in accordance with regulators' wishes—in no small part because the cost of intransigence can be so high. A university like USC, dependent on federal dollars, is in no good position to push back against the government's view. If students like Matt Boermeester are collateral damage, that's their problem, not the university's.

. . .

In 1944, the Supreme Court in *Hearst* and *Skidmore* granted administrative agencies broad deference in interpreting the statutes that give them authority. The following year, the Court considered a case in which an administrative agency interpreted its own regulation. *Bowles v. Seminole Rock & Sand* involved government price controls instituted during World War II.

Congress had enacted the wartime Emergency Price Control Act three years earlier. The law created an Office of Price Administration and gave its administrator the power to freeze prices and set price maximums during the war effort. In 1944, the Supreme Court upheld the price-control act as constitutional.

Under its broad authority, the Office of Price Administration in April 1942 issued Maximum Price Regulation no. 188, which froze prices for many sectors of the economy at their level the previous month. The agency administrator, Chester Bliss Bowles, brought an action against the Seminole Rock & Sand Company for violating the regulation.

Seminole Rock sold crushed stone. In March 1942, it delivered such stone to Seaboard Air Line Railway at a cost of 60 cents per ton, under a contract entered into the previous October—before the Japanese attack on Pearl Harbor. But in January 1942, after Pearl Harbor but before the issuance of Regulation no. 188, Seminole Rock had entered into another contract with a government contractor for future delivery of stone at $1.50 a ton. The government later maintained that Seminole could not sell any stone at a price higher than the 60 cents at which it had actually delivered its product in March. The company argued that the $1.50 contract price it had agreed to in January was its price ceiling.

Whatever the merits of the price-control scheme, it's hardly surprising that the Supreme Court refused to go against the government's position in wartime. And the government's reading of its regulation was the best one. The express language of Regulation no. 188 defined the price ceiling as the "highest price which the seller charged to a purchaser of the same class for delivery of the article or material during March, 1942"—and Seminole Rock had in fact "charged" 60 cents for the actual "delivery" of crushed stone "during" that month. The Supreme Court's decision upholding the government's position did allude to the "relevant interpretations of the Administrator," but also emphasized that the plain reading of the text "clearly applie[d]" to the case's facts.

Yet Justice Frank Murphy's opinion framed the Court's decision with verbiage that underpinned a sweeping discretion for federal administrators to interpret their own regulations:

> Since this involves an interpretation of an administrative regulation a court must necessarily look to the administrative construction of the regulation if the meaning of the words used is in doubt.... [T]he ultimate criterion is the administrative interpretation, which becomes of controlling weight unless it is plainly erroneous or inconsistent with the regulation.

Strictly speaking, the Supreme Court's "look" to the agency's "construction" of its own rule wasn't necessary, by its own analysis: if the text of the rule *clearly* applied to Seminole Rock, as the Court said, then the meaning of that text was *not* "in doubt." But even if the Court's "plainly erroneous" standard of review was not necessary to decide the case, its announced framework survived. By expressly making the administrative agency's own interpretation of its regulations the "ultimate criterion," the *Seminole Rock* case would implicitly empower administrators to play fast and loose with their regulatory dictates.

• • •

After handing down its decision in *Seminole Rock*, the Supreme Court repeatedly invoked it to defer to agency "interpretations" of their own rules and regulations. As Justice Clarence Thomas pointed out in a 2015 opinion questioning the doctrine:

> [*Seminole Rock*] developed a doctrine of deference that has taken on a life

of its own. It has been broadly applied to regulations issued by agencies across a broad spectrum of subjects. It has even been applied to an agency's interpretation of another agency's regulations. And, it has been applied to an agency interpretation that was inconsistent with a previous interpretation of the same regulation. It has been applied to formal and informal interpretations alike, including those taken during litigation.

In Justice Thomas's view, deferring to agencies' interpretations of their own regulations is a judicial abdication inconsistent with the Constitution's expectations of the judicial branch. The practice improperly permits an "accumulation of governmental powers" in administrative agencies. It "allows agencies to change the meaning of regulations at their discretion and without any advance notice to the parties." And in so doing, the Supreme Court's deferential standard "turns on its head the principle" underlying *Marbury v. Madison*, the seminal decision first invoking the federal courts' judicial review of other branches' decisions for constitutional soundness—namely "that the United States is 'a government of laws, and not of men.'"

When Justice Thomas referenced the Supreme Court's decision to defer to an executive-branch interpretation of its own regulation expressed during the course of litigation itself, he was talking about *Auer v. Robbins*, a 1997 case that involved the Fair Labor Standards Act of 1938 (FLSA). That law requires employers to pay higher-rate overtime wages to employees who work more than forty hours per week. The overtime-pay requirement applies, in the statute as amended, to public-sector employees. But the statute also expressly excludes from the requirement any "bona fide executive, administrative, or professional" employee.

The plaintiffs in *Auer* were a police lieutenant and several police sergeants who worked for the St. Louis Police Department. They claimed they were owed overtime wages—but the police department argued that as supervisory employees they were exempt from the overtime-pay rule.

In determining whether an employee was or was not exempt from the FLSA's overtime rule, the Department of Labor in 1940 adopted a "salary-basis test," essentially deciding that salaried as opposed to hourly employees fell under the statutory exemption. As codified in a regulation from 1954, the agency clarified that an employee was exempt from the overtime-pay requirement if "he regularly receives each pay period on a weekly, or less frequent basis, a predetermined amount constituting all or part of his compensation, which amount is not subject to reduction because of variations in the quality or quantity of the work performed."

Although the police lieutenants and sergeants in *Auer* received fixed salaries rather than hourly wages, they argued that they were nevertheless entitled to overtime pay. Their rationale? The police department's manual specified that various *disciplinary actions* for police officers—including sergeants and lieutenants—could result in docked pay. Thus, the sergeants and lieutenant argued, their compensation was "subject to reduction because of variations in the quality...of the work performed." And therefore, they claimed, they were not salaried employees after all.

Rather than addressing whether the Department of Labor regulation was consistent with the underlying statute, the Court simply invoked *Chevron* deference: "Because Congress has not directly spoken to the precise question at issue, we must sustain the Secretary's approach so long as it is based on a permissible construction of the statute." And rather than deciding directly whether the police officers' interpretation was consistent with the regulation, the Court simply invoked *Seminole Rock* deference—relying on the secretary of labor's interpretation, as expressed in a legal brief submitted during the litigation: "Because the salary-basis test is a creature of the Secretary's own regulations, his interpretation of it is, under our jurisprudence, controlling unless plainly erroneous or inconsistent with the regulation."

• • •

On the surface, the idea that an agency that developed a rule is best positioned to interpret it seems reasonable. But as Justice Thomas opined, giving the power both to craft and to interpret a regulation concentrates power in the executive. It's also an invitation to lawlessness. *Chevron* allows the executive branch to change the legal meaning of statutory terms without any redefinition from Congress—as we have seen in the context of regulating smokestacks, Internet providers, and wetlands. But *Seminole Rock* and *Auer* go even further and permit the executive branch to decide to change its own prior positions without any formal rulemaking at all. These doctrines enable the executive branch to make an end run around the requirements specified by Congress in the Administrative Procedure Act (APA), namely open hearings and notice-and-comment periods to formulate new regulations.

Hearings and comments shape the process for administrative rulemaking, and form the record for legal challenges that can be raised against final promulgated regulations. But not if agencies are able to evade the rulemaking process altogether. The APA specifies that the hearing and notice-and-comment requirements do not apply to "interpretative rules, general statements of policy, or rules of agency organization, procedure, or practice." And with courts deferring to agencies' interpretations of their own rules, it becomes all too easy for agencies to avoid the rulemaking process established by Congress and effectively to rule by fiat.

Unsurprisingly, when afforded this option, agencies began to take it. The Supreme Court issued its *Auer* decision on February 19, 1997, and only nine days later the Food and Drug Administration (FDA) placed a report in the *Federal Register* entitled "Development, Issuance, and Use of Guidance Documents." According to the legal scholar Richard Epstein, this was the "first full blown administrative account of the term 'guidance,'" a term nowhere found in the APA. The FDA's published approach specifies that its guidance documents "do not establish legally enforceable rights or responsibilities." But precisely because the agency has issued a guidance rather than a formal regulation, there's no ability to challenge the agency determination in court. Thus, a company under regulation would have to wait for a formal enforcement proceeding after the fact, knowing that courts are ready to defer to the agency's guidance as a regulatory interpretation. For a pharmaceutical company embarked on a multibillion-dollar drug development, there's simply no way to avoid following the agency's wishes.

Defenders of the deferential doctrines in *Chevron* and *Auer* typically invoke administrative agencies' expertise and the need for flexibility to adapt to changing circumstances. But such considerations are more applicable to the *policy judgments* of agency experts—which by congressional direction are to be given deference unless "arbitrary and capricious" (even if the Supreme Court has tended to mangle that command with "hard look" reviews of deregulatory policy changes). In contrast, interpreting *words*—the stuff of written regulations—is precisely the core competence of legally trained judges. And if regulators think judges' linguistic interpretations have led to a policy error, they can always go through a formal rulemaking process, under the Administrative Procedure Act, and change course with a new regulation. The point is that individuals and businesses need to be *on notice* of regulatory commands so that they can order their affairs and comply with the law. That course is consistent with the rule of law—and the transparent, considered process for drafting regulation that Congress has set forth.

By deferring to agency interpretations, in the absence of any formal rule-making process under the Administrative Procedure Act, the courts have invited the executive branch to create rules on a whim. Eschewing actual regulatory process, the executive branch can flip positions by mere "interpretive guidance." This practice has raised the stakes of presidential elections.

Indeed, there was a political undercurrent in *Auer* not discussed in the Supreme Court's opinion: placing more workers under Department of Labor supervisory authority was the policy position that many in the Clinton administration hoped to advance. In the wake of *Auer*, rules for overtime wages and hours became a political football, changing from one administration to the next. In 1999 and 2001, the Clinton Labor Department issued opinion letters advising that mortgage loan officers do not qualify as "executive, administrative, or professional" employees exempt from regulatory rules for hourly employees. The Bush administration, after a notice-and-comment rulemaking that revised underlying regulations, issued a letter in 2006 reversing the position. Four years later, the Obama Labor Department, without any further rulemaking, again reversed course and restored the Clinton-era interpretation. The Supreme Court rubber-stamped the change—though Justice Thomas pointedly observed, "If courts accord 'controlling weight' to both the 2006 and 2010 interpretations, the regulated entities are subject to two opposite legal rules imposed under the same regulation."

• • •

Beyond permitting flip-flops, the deferential standards that courts employ to review agency interpretations of their own regulations have empowered executive-branch officials to pronounce sweeping policy shifts, unimpeded by formal process or judicial review. Thus was the Obama administration able to retrofit Title IX of Congress's 1972 education law, which simply prohibits discrimination on the basis of sex in educational programs or activities, to meet its policy goals—without any notice-and-comment rulemaking process whatsoever.

As noted at the beginning of this chapter, the Obama administration's Department of Education employed a simple "dear colleague" letter to overhaul college and university practices for handling claims of sexual assault—much to the detriment of Matt Boermeester and many other individuals accused under evidentiary standards that give little protection to the accused.

Reasonable minds may differ as to exactly how universities should adjudicate sexual assault claims. Sexual assaults are sadly commonplace in modern university settings, given the proximate cohabitation of young adults—who have not-fully-formed moral compasses, raging hormones, and varying sexual mores, and who often consume substantial quantities of alcohol and other mind-altering substances. There's certainly a strong case to be made that colleges and universities should develop processes for adjudicating assault claims to help create a safe environment for students and employees, and that such processes need not afford the accused individuals the full panoply of protections that criminal defendants are offered in criminal trials—just as employers should not be required to afford full criminal-law protections to employees accused of misconduct before making termination decisions.

The point here, though, isn't where the line should be drawn in formulating this or that adjudicating procedure on a university campus. It's *who* should be drawing that line. If Congress wants to condition its funding of educational institutions on having a certain procedure for adjudicating sexual assault claims, it certainly may do so—whether or not its judgment is wise. But on what basis should such judgment fall to the unelected assistant secretary for civil rights in the U.S. Department of Education? To be sure, this political position is appointed by and serves at the pleasure of the elected president, unlike the heads of independent agencies discussed in Chapter 2. And the president's nominee must be confirmed by the Senate. Yet the Senate's confirmation of a nominee in this role is hardly the equivalent of affirming any and all policy judgments the official might subsequently make. And the confirmation process has no role for the House of Representatives whatsoever.

The 2011 letter from Russlynn Ali was not the Obama administration's only foray into Title IX guidance-letter adventurism. On May 13, 2016, Ali's successor as assistant secretary for civil rights, Catherine Lhamon, issued another Title IX "dear colleague" letter jointly with Vanita Gupta, the acting assistant attorney general for civil rights in the Department of Justice. (Gupta was the third of three individuals "acting" in this role during President Obama's second term, none of whom were confirmed by the Senate.) The 2016 letter advised colleges and universities that under the 1972 statute prohibiting sex discrimination, they had to "treat students consistent with their gender identity even if their education records or identification documents indicate a different sex." Among other things, the letter prescribed that all school staff and contractors call students by their preferred pronouns, and mandated that schools' separate-sex housing, restrooms, and changing facilities be open to students based on gender identity rather than strictly on biological sex. Concurrent with the release of the Lhamon-Gupta letter, the Department of Education released a nineteen-page guidance document covering these issues for secondary schools.

As with the handling of sexual assault claims, how schools should accommodate students with alternative gender identities is a policy question about which reasonable people might disagree. Again, though, who decides how to answer the question? The 1972 statute enacted by Congress stated expressly: "nothing contained herein shall be construed to prohibit any educational institution receiving funds under this Act, from maintaining separate living facilities for the different sexes." And the subsequent regulations formally developed through notice-and-comment rulemaking expressly said that schools receiving federal dollars "may provide separate toilet, locker room, and shower facilities on the basis of sex," as long as "such facilities provided for students of one sex" are "comparable to such facilities provided for students of the other sex." Nothing in the statute or the formally adopted regulations defined "sex" as "gender identity." The unelected appointees in the Obama administration did that themselves.

The judiciary's deference to executive-branch agencies' interpretations of their own regulations enables the kind of concentrated decision making represented by the Lhamon-Gupta letter. A lower-level official in the Education Department had already pronounced on the issue of Title IX and gender identity the previous year. It was in response to an inquiry by Emily Prince, an attorney whose self-described focus is using "bureaucratic processes to push for greater justice" in the field of "trans rights." The official replied on January 7, 2015, with a three-page letter that advised:

> Title IX regulations permit schools to provide sex-segregated restrooms, locker rooms, shower facilities, housing, athletic teams, and single-sex classes under certain circumstances. When a school elects to separate or treat students differently on the basis of sex in those situations, a school generally must treat transgender students consistent with their gender identity.

The official supported this claim about the meaning of Title IX regulations by referencing a "question and answer" document from December 2014 authored by none other than Catherine Lhamon, the assistant secretary for civil rights.

The January 2015 letter noted that the Department of Education's Office of Civil Rights "refrains from offering opinions about specific facts, circumstances, or compliance with federal civil rights laws without first conducting an investigation." But that did not stop federal courts from embracing the letter as the department's official interpretation, and deferring to it under *Auer* in unrelated litigation.

In June 2015, a Virginia student sued the local school board for discrimination. The student had been "diagnosed with gender dysphoria, a medical condition characterized by clinically significant distress caused by an incongruence between a person's gender identity and the person's birth-assigned sex." The student identified as male. The school board had adopted a policy that the use of "male and female restroom and locker room facilities" would be determined by the students' "biological genders," while "students with gender identity issues" would be provided with "an alternative appropriate private facility." The student sued, and the U.S. Court of Appeals for the Fourth Circuit ruled in the student's favor—after it "accorded controlling weight" to the January 2015 letter, which it characterized as the Department of Education's "interpretation of its own regulation...entitled to *Auer* deference."

The story doesn't end there. As with the Department of Labor's wage-and-hour interpretations, the gender-identity determinations made by the Department of Education and the Department of Justice flip-flopped upon a change of administration. On February 22, 2017, scarcely a month after Donald Trump was inaugurated as president, the new acting assistant secretary for civil rights in the Education Department and the acting attorney general for civil rights in the Justice Department changed course. They withdrew and rescinded the "dear colleague" letter issued by their predecessors nine months before, as well as the January 2015 letter that the Fourth Circuit Court had given *Auer* deference. On March 6, 2017, the U.S. Supreme Court vacated the Fourth Circuit's decision and sent it back to the lower court "for further consideration in light of the guidance document" issued twelve days earlier.

• • •

Two days after the new Education and Justice administrators repealed their predecessors' letter, President Trump issued Executive Order 13777, which set up a process for regulatory reform. The president's order sought "the termination, consistent with applicable law, of programs and activities that derive from or implement Executive Orders, guidance documents, policy memoranda, rule interpretations, and similar documents." The attorney general, Jeff Sessions, issued a memorandum in November 2017 stating that the Department of Justice would no longer publish guidance documents and opinion letters—such as the one cosigned the previous year by Vanita Gupta—that "effectively bind private parties without undergoing the rulemaking process."

There is nothing to stop any future attorney general, in a future administration, from reversing this position and reverting to a regulation-through-guidance approach. But the ability to gain substantial deference from the courts will be more constrained. In 2019, the Supreme Court considered another case involving deference to administrative agencies' interpretations of their own regulations, *Kisor v. Wilkie*. Although it did not overturn *Auer*, the Court did take steps to rein it in.

James Kisor was a Vietnam War veteran. In 1982, the Department of Veterans Affairs denied his claim for benefits after he alleged that his wartime service had caused him to suffer from post-traumatic stress disorder (PTSD). He sought to reopen his case in 2006. In the second effort, he submitted a new psychiatric report, which the agency credited in granting his claim. But the department granted him benefits starting only in 2006, when Kisor relaunched his case; it did not give him retroactive benefits dating back to when he had filed his initial claim in 1982.

In ruling that Kisor's claim was not retroactive to 1982, the department cited its own interpretation of its own regulations. The Veterans Affairs regulation, developed with notice-and-comment rulemaking and recorded in the *Federal Register*, specified that reopened claims granted relief could be made retroactive if the individual claiming relief presented "relevant official service department records" in the second instance that had not been presented the first time around. In his 2006 petition, Kisor had presented, in addition to his new psychiatric report, two new service records showing he had served in Vietnam. The department claimed that although these *were* new "official service department records" they were *not* "relevant," since the earlier decision denying benefits had been based on skepticism of Kisor's PTSD claim, not his service in combat.

The department's position made sense. Since the government had never questioned Kisor's military service itself, it's hard to fathom how a document attesting to that service was somehow relevant in the context of whether his claim should be made retroactive. Kisor, however, sought a broader interpretation of "relevant." He argued that because his service in Vietnam was relevant to his claim—which it certainly was, albeit not to the department's decision denying it—his inclusion of the new documents in his resubmission should trigger retroactive payments. The U.S. Court of Appeals for the Federal Circuit decided that the regulation was ambiguous and could support either Kisor's reading or that of Veterans Affairs; so it affirmed the department's decision, granting it deference under *Auer*.

The Supreme Court laid down a decision in June 2019. All the justices were in agreement that Kisor was not entitled to retroactive pay, but they split on whether to preserve *Auer*. Four justices joined Elena Kagan's opinion upholding *Auer*; four justices joined Neil Gorsuch in deciding that *Auer* should be overruled. Chief Justice John Roberts joined Justice Kagan's opinion in deciding that *Auer* should not be overruled as a matter of *stare decisis* (Latin for "to stand by things decided"), the doctrine by which the Supreme Court defers to its own prior opinions. So *Auer* survived. But it was somewhat narrowed. Justice Kagan's opinion introduced the concept of "genuine ambiguity," purporting to say in essence that a regulation must really, *really* be ambiguous before courts should give deference to an agency's interpretation. Citing a footnote in *Chevron* suggesting that deference did not imply that courts should abandon the "traditional tools of statutory construction," she implored lower courts to "carefully consider" the "text, structure, history, and purpose of a regulation, in all the ways it would if it had no agency to fall back on."

To know whether this limitation, in practice, will truly cabin the scope of deference given to agencies' interpretations of their own regulations, we'll have to wait for yet more litigation.

CHAPTER 5

Criminalizing Everything

Bobby Unser had a celebrated career as a racecar driver: he's one of only two people to have won the Indianapolis 500 in three different decades. As one might expect, Mr. Unser was a vehicle enthusiast both before and after his retirement from competitive racing. Among the pastimes he enjoyed was riding snowmobiles at and around his New Mexico ranch. He and a friend were doing just that on December 20, 1996, and it nearly cost them their lives. The fateful events of that day also left Unser forevermore branded a federal criminal.

Unser's friend, Robert Gayton, was an auto mechanic but not an experienced snowmobiler. So they planned to keep their excursion short. They took their snowmobiles into the Jarosa Peak area of the Rio Grande National Forest—a legal place to ride a snowmobile.

The day was crystal clear. But about an hour after Unser and Gayton began their journey, they faced a severe "ground blizzard" generated by wind gusts. Exposed at 11,000 feet, with next to no visibility, the men quickly tried to get down off the mountain.

About thirty minutes after they began fleeing the blizzard, Gayton lodged his snowmobile in an embankment. Then, Unser's snowmobile broke down. The men hiked down the mountain below the tree line and built a snow cave for the night.

The next day, they continued hiking, and pressed on through the second

85

night. Around daybreak, they reached a barn with a space heater. They had trekked some twenty miles, often through chest-high snow, and endured vomiting, dehydration, hypothermia, and frostbite.

They were lucky to survive, but Unser's ordeal had just begun. When he went to the U.S. Forest Service to try to locate his abandoned snowmobile, agents informed him that in fleeing the blizzard he and Gayton had wandered into a protected national wilderness area. Although he had done so unknowingly and under duress, the agents told Unser that his was a "strict liability" crime requiring no intent or knowledge of wrongdoing.

Like Peter Gleason, the doctor we met earlier who tragically took his own life after being charged with a "drug misbranding" offense, Unser was not accused of violating a crime specified in a statute that had been considered and voted upon by Congress. Instead, he had run afoul of a regulation promulgated by the secretary of agriculture, to whom Congress had delegated broad authority to "make provisions for the protection against…depredations upon the public forests" and to regulate their "occupancy and use." In an all-too-common formulation, this congressional grant of authority then makes *any* violation of the regulation promulgated under the rule a criminal offense by default.

Unser fought the government prosecution. But the agents had correctly advised him that he was guilty even if he had not knowingly done anything wrong—and he was convicted. He was assessed a modest fine of $75—much less than it cost him to litigate his case. But although the punishment was a "slap on the wrist," he will always have a federal criminal record. And under the default grant of criminal lawmaking authority, he could have faced up to six months in prison and a $5,000 fine. Not an enormous stay in prison—but a very real depravation of liberty; and not a massive fine—but a very real hardship to the average American without the net worth of an IndyCar racing champion.

And unfortunately, the labyrinthine *Federal Register* also ensnares many ordinary citizens who unknowingly violate the law. As previously mentioned, an estimated 300,000 criminal offenses lie within the complex tangle of regulations; no one knows exactly how many for sure.

For Bobby Unser, the operative violation fell under Section 16(a) of Part 261 of the 36th Title of the Code of Federal Regulations. An experienced attorney, consulted before the fact, might have advised Unser about his legal obligation to stay out of a specific unmarked portion of a protected national forest. But most snowmobilers—even sports enthusiasts as well-heeled as Unser—are unlikely to consult attorneys before venturing out. And legal questions are unlikely to be at the front of their minds during a life-threatening blizzard.

Most small-business owners, entrepreneurs, and family farmers do not maintain a retinue of attorneys on call to keep all the federal regulatory ducks in a row. The biggest of big businesses, of course, have teams of in-house compliance officers who coordinate efforts with outside counsel to navigate the regulatory thicket. In a very real sense, then, the proliferation of federal rules waiting to trip up the unsuspecting violator serves as a regulatory barrier to entry, protecting big businesses against upstart competitors. Those small upstarts typically lack the wherewithal to hire top-flight attorneys to fight back.

· · ·

America's Founding Fathers were well aware of the dangers that lay in a proliferation of laws. In *Federalist* no. 62, James Madison argued that the Senate should serve to check against overly "mutable" laws and an expansion of the number of laws beyond what the populace could easily understand. Madison inveighed: "It will be of little avail to the people that the laws are made by men of their own choice, if the laws be so voluminous that they cannot be read." In Madison's view, "Law is defined to be a rule of action; but how can that be a rule, which is little known, and less fixed?"

Madison's admonition flowed from the Enlightenment understanding of the "legality principle," as characterized by the Latin maxim *nulla poena sine lege*, "there is no penalty without a law." By the time of the Enlightenment, the legality principle was thought to be a necessary adjunct to the Roman law maxim *ignorantia juris non excusat*, "ignorance of the law is no excuse." Thus, the Framers enshrined in the nation's founding document a prohibition of *ex post facto* laws—banning retroactive punishment. (Courts have limited this prohibition to the criminal-law context: *nullum crimen sine lege*.)

As Madison's exposition in *Federalist* no. 62 suggests, Enlightenment thinkers understood that merely enacting or announcing a law did not effectively put the populace on notice of criminality. The Roman emperor Caligula had famously posted his edicts high on building columns so that ordinary citizens were *not* able to read them.

The Framers' insistence that laws be known hardly implied that they needed to be codified with specificity: the principal crimes at the time of the founding were "common law" crimes handed down in judicial rulings over time, not crimes specified in any legal statute. But these were so commonly understood to be criminal as to put the ordinary citizen on notice. There were only nine major felonies under the common law: murder, manslaughter, rape, mayhem (intentional maiming), robbery, burglary, larceny, arson, and sodomy. Apart from the last, which is no longer deemed criminal under the Supreme Court's interpretation of constitutional privacy protections, these common-law prohibitions basically boil down to: respect other people's bodies and property. (They might also be deemed variants of the Decalogue's prohibitions on killing and stealing.) Various common-law misdemeanor offenses covered lesser versions of the same principles, such as assault, battery, and false imprisonment, as well as perjury and other frauds.

These common-law crimes all encompass conduct that is *obviously* blameworthy—at least if we carve out the old victimless sodomy laws historically deemed an affront to God. Indeed, William Blackstone, the natural-law chronicler whose *Commentaries* from the 1760s greatly influenced the American Founders, viewed the common-law crimes as "natural law" prohibitions that needed no authorization from the king. He distinguished these *malum in se* crimes ("bad in and of themselves") from *malum prohibitum* crimes ("bad by way of prohibition"), a distinction observed in British courts at least as early as 1496, under the rule of Henry VII.

If "bad because it's prohibited" sounds circular, that's because it is. The flip side of the legality principle is the English common-law maxim, "Everything which is not forbidden is allowed." But if too much is forbidden, no one can know for sure what is truly permissible. Which is precisely why Madison and other thinkers worried about making prohibitions so numerous.

In the Crimes Act of 1790, the First Congress specified thirty federal crimes, which included some ordinary common-law crimes that fell within federal jurisdiction as well as other offenses specified in the new constitution, such as treason, piracy, and counterfeiting. It would be hard to argue that anyone committing one of those core crimes would have done so through innocent mistake.

But that's hardly the case for today's 300,000 criminally enforceable federal regulations, covering some 80,000 pages in the *Federal Register*. Harvey Silverglate, a legal analyst and litigator, estimates that the average American commits three federal felonies a day. In general, that average American has no idea he is violating the law.

• • •

The distinction between *malum in se* and *malum prohibitum* gets a humorous treatment in the movie *Legally Blonde*, with Reese Witherspoon starring as Elle Woods, a bright sorority girl turned Harvard law student. She faces a colloquy with her criminal-law teacher for which she is unprepared:

> *Professor Callahan:* Would you rather have a client who committed a crime *malum in se* or *malum prohibitum*?
>
> *Elle:* Neither.
>
> *Professor Callahan:* And why's that?
>
> *Elle:* I would rather have a client who's innocent.
>
> *Professor Callahan:* Dare to dream, Miss Woods.

Miss Woods's rival Vivian Kensington goes on to answer the question, showing that she's done her reading: "*Malum prohibitum*, because then the client would have committed a regulatory infraction as opposed to a dangerous crime."

In some important respects, though, Miss Kensington also gets it wrong, at least if her desire is to win a verdict acquitting her client. To be sure, many a dangerous criminal might face a longer *sentence* than one who faces a sentence for a *malum prohibitum* offense—though that is hardly a certainty, if we're talking about a federal crime applying statutory maximums and the principles of the federal sentencing guidelines. But a client of Miss Kensington's facing prosecution for a *malum prohibitum* offense would also be unable to invoke certain longstanding legal protections that apply to a more traditional *malum in se* criminal defendant.

In the traditional understanding, convicting a criminal required the state to show a bad act (*actus reus*) undertaken with a guilty mind (*mens rea*). The latter requirement, *mens rea*, does not mean specific knowledge of criminality under the law, but rather "moral turpitude." In Blackstone's formulation, "an unwarrantable act without a vicious will is no crime at all." The notion as it had evolved in Anglo-American legal practice was that criminal law was different from ordinary torts punishable through private lawsuits: a crime was an offense against the broader society, punishable by the state, and carrying a degree of opprobrium. Whereas civil lawsuits could be brought against those who accidentally injured a neighbor, a crime required ill intent. "Even a dog distinguishes between being stumbled over and being kicked," observed the Supreme Court justice Oliver Wendell Holmes.

Traditionally, the "guilty mind" requirement served to insulate individuals from criminal sanctions for unintentional acts. Consider the 1877 British case *Regina v. Faulkner*. A sailor, Mr. Faulkner, burned up his ship when he struck a match that ignited rum in the vessel's hold. The appellate court overturned his conviction for arson, reasoning that there was no evidence he had actually intended to burn the ship or acted in "reckless disregard" of the risks of a rum-flame explosion. That's *even though* Faulkner was up to no good, as he had been pilfering the ship's rum at the time he lit a match in an effort to see in the dark hold.

There is no such protection in the modern understanding of *malum prohibitum* regulatory crimes, as Bobby Unser discovered.

So did Lawrence Lewis, who in 2007 became a federal criminal. Lewis grew up in the projects of Washington, D.C., and worked his way from a position as school janitor to one as the chief engineer at a military retirement home. One day the retirement facility under his charge began to flood. It was full of sick veterans. To mitigate their risk, Lewis diverted a sewage backup into a storm drain he thought led to the sewage treatment plant. Unfortunately, the drain instead led to a creek, which fed into the Potomac River.

Mr. Lewis's action violated a regulation that had been promulgated by the Environmental Protection Agency, under a broad grant of authority given in the Clean Water Act. Like the secretary of agriculture's regulation violated by Mr. Unser, the EPA rule did not require any showing of intent or "moral turpitude." As in Unser's case, the fact that Lewis was acting under duress counted for naught. He was convicted.

• • •

The rise of *malum prohibitum* "public welfare" offenses traces to the early twentieth century, in the Progressive Era. New York enacted landlord-tenant regulations that carried criminal penalties for landlords who had acted without any criminal intent. In 1915, the New York Court of Appeals affirmed the practice, arguing that standards applicable to "the prosecution of minor offenses" did not need to incorporate the mental-state standards that governed "infamous crimes."

The U.S. Supreme Court signed off on intent-free regulatory crimes in 1952, in *Morissette v. United States*. Mr. Morissette, a World War II veteran living in Michigan, operated a fruit stand in the summer and recycled junk metal in the winter. One day in the winter of 1948, he went deer hunting. He saw no deer, but he did happen upon a pile of spent metal shell casings, which he loaded on his truck and sold at a nearby farm for $84. Unbeknownst to Morissette, the casings were left over from U.S. Air Force bombing exercises. He was convicted of violating 18 U.S.C. § 641, which forbids "knowingly" converting government property for private gain.

Morissette testified that "he believed the casings were cast-off and abandoned, that he did not intend to steal the property, and took it with no wrongful or criminal intent." He was convicted nonetheless.

In affirming his conviction, the Supreme Court emphasized the historical *mens rea* requirement, noting that traditionally crime was "generally constituted only from concurrence of an evil-meaning mind with an evil-doing hand." But the Court observed that newer laws governing "public health, safety or welfare" tended to invoke not only civil penalties but also "criminal sanctions to be applied by the familiar technique of criminal prosecutions and convictions." The Court reasoned that these new laws were offenses against the "authority" of the state and that upholding these intent-free crimes was necessary to maintain "the efficiency of controls deemed essential to the social order as presently constituted."

The new "public welfare" criminal-law doctrine flipped the old understanding on its head. Whereas the old common-law crimes were *intuitively* criminal—injuring another person, or stealing or destroying someone's property—the new class of offenses involved conduct that was blameworthy solely due to a statutory command itself, and thus were all the more likely to trap the unknowing violator.

Over time, public-welfare crimes became the norm. In 2010, the National Association of Criminal Defense Lawyers and the Heritage Foundation studied every law with criminal penalties enacted by the 109th Congress (2005 and 2006). They found that 57 percent of the 446 nonviolent crimes proposed in the 2005–6 Congress lacked an adequate criminal-intent requirement. Twenty-three percent had no criminal-intent requirement whatsoever. In certain state jurisdictions, the problem might be even worse. The Mackinac Center for Public Policy in Michigan studied that state's criminal laws in 2014 and found that 59 percent of misdemeanors in the statute books contained no criminal-intent provision. And even though the jettisoning of *mens rea* protections was legally justified on the rationale that public-welfare offenses were "minor offenses" rather than "infamous crimes," modern American legislatures regularly enact intent-free felonies as well—including 27 percent of all statutory felonies in Michigan, by Mackinac's count.

Even when legislators have specified some form of criminal intent, courts have regularly embraced cramped readings of statutory text that do little to help morally innocent criminal defendants. Consider the way courts typically read the requirement that a defendant's act be "knowing." As a general rule, courts merely require that prosecutors establish basic intent to do some-thing—not an awareness of doing anything wrong. So to establish that a defendant has "knowingly filed a false report" in violation of a statute, a pros-ecutor need not prove that the defendant knew the report was false. Merely establishing that the defendant knew he was filing the report will suffice.

•　•　•

Individuals can be convicted of public-welfare offenses even when they do not affirmatively act. Traditionally, liability for "negative acts" was quite rare—as suggested by the law's insistence on not only a guilty mind but a guilty act (*actus reus*).

There have been some longstanding exceptions. In the law of criminal conspiracy, a defendant can be prosecuted based solely on the actions of a co-conspirator, so long as the government can show that the defendant was part of the conspiracy itself. A criminal defendant can be convicted of "felony murder"—and even subject to capital punishment—for another's unlawful killing, if the defendant participates in a common criminal endeavor, such as a multiparty robbery. But note that in each of these examples the criminal defendant is knowingly engaged in a criminal activity of some sort.

In general, then, a crime requires a criminal act. Ordinarily, a *failure* to act is not a crime: the criminal law generally does not impose any affirmative duty to help another person. Some states do impose a limited "duty to rescue," making it a misdemeanor not to summon law enforcement or aid if one sees someone in peril. But most do not have such rules, and our general intuition runs against them. That is why the two-part finale of the popular television series *Seinfeld* found humor in portraying its stars on trial for violating a "Good Samaritan" law by their inaction.

Again, however, the criminal law's general requirement that a crime involve an affirmative act falls away for *malum prohibitum* public-welfare offenses. Consider the case of Edward Hanousek, Jr. In the 1990s, Hanousek served as the White Pass & Yukon Railroad's "roadmaster," which meant he was in charge of "the safe and efficient maintenance and construction of track, structures and marine facilities of the entire railroad." Like Lawrence Lewis, Hanousek fell afoul of the Clean Water Act—in his case, for negligently spilling more than 1,000 gallons of oil into Alaska's Skagway River.

But here's the rub: the oil spill was caused not by Hanousek but by a subcontractor, Shane Thoe, who had backed a digger vehicle into a pipeline carrying heating oil. Thoe had been hired by the railway before Hanousek even started his job. Hanousek was not even at the worksite when the spill happened. And in moving the heavy equipment off the work platform, Thoe was violating express instructions.

Still, Hanousek was charged with and convicted of the "negligent discharge" of the oil. He was sentenced to six months in prison. (Hanousek was also indicted for a more serious felony offense, allegedly lying to Coast Guard officials, but acquitted of the charge by a jury.)

The Supreme Court declined to review Hanousek's conviction, though Justice Clarence Thomas wrote a dissent, joined by Justice Sandra Day O'Connor. Justice Thomas excoriated the lower courts for broadly construing as public-welfare offenses crimes with far more serious punishments than the "minor offenses" originally subjected to the strict-liability criminal doctrine. The relevant portion of the Clean Water Act for Hanousek's prosecution threatened violators with up to six years in prison and $100,000 *per day* for any violation.

But Hanousek's prosecution flies in the face of the traditional understanding of the criminal law in another way, too: it imputes to him, as a company manager, criminal liability for the actions of an employee. At the time of the American founding, and for a long time thereafter, an underling's act would not make a supervisor criminally liable unless the act had been done at the supervisor's "command or direction," or at least with his consent. In the seminal pre-founding case, the British courts in 1730 absolved a prison warden, Mr. Huggins, for the death of a prisoner under his care, since it was his deputy who had been actively in charge of the prisoner's care.

In Hanousek's case, the evidence presented in court did not show that the violation had been done at his command or direction or with his consent. Unfortunately for him, the general rule had changed in the aftermath of the New Deal.

In 1943, the Supreme Court considered the criminal conviction of Joseph Dotterweich, the president and general manager of the Buffalo Pharmacal

Company. Dotterweich was charged with "drug misbranding" under the Food, Drug, and Cosmetic Act—the predecessor statute to the one that later ensnared Dr. Gleason. Under section 301(a) of that statute, any "person" who introduced a "misbranded or adulterated drug" into interstate commerce was guilty of a misdemeanor. The state expressly defined "person" to include corporations. It did not specify any criminal-intent requirement—nor did it give any indication that the statute would make owners or supervisors guilty of the offense without evidence of giving a command or direction.

The government prosecuted Dotterweich, as well as his company, for the offense. Ultimately, Dotterweich's conviction was upheld by the Supreme Court. Justice Murphy issued a blistering dissent, in which he observed, "in the absence of clear statutory authorization, it is inconsistent with established canons of criminal law to rest liability on an act in which the accused did not participate and of which he had no personal knowledge." He acknowledged that imputing criminal liability to "corporate officers may be consistent with the policy and purpose of a public health and welfare measure," but insisted that such liability should attach only upon a clear and unambiguous statement by Congress in the statutory text.

But Murphy was in the minority. In short order, the courts imported the "vicarious liability" doctrine of tort law and created the "responsible corporate officer" doctrine in criminal cases. This doctrine holds supervisors criminally responsible for their charges' actions even when an employee is acting against an express order or command—as was the case of the contractor Thoe working under Hanousek.

• • •

There are far more rules on the books than anyone can possibly read or understand, and individuals who meant to do nothing wrong are held liable for violating them. But no prosecutor or agency official with enforcement power can possibly hope to enforce every legal violation. In the general case, prosecutorial discretion and its equivalents serve as important checks against state abuse of regulations.

But reliance on prosecutorial discretion as an exclusive backstop to protect the innocent is dangerous. Well-meaning prosecutors and agency enforcers will assess differently the appropriate rules to enforce among the plethora of offenses, and the sanctions to impose. Wide variance in treatment of comparable cases across jurisdictions is almost inevitable. In the worst-case scenario, granting ultimate discretion to enforcers of the law to choose targets among a populace committing three felonies a day empowers those unelected officials to play favorites—and to target enemies.

At the federal level, prosecutorial discretion has not prevented absurd prosecutions, and convictions. Vague laws empower prosecutors to "throw the book" at offenders by applying the express terms of the law to target conduct far beyond what legislators had in mind when they enacted the law. For instance, a fisherman who threw three fish back into the sea was convicted of violating a statute against document shredding, because a "fish" is a "thing." A Florida seafood importer was sentenced to eight years in prison for transporting lobsters in plastic bags rather than cardboard boxes—a crime only because of an obscure provision of the Honduran regulatory code in combination with a federal law that effectively delegated criminal lawmaking to foreign countries.

A proliferation of crimes with a host of onerous penalties puts innocent individuals at risk, even when they're trying to do the right thing. And loose liability standards—including those that impute criminality to owners and supervisors for subordinates' conduct, even when it contradicts express instructions—give enormous leverage to government enforcers in the executive branch. Little wonder that most criminal defendants settle on the government's terms. And when the defendant includes a corporation as well as an individual, the unelected government's regulatory power is multiplied yet more. That's the story of the next chapter.

CHAPTER 6

Offers You Can't Refuse

In June 2016, the FedEx package-delivery company went to trial in federal court in California. It's hardly unusual to see multinational corporations in the courtroom. But it is almost unheard of to see a large business facing trial as a *criminal defendant.*

What's even more unusual: some two years after obtaining an indictment, and one week into the trial, the federal government dropped all charges. The judge in the case, Charles R. Breyer, had expressed skepticism, and called the case a "novel prosecution." Presumably, prosecutors concluded that their case was unlikely to secure a verdict against the company.

What exactly was FedEx's purported crime? According to the U.S. attorney for the Northern District of California, the company had delivered packages that contained pharmaceuticals illegally ordered from Internet pharmacies. To be sure, there are federal laws regulating interstate pharmaceutical sales. But as Judge Breyer suggested, the government had failed to show any ill intent on the part of FedEx or its employees. And the prosecutors were essentially asking FedEx to snoop on its customers and open their packages—which has privacy-law implications, in addition to being bad for business.

What makes the FedEx case even more remarkable is that the company's main private competitor, United Parcel Service (UPS), had agreed three years earlier to settle a nearly identical claim—initiated by the same prosecutors, and involving the same alleged conduct. In exchange for an agreement not to

97

prosecute, the government and UPS entered into a "non-prosecution agreement" under which the company forfeited $40 million to the government. In addition to the payout, UPS agreed to several changes in corporate behavior. Among these were hiring a new high-level "compliance" officer reporting to the chief executive and hiring an "independent" auditor paid by the company but reporting to the U.S. attorney.

Given the novelty of the government's case, why would UPS have agreed to such terms? Consider that in the FedEx prosecution, the government sought $1.6 billion in fines—an astronomical sum, when the indictment alleged only $600,000 in shipping payments over a ten-year period. We don't know that federal prosecutors were threatening UPS with fines of that magnitude before it agreed to its deal, but it's not unreasonable to assume they were. And with a prospective penalty on that order presumably looming for UPS, a $40 million forfeiture and a couple of new hires would seem positively cheap. The Justice Department lost the FedEx case, but in seeking penalties forty times higher than it had earlier settled for with UPS, prosecutors sent a clear message about the stakes involved for companies that might refuse to deal in the future.

Most companies don't take the risk that FedEx did in going to trial. What the government can do to a company in court, in many instances, is destroy it. Criminal prosecution can imperil companies' ability to raise financing in debt and equity markets. Moreover, under federal statutes, a criminal conviction—or, in many cases, even an indictment—could bar contractors from government business, exclude medical companies from federal reimbursement, or cost financial companies their licenses. Thus, most companies have little choice but to agree "voluntarily" to the government's terms. Essentially, like Don Corleone in *The Godfather*, the Justice Department tends to make companies "offers they can't refuse."

• • •

Facing extraordinary pressures to avoid trial is of course not unique to corporate criminal defendants. The overwhelming majority of individual criminal defendants, too, tend to enter into plea bargains. And as we discovered in the last chapter, a lack of ill intent is little protection from a modern-day prosecution in America.

Still, individual plea bargains must be approved by a judge. Non-prosecution agreements, such as that reached between federal prosecutors and UPS, do not involve the formal filing of charges and thus never come before a judge.

Prosecutors sometimes settle with companies after formally filing charges, in what is called a "deferred prosecution agreement." But the difference is one of form, not substance. Such agreements regularly specify that the prosecutor alone is empowered to determine whether a company has breached its terms, with no judicial review. Companies typically waive all statutory, constitutional, and procedural rights. The agreements typically prohibit corporations from contradicting the prosecutors' statements of alleged fact in the future—even in private civil litigation.

Serving as effective judge and jury has given enormous power to federal prosecutors. Knowing that a defendant cannot afford to fight back can tend to give at least some prosecutors a broad view of their powers. As we shall see, such federal prosecutors have regularly held companies to account for alleged conduct that appears to be legal under the laws enacted by Congress.

The prosecutor-run shadow regulatory state covers a vast swathe of American business. Over the last decade, one in five of the Fortune 100 companies—the largest businesses by revenues—have been operating under deferred prosecution or non-prosecution agreements like those governing UPS. Payouts under these agreements over that time total more than $50 billion—and many multiples of that in follow-on civil administrative settlements, monies paid to state governments involving the same or similar conduct, and piggyback civil lawsuits. These payouts are not necessarily tied to statutory fines. And in at least some cases, the executive branch has used such agreements to funnel funds to preferred constituencies, in an effective end run around Congress and its power of the purse.

Beyond these payouts, the threat of government enforcement action has given the executive branch vast, and largely unchecked, power to regulate commerce. Through deferred prosecution and non-prosecution agreements, prosecutors have required companies to fire key employees, including chief executives; modify compensation, sales, and marketing plans; and create new board committees. Agreements like those at UPS—to hire new corporate officers and to retain independent monitors reporting back to the government—are commonplace.

Speaking before the Organization for Economic Cooperation and Development (OECD) in 2014, the U.S. assistant attorney general, Leslie R. Caldwell, made the obvious point that "companies cannot be sent to jail." So it makes sense, from her perspective, to tell companies: "you will also have a monitor and will do all sorts of other things for the next five years, and if you don't do them…then you can still be prosecuted." In her view, a deferred prosecution agreement is "a more powerful tool than actually going to trial."

But none of these remedies have statutory authorization. None have been developed through regulatory rulemaking under the Administrative Procedure Act. None would be a permissible remedy in court.

• • •

Federal deferred prosecution and non-prosecution agreements with corporations are novel. The first was entered into between the Justice Department and Salomon Brothers in 1992, the last year of the George H. W. Bush administration. Since then, their numbers have grown dramatically. Eleven such agreements were negotiated during the first Clinton administration, 130 during the George W. Bush administration, and 334 during the Obama administration. The number of new agreements fell slightly, to forty-six, in the first two years of the Trump administration—a number that is sufficiently large to infer a difference in degree, not in kind. (As one might expect, given administration priorities, some of the new agreements in the Trump years target corporations over alleged immigration-related offenses.)

Historically, corporations, as a general rule, could not be prosecuted criminally at all. As discussed in the last chapter, a crime involved a guilty mind as well as a guilty act. Corporations, as collective entities, have no moral compass, can possess no "criminal intent," cannot be sworn in to a court of law, and cannot be imprisoned. Thus, criminal law was exclusively the domain of *individual* wrongdoing. The Roman law maxim, *societas delinquere non potest*, roughly translates as "the company may not engage in criminal activity." This general principle still heavily governs European democracies. Germany, to this day, does not hold corporations criminally responsible for the actions of its employees or directors.

So too was this the general rule in the American colonies at the time of the Revolutionary War. A few cases in the seventeenth and eighteenth centuries had permitted the British Crown to prosecute a *municipal* corporation for failing to clean up a road or throughway. At this time, the corporation was the principal form of organization for local government entities. (By 1900, there were more than 10,000 municipal corporations in the United States.) The practice of prosecuting such entities to prompt quasi-governmental action, at a time when government was rather rudimentary, carried over into the new republic.

In 1834, for example, the State of New York indicted the city of Albany, a chartered corporation, along with the city's mayor and alderman. Albany's crime was allowing an adjoining stretch of the Hudson River to become "foul, filled and choked up with mud, rubbish, and dead carcasses of animals."

Notably, these early criminal prosecutions against municipal corporations did not punish acts of commission but rather acts of omission. The criminal indictment was meant to spur municipal corporations to act. And it was still the general rule that a corporation could not be liable "for any crime of which a corrupt intent or *malus animus* is an essential ingredient."

By the mid-nineteenth century, American courts began permitting commercial companies, on occasion, to be indicted under nuisance laws that had previously been applied to municipal corporations. They also allowed prosecution for affirmative acts, not only for a failure to act. In 1852, the New Jersey Supreme Court affirmed the indictment of the Morris & Essex Railroad for obstructing a public roadway with a building and railcars. But the court emphasized that a corporation could not be prosecuted for crimes requiring the state to show "a corrupt intent."

By the turn of the century, some courts started loosening this stricture, too. In 1899, the Massachusetts Supreme Judicial Court permitted the indictment of a media company, Telegram Newspaper, for contempt of court. The judges reasoned that the same principles that enabled a court to find a company liable in tort for its employees' actions should also make a corporation criminally liable. The U.S. Supreme Court would soon adopt similar logic in a case that ushered in the modern era of corporate criminal liability.

• • •

As discussed in Chapter 1, Congress responded to the growth of interstate commerce in the late nineteenth century by enacting legislation—the Interstate Commerce Act of 1887 and the Sherman Antitrust Act of 1890—that laid the groundwork for the federal regulatory state. The original Interstate Commerce Act lacked criminal penalties, but a successor statute regulating railroads, the Elkins Act of 1903, established such penalties for violating regulations that forbade the railways from giving price rebates to large customers.

It's not clear that Congress contemplated whether these criminal provisions should apply to corporations themselves. But the Elkins Act contained broad definitional provisions that implied it. The new statute provided that "the act, omission, or failure to act" of anyone "employed by" a railroad was to "be deemed" the *railroad's* "act, omission, or failure to act."

Thus, it's hardly surprising that the Supreme Court held that the New York Central & Hudson River Railroad Company could be held criminally liable under the new law in 1909. The Court observed that there were "some crimes which, in their nature, cannot be committed by corporations." But it saw no problem in holding corporations criminally responsible for "rebating under the Federal statutes...wherein the crime consists in purposely doing the things prohibited by statute." Like the Massachusetts Supreme Judicial Court in *Telegram Newspaper*, the Court drew an analogy to the tort-law doctrine holding companies civilly liable for employees' actions.

The Supreme Court's decision in *New York Central & Hudson River Railroad* merely held that it was *constitutionally permissible* for *Congress* to ascribe criminal liability to a corporation on the basis of the actions of its employees or agents. But other courts subsequently borrowed from the Court's rationale in the case to find corporations criminally liable—even when legislatures had *not*, as in the Elkins Act, given any explicit statutory authority for applying the crime in question to corporate entities on the basis of their employees' actions.

Without any act of Congress, then, courts have assumed that crimes written into law for individuals apply to corporations, regardless of whether any statutory language supports that construction. It is now the standard federal rule that corporations are liable under criminal law for the crimes of corporate employees. Even for offenses of low-level employees. Even for actions that are contrary to corporate policy. And even if the individual employees in question lacked the level of knowledge that is necessary to confer personal criminal liability.

• • •

The U.S. Sentencing Commission is one of those groups created by Congress with the task of writing rules that the Framers intended for the legislature to write. Charged with writing "guidelines" to ensure consistency in sentencing for federal crimes, the commission in 1991 recommended the awarding of "credit" to corporations for "cooperating" in criminal investigations. In the process, it jump-started the modern practice of threatening to prosecute corporations as entities for major crimes, and deferring such prosecutions by agreement.

The commission hoped that the prospect of a reward for cooperation would induce companies to ferret out criminal misconduct on their own. Rather than the government reacting to crimes after they occurred, the idea was to deputize corporations to police themselves—and their employees. The objective was to increase compliance with the law. And due to businesses' sensitivity to criminal sanctions, they could be expected to cooperate.

In late 1992, in the waning days of the George H. W. Bush administration, the investment bank Salomon Brothers reached the first non-prosecution agreement with the federal government. But the practice was initially little used: over the first decade after the sentencing guidelines were adopted, the Justice Department reached non-prosecution agreements only fourteen times.

That changed after 2002. On March 7 of that year, the federal government indicted Arthur Andersen, at the time one of the United States' "Big Five" accounting firms. Andersen had served as the auditor of Enron, a large energy trading company that had collapsed in 2001, along with the "dot-com" stock market bubble. Enron had cooked its books. Andersen had certified its financial misstatements.

Andersen was not indicted for Enron's misstatements. Instead, the government indicted the accountancy on a single criminal count of withholding, altering, or destroying documents "with the intent to impair their availability in an official proceeding."

The government presented no evidence that Andersen partners had conspired to destroy evidence. Rather, its case was circumstantial. An in-house lawyer at Andersen had caught wind of a looming investigation of Enron by the Securities and Exchange Commission. Some time later, an Andersen partner reminded a general training session of the firm's "document retention" policy. He urged them to comply with it. Of the eighty-nine employees at the session, ten worked on the Enron account. Andersen employees subsequently began shredding documents. Some of the shredding continued even after the firm received a letter from the SEC announcing the opening of an investigation into Enron's accounting.

Andersen's trial commenced two months after its indictment. A guilty verdict was returned on June 15. Andersen's criminal punishment was mild: a $500,000 fine and five years' probation.

The firm appealed, and ultimately prevailed in court. In 2005, the Supreme Court unanimously overturned Andersen's conviction. The justices objected to a jury instruction that "failed to convey the requisite consciousness of wrongdoing." They emphasized that interpreting federal criminal statutes required restraint, "both out of deference to the prerogatives of Congress, and out of concern that 'a fair warning should be given to the world in language that the common world will understand, of what the law intends to do if a certain line is passed.'" Andersen's indictment was dismissed. The sole individual Andersen employee to have been convicted of wrongdoing, David Duncan, withdrew his guilty plea and settled with the SEC without admitting any wrongdoing.

But while Duncan clearly benefited from the Supreme Court's ruling, the firm's ultimate victory was in name only. Andersen's felony conviction was essentially its death knell: SEC regulations prohibit convicted felons from representing publicly traded companies. Prior to its indictment, Andersen had 85,000 employees worldwide, 28,000 of them in the United States. By the end of 2002, it had only 3,000 employees left. When Andersen won its case on appeal, only a couple hundred remained, to wind down the accountancy's affairs.

The Arthur Andersen case changed the way federal prosecutors and companies interact. When another large accounting firm, KPMG, faced its own criminal indictment over its marketing of tax shelters, it unsurprisingly decided to "cooperate" with prosecutors. The firm entered into a deferred prosecution agreement in August 2005, agreeing to pay a fine of $456 million—almost a thousand times the fine levied against Arthur Andersen after its trial. KPMG also agreed to "special oversight" conditions, which have become commonplace in the structuring of DPAs.

And KPMG was not alone. Accounting firms are peculiarly susceptible to criminal charges. But so too are military and other government contractors (which can be "debarred" from doing government business), health-care companies (which can be "excluded" from Medicare and Medicaid reimbursement), and financial companies (which can lose government licenses allowing them to participate in securities exchanges and other regulated markets).

In 2003, the year following Andersen's conviction, federal prosecutors entered into six deferred prosecution agreements with corporations. That number grew to eight in 2004, fifteen in 2005, twenty-six in 2006, and forty in 2007—all this during the relatively pro-business Bush administration. The growth continued during the Obama presidency, and has scarcely abated under President Trump. By 2015, the number of federal deferred prosecution agreements reached with business topped one hundred for the first time.

• • •

On the one hand, it is heartening that federal prosecutors want to avoid the risk of causing an Andersen-style corporate collapse. The firm's demise cost thousands of employees their jobs. It also reduced competition in the marketplace, cutting large companies' choice of auditor from a "Big Five" to a "Big Four." And that's before getting to the question of fundamental fairness, given that the company ultimately won its legal appeal.

But the subsequent explosion of "cooperation" agreements between federal prosecutors and large companies has given the prosecutors unprecedented and essentially unchecked regulatory powers. After the Affordable Care Act was passed in 2010, prosecutors in the Obama Justice Department frequently targeted health-care companies for regulatory violations. In the process, they gained substantial control over various aspects of those companies' operations through non-prosecution agreements or the equivalent.

Federal prosecutors have often targeted pharmaceutical companies for promoting "off-label" uses of their products—a no-no discussed in Chapter 1. Doctors regularly prescribe drugs for off-label uses, but the FDA considers it "misbranding" for drug companies or their agents to promote such uses.

On July 2, 2012, the U.S. Attorney's Office for the District of Massachusetts reached a sweeping agreement with the American subsidiary of GlaxoSmith-Kline, a British multinational health-care company. The federal Department of Health and Human Services claimed that the company had illegally "misbranded" its antidepressant drugs Paxil and Wellbutrin for off-label uses. The company had sponsored a series of continuing medical education programs including lectures, lunches, and dinners. Participants discussed research about prescribing Paxil to children and adolescents, and Wellbutrin for weight loss and sexual dysfunction, uses not reviewed by the FDA.

The deputy attorney general, James M. Cole, trumpeted the government's agreement with Glaxo as "unprecedented in both size and scope," and the "largest health care fraud settlement in U.S. history." Glaxo coughed up $3 billion in fines and payments, which was divvied up between the federal and state governments. Agreements that prosecutors in the Obama administration reached with other drug manufacturers on misbranding claims didn't fall too far behind: Pfizer settled for $2.3 billion, Abbott Laboratories for $1.5 billion, and Eli Lilly for $1.4 billion. Beyond the money, the companies agreed to multiyear "corporate integrity agreements," which included stringent provisions requiring them to make "major changes" to business operations.

In addition to the allegations of criminal conduct and the astronomical settlement values, the Pfizer, Abbott, and Lilly agreements are all striking in that no individuals were prosecuted in connection with the alleged underlying conduct. In Glaxo's case, the Justice Department accused its general counsel, Lauren Stevens, of obstruction of justice and making false statements to the government. But a federal judge dismissed the case, with withering criticism of the government's actions in both the investigation and the prosecution.

The routine use of such "misbranding" settlements and the absence of any individual criminal indictments for the underlying conduct have largely insulated the government from testing its criminal-law theories. In a 2012 decision, the U.S. Court of Appeals for the Second Circuit overturned the federal prosecution of a pharmaceutical sales representative on constitutional grounds. The sales rep had communicated truthful information about an off-label drug use. The court ruled that "criminalizing the truthful off-label promotion of FDA-approved prescription drugs" was an unconstitutional limitation on free speech, in violation of the First Amendment. Alas, this decision came one year too late for Dr. Gleason. And the FDA announced it would not be altering its future off-label drug misbranding enforcement—i.e., that companies and individuals are still subject to the same sorts of prosecution.

Because the FDA decided not to appeal that decision, it's not clear whether the Supreme Court would agree with the Second Circuit. And it's not clear that the free-speech logic that the court applied to an individual would extend to a corporation. But no pharmaceutical company is likely to test such theories. Consider the "side letter" that federal prosecutors gave to Glaxo in its settlement, waiving the government's authority to debar the company from Medicare or Medicaid reimbursement. Such side letters are common in these agreements, and they highlight the "sword of Damocles" hanging over companies that might face prosecution.

• • •

What happens to the billions of dollars extracted from Glaxo, Pfizer, Abbott, Lilly, and other companies in settlements with government prosecutors? It doesn't necessarily go into the general public coffers. Agreements between the federal government and companies sometimes specify how a company should spend money internally, on new personnel or programs. But sometimes the money that prosecutors extract from companies goes to third parties.

The Obama administration entered into many eye-popping multibillion-dollar settlements with private businesses it was investigating. None was bigger than those reached with various banks and other financial institutions. That makes some sense: the 2008 financial crisis could be linked to various misdeeds, real or alleged, by such institutions. Bank of America alone dealt with more than fifty settlements, fines, and penalties totaling more than $90 billion. The largest Bank of America settlement was reached in August 2014. The settlement's total price tag was $16.65 billion. It followed on the heels of similar agreements, announced earlier in 2014, with JPMorgan Chase ($13 billion) and Citigroup ($7 billion), over the same alleged conduct.

None of these giant settlements directly involved mortgage-lending abuses that did occur, at least during the latter stages of the housing bubble. Rather, they resolved claims that the banks concealed the risks of mortgage-related *securities*. The purported victims of these sales were not ordinary investors. Rather, the investors that allegedly did not understand the risks of the mortgage-backed securities they were buying were sophisticated parties—insurance companies, pension funds, and university endowments.

What is most remarkable about the settlements reached with the banks is the degree to which they ordered the companies under investigation to redistribute money to third-party groups. Almost half the "fines" imposed were not payments to the government but rather "consumer relief" payments directed by the Department of Justice.

The Bank of America settlement, for example, forced the bank to allocate $7 billion to "consumer relief" credits. This included potentially more than $5 billion to write down the principal owed by consumers on their mortgages and home equity loans. Such a demand is extraordinary given that institutional investors, rather than homeowners, were the purported victims of the alleged fraud. Whether or not writing down the loans of underwater consumers made sense as a policy matter was hotly debated. But the administration was able to avoid subjecting its judgment to public debate on the matter—and avoid going to Congress—by strong-arming banks to its will.

The Bank of America settlement also ordered the bank to underwrite new "affordable housing" developments, and to give grants to community-development and housing groups, legal aid groups fighting foreclosures, and various government-sanctioned housing-activist groups. The settlement was structured to encourage the bank to pay more than the required minimums under its terms. For each dollar the bank gave out to favored community-development and housing-activist groups, the bank received a $2 credit against its other settlement obligations.

It's perhaps unsurprising that the Obama Justice Department would have liked giving money to housing and community activists. Upon graduating from Columbia University, Barack Obama had famously headed to Chicago to work as a community organizer.

Groups such as those funded in the Obama administration's banking settlement can vary in form, structure, and mission. Many exist in a symbiotic relationship with government and depend significantly on government funding. A 2009 audit of the Association of Community Organizations for Reform Now (ACORN), a large community-organizing umbrella group, determined that it had received $53 million in federal funds over the preceding fifteen years.

ACORN dissolved just one year later, after being exposed for illegal practices. The 2010 Republican takeover of the House of Representatives meant that funding for community-organizing groups came under increasing congressional scrutiny. So the Obama administration had a problem with its funding priorities in this area. Under the federal government's constitutional design, the funding power—the "power of the purse"—resides with Congress, not the executive branch.

Indeed, the taxing and spending power is the core of the congressional function. But in an aggressive end run around this authority, the Obama administration allocated billions to outside third-party groups through legal settlements. Bank settlements totaled $46 billion between 2013 and 2016 alone. In June 2017, the new attorney general, Jeff Sessions, announced that the Justice Department was suspending the practice. Yet absent congressional action, nothing prevents a future administration from bringing it back.

• • •

Through the threat of its enforcement power, the federal government has assumed a shadow regulatory power that in some ways is more unlimited than its ordinary administrative authority. The judiciary at least *looks at* administrative rulemaking—even with broad grants of legislative authority and deferential review under *Chevron.* But non-prosecution agreements never come before a court, and judges review deferred prosecution agreements only to check that the government has done things punctually as specified by the Speedy Trial Act. Even more than usual, the executive branch acts as its own judge and jury.

With no real checks on their authority, federal prosecutors have often stretched statutes beyond what Congress authorized.

Consider the Foreign Corrupt Practices Act (FCPA). Enacted in 1977, the FCPA is intended to prevent American-based businesses from paying foreign officials to award government contracts, to procure preferred regulations, or to look the other way in enforcement. The statute is a good-government measure. It's implicitly rooted in American idealism. Congress was acting on the plausible belief that American interests are fostered, in the long run, by the rule of law abroad. But Congress, in enacting the FCPA, made exceptions. The statute specifically exempts "facilitating payments" designed "to expedite or secure the performance of a routine governmental action by a foreign official." Congress clearly meant to acknowledge the reality that some low-level officials in foreign countries, such as customs officials, regularly take small cash payments—just as they did in the New York Customs House under Chester Arthur in nineteenth-century America. Yet federal prosecutors have entered into non-prosecution agreements with companies that self-reported just such low-level corruption. Notwithstanding the "safe harbor" in the statute actually enacted by Congress, the companies have had little choice but to comply with the prosecutors' terms.

Prosecutors have also aggressively assumed jurisdiction under this and other statutes, even against *foreign* companies acting in foreign countries. Among the thin jurisdictional reeds asserted by American prosecutors were a company doing business in U.S. dollars, and a company sending emails that were routed through an Internet server based in the United States. These standards, of course, could encompass essentially all business activity worldwide. But many federal prosecutors *do* view themselves as world policemen. Once at a conference, I challenged a senior Justice Department official about such overreaching jurisdictional claims. He replied that the U.S. federal government assumed a regulatory role over such cases only because foreign governments did not.

Yet there is a cost to delegating so much regulatory power to prosecutors. Most prosecutors are well-intentioned. Still, they usually have none of the specialized expertise that the rulemaking and enforcement officials in administrative agencies possess. Lawyers with English degrees are assuming broad regulatory authority over commercial enterprises they little understand. Even when they are prosecuting valid claims, the quasi-regulatory powers they assume can have broad and potentially harmful consequences.

To take one example, the London-based bank HSBC entered into a deferred prosecution agreement with the federal government in December 2012. The agreement alleged that the bank had violated the federal Bank Secrecy Act—an actual oversight program established by Congress, unlike the made-up oversight program the Justice Department asserted in the FedEx case. Congress's statute requires banks to maintain an effective program against money laundering. If the facts alleged in the agreement are to be believed, HSBC failed in its obligations, which permitted drug traffickers in Mexico and Colombia to launder hundreds of millions of dollars.

Because its U.S. banking license was at stake, HSBC had little negotiating leverage, and so the bank agreed to sweeping management changes under prosecutorial pressure. The bank shook up its executive team and replaced almost all senior management. It cut and deferred executive bonuses. It implemented a new compensation system tying bonuses for senior executives to regulatory-compliance standards. It hired a compliance officer reporting back to the government for a period of five years. And it made other changes to reporting and compliance standards, management structure, and general business practices.

In addition, facing the Hobson's choice of losing its banking license, HSBC decided to pull out of numerous emerging-market countries. The bank abandoned an array of business activities in Asia and Latin America: it sold forty-two businesses, exited 109 correspondent relationships, and pulled out of nine countries entirely. Developing countries such as Angola and Myanmar, desperately dependent on outside capital, implored the bank not to leave—but to no avail. Based on the decisions of prosecutors in Washington—under no regulatory directive from Congress and no administrative rulemaking—some of the world's poorest nations lost a global lender that helped fill a critical gap in their emerging infrastructure.

CHAPTER 7

Litigation Nation

Among the historic sites on Route 66 in California is the Aztec Hotel in Monrovia. Listed in the National Register of Historic Places, the 1925 hotel is a landmark example of Mayan Revival architecture. Over the years, the Aztec Hotel hosted Hollywood stars including Marilyn Monroe and Clark Gable, as well as the legendary Western lawman Wyatt Earp.

A California businesswoman, Kathie Reece-McNeill, bought the historic property in September 2000, intending to restore the hotel to its former glory. She didn't anticipate the barriers that would be thrown in her way—barriers constructed neither through administrative rulemaking nor with government enforcement actions, but rather by our third group of unelected regulators, the litigators.

While renovations were in process, Reece-McNeill underwrote a guest's extended stay at the hotel as a favor to a friend. The guest's mother was disabled. In April 2003, the hotel was hit with a lawsuit by a California disability lawyer alleging that the vintage hotel's bathroom and parking lot were not compliant with modern rules governing disability access.

The lawyer, Mark Potter, was among the Golden State's "frequent filers," a group of California disability attorneys who maintain a list of repeat plaintiffs and file similar claims on behalf of the same individuals against multiple businesses. Each individual demand is modest, but multiplied across hundreds of small businesses with little capacity to fight back, they generate hefty profits for the lawsuit mills.

Unlike most defendants, Reece-McNeill decided not to accept Potter's offer to settle his suit for a "meager" $18,000. On the legal merits, she was right: she ultimately prevailed when she took the case to court. But her victory proved Pyrrhic, as she ended up spending more than $100,000 litigating her defense. Reece-McNeill learned a bedrock lesson of American litigation: even when you win, you lose, because the general "American Rule"—in contrast to most of the rest of the developed world—does not require the loser in a lawsuit to reimburse the winner's legal costs.

In 2011, the Aztec Hotel was in bankruptcy court, and Reece-McNeill lost control of the property she had spent a decade trying to renovate. Her story, and the whole of disability law, only scratch the surface of the uniquely American litigation phenomenon. In modern America, the state can regulate private behavior without a government agent—an administrator or a prosecutor—acting affirmatively to do so.

• • •

When people hear talk about "wealth redistribution," they tend to think of elected legislators raising taxes on those most able to pay and "transferring" those funds to those with greater need—as we see in well-known programs like Medicaid and food stamps. Yet American federal and state governments also regularly transfer monies from one group of citizens to another without collecting payments through any taxing authority or distributing them from any government office. Defenders of the American system of tort litigation call it a "private" law system, but it bears little resemblance to the private ordering we see in the consensual relationships of business, friendship, or club. In both the ordinary wealth-redistribution system and the tort-litigation system, the government forces people to pay up—but the tax collector in the tort system is a plaintiffs' lawyer.

Tax collection is always inefficient. People and businesses have to pay for accountants or services to help them. Those owing a lot of taxes spend a lot of money trying to avoid paying extra tax. Economists call this a "dead weight loss." And taxes necessarily change incentives. When taxes go up, investors and businesses avoid making investments in new projects, because the money coming back in after taxes won't be enough to cover the risk that the investment won't pan out. But for all the inefficiencies of the regular tax system, the tort-tax system is astronomically more wasteful. Imagine if, at tax time, you had to pay almost as much money to your accountant as you paid the government. That's exactly what we see in tort litigation: only fifty-seven cents on every dollar goes from the defendant in a tort lawsuit to the plaintiff—and that's before the plaintiff pays his lawyer. The rest goes to attorneys on the other side, as well as to insurance policies for businesses, doctors, and drivers who cannot afford to risk losing it all in the litigation lottery.

That lottery is expensive. Economists estimate the direct costs of the tort-litigation system—payments from one party to another, plus the fees paid to lawyers on both sides and to insurance companies processing claims—at over $400 billion annually. That's about 2.3 percent of U.S. economic output—equivalent to almost a 10 percent bump up on regular taxation collected through the federal, state, and local governments combined. The "tort tax" costs significantly more than all U.S. corporate income taxes, and the cost of tort litigation in the United States is about three times the comparable litigation costs in the average European country as a percentage of the economy. Obviously this hurts American firms' competitiveness with foreign rivals.

The tort tax of course flows through to the average American consumer as well—pushing up the cost of housing, driving, health care, and many other of our big-ticket expenses. And the effects of our litigation system far exceed the direct costs levied through the tort tax itself. Like the threat of prosecution or other government enforcement actions, the threat of litigation influences behavior. Doctors and hospitals often order unnecessary or unnecessarily expensive tests due to the fear that if things go badly for a patient, a lawyer can convince a jury that the extra test might have made a difference. If juries could be trusted to perform rational cost-benefit analyses of medical procedures, this would be a good thing. But in practice, juries understandably tend to respond to sad cases and try to help those in dire circumstances—it's just the insurance company paying, right? The former senator and vice-presidential nominee John Edwards amassed a small fortune trying medical malpractice cases before beginning his political career; he was one of the best at tugging on heartstrings—telling jurors he could hear a baby born with a birth defect speaking through him, asking for their help.

Although the broader administrative state has plenty of foreign parallels, tort litigation in the United States is unique. Many of the most distinctive features of American civil litigation have essentially no parallel in other developed nations. Among these are civil juries deciding complex liability trials, broad rights to "discover" documents and depose witnesses before trial, and the American Rule in which the winner of a lawsuit does not recoup costs from the other side.

Most of our idiosyncratic system of tort taxation and regulation was never voted upon by elected legislators at all. To some degree, the power of litigation as an American regulatory force owes to the shoehorning of old legal doctrines from a different era into a modern economic context to which they are ill-suited. We inherited from England a "common law" tort system that evolved over centuries as the King's Bench emerged to replace trial by ordeal with trial by jury. (What is a "trial by ordeal"? Think burning or drowning: if the accused survives, God is telling us the accused is innocent.) But as we shall see, the vast reach of U.S. civil litigation is not merely an accident of English law. Some features, like the American Rule, did develop essentially by accident years after our constitutional founding, but others resulted from the extensive delegations of power by Congress to the courts in the twentieth century. And strangely, the courts in turn delegated authority to *law professors*, who aggressively and foolishly remade the rules to fit as-yet-untested theories.

● ● ●

At America's constitutional founding, Antifederalist critics of the new plan of government decried its lack of a formal bill of rights. For some Antifederalists, one of the rights lacking was protection for civil juries. Alexander Hamilton acknowledged that most delegates at the Constitutional Convention viewed jury trials in general as "a valuable safeguard to liberty" if not "the very palladium of free government." The 1776 Virginia Declaration of Rights had upheld jury trials as "sacred" in "controversies respecting property," including "suits between man and man." Hamilton himself took a different view. In *Federalist* no. 83, he wrote that he could not "readily discern the inseparable connection between the existence of liberty, and the trial by jury in civil cases"; the key purpose of a jury was to protect against the tyranny of *government* officials, which involved criminal prosecutions, not disputes between two private parties.

Some of the Antifederalists observed, correctly, that the government could be a party in civil forfeiture actions, not only in criminal prosecutions, and they worried about the new government seizing ships "for non-compliance with, or breach of the laws of the customs, or those for regulating trade." This risk could be mitigated, they reasoned, by forcing the government to prove its case before a jury of peers. Just as ordinary folks sitting in a jury box would stop the government from abusing its powers to throw accused criminals in jail unjustly, juries could stop the government from using courts in civil actions to take people's property. Much of the Antifederalist fear of losing civil juries also revolved around debtor-creditor relations: those who owed large sums after the war hoped that juries might throw them a lifeline.

Ultimately, the Antifederalist critics won out on this point: the Seventh Amendment to the Constitution included the "right of trial by jury" for "Suits at common law, where the value in controversy shall exceed twenty dollars." This is one of the few provisions of the Bill of Rights that the U.S. Supreme Court has *not* applied to state governments over the last century or so. As Hamilton observed, the states at the time of the founding had broadly divergent legal systems; and virtually all of them had special courts, like those in England, that handled certain types of legal disputes without juries— among these, probate courts handling inheritances, admiralty courts handling maritime disputes, and chancery courts overseeing complex contractual and business matters. (Federal courts also eschew juries for certain of these matters.) Many state constitutions have parallel civil-jury provisions—and some state supreme courts have applied those broadly, to overturn hosts of tort-reform laws enacted by the states' elected legislatures. In essence, these often-unelected courts are saying they—and only they—can cut tort taxes or trim tort regulations.

Although civil juries were enshrined in the Constitution, legal rights at the time were remarkably limited in comparison with what we see today. The ability to sue the manufacturer of a product in court did not exist before the twentieth century. As today, doctors (and lawyers) could be hauled into court for breaching their duties to patients (or clients). But a plaintiff in that era had to be alive to pursue a claim, and not too many patients with serious conditions lived to tell the tale—nor could many people credibly argue that the medical standards available at the time could have led to an easy cure. Witnesses could be compelled to testify in American courts at the time of the nation's founding. But neither defendants nor plaintiffs—the alleged wrong-doers and allegedly injured victims themselves—could appear as witnesses in court. As "parties of interest," they were deemed likely to commit perjury.

A leading legal historian has described the state of tort law at the time of the American founding as "rudimentary," observing that "the central feature of contemporary tort law—the law of negligence—was largely lacking." As late as 1871, the future Supreme Court justice Oliver Wendell Holmes criticized a new torts treatise as "not a proper subject for a law book."

The post–Civil War years, however, saw the nation's first litigation explosion. Tort law, deemed too insignificant for a book just a few years before, gobbled up an increasing share of the legal system's time—and the economy's money. Over a forty-year period, tort litigation increased by an order of magnitude, from 4.2 percent of New York City trial courts' dockets in 1870 to 40.9 percent in 1910. Tort law had long allowed plaintiffs to recover from defendants who trampled them on horseback—the fact pattern of *Gibbons v. Pepper*, an English case of the late seventeenth century. But from 1880 to 1900, the number of cases in Boston alleging injury from a horse-drawn carriage had jumped 6,500 percent. By the early twentieth century, bar leaders complained that the rash of tort cases were "blocking…calendars with a mass of litigation so great as to impede administration in all other branches of law."

What led to this surge in lawsuits? Part of the answer, to be sure, lay in urbanization. As more people left farms for cities, there were more opportunities to bump into each other—and, as in Boston, get run over by a horse and buggy. But the city of Boston grew just under 55 percent from 1880 to 1900, not 6,500 percent. The biggest factor explaining the explosion in lawsuits is that nineteenth-century courts had relaxed earlier doctrines limiting how cases could be brought, what theories enabled or limited recovery, what evidence could be produced, and—critically—what fees lawyers could be paid.

• • •

To use the power of government courts to recover compensation from another party in the early years of the American republic required navigating a complex series of "writs," or pleadings, to get one's case considered. Plaintiffs had to file different actions for direct and indirect harms. They could not file an action for both, and it was not always easy to determine what action applied. Thus, law students' tort-law books discuss early cases with strange fact patterns involving injuries caused by lighted explosive squibs and runaway hot-air balloons. In the early nineteenth century, courts began to relax the rules governing these causes of action, expanding the types of injuries that could get relief under the indirect cause of action ("trespass on the case")—jump-starting the emerging law of accidents.

When they expanded the scope of legal actions to recover from indirect harms, courts also decided that plaintiffs could not recover damages from defendants for harms caused by accident unless the defendant was "negligent" in exercising due care to avoid injuring others. The early cases also forbade plaintiffs from recovering from defendants if the plaintiffs themselves had been negligent—and left the question to the judge, not the jury.

Those who voluntarily chose to assume risks—such as workers in dangerous professions—could not come back later and complain that their employer should have provided a safe workspace. In the seminal 1842 case *Farwell v. Boston & Worcester Railroad Corporation*, Lemuel Shaw, the chief justice of the Massachusetts Supreme Judicial Court (and father-in-law of Herman Melville), articulated this principle: "[T]he plaintiff was employed by the defendants as an engineer, at the rate of wages usually paid in that employment, being a higher rate than the plaintiff had before received as a machinist. It was a voluntary undertaking on his part, with a full knowledge of the risks incident to the employment."

Over time, courts and some state legislatures began to remove, or at least lower, some of these bars to recovery. The common-law requirement that a plaintiff be alive to access the courts was jettisoned first—eventually, all states allowed recovery for "wrongful death." By the late nineteenth century, courts had also relaxed the bar on recovery when plaintiffs were themselves somewhat at fault; most states left the question to the jury, not the judge.

Courts later began to limit Judge Shaw's "assumption of risk" principles and permit more lawsuits for workplace injuries. In some cases—beginning with Massachusetts in 1887—state legislatures acted directly to supplant the old common-law rules and allow employees to sue over workplace injuries when juries deemed the employer negligent in failing to provide a safe workplace. Congress followed suit with the Federal Employers' Liability Act in 1908, which remains in effect today, in modified form. The workplace-injury changes owed in no small part to understandable sympathy for those maimed and killed in emerging industrial workplaces. (And make no mistake: these workplaces were very dangerous, and early railroads and coal mines had shockingly high fatality rates.) Ultimately, Progressive Era reformers pushed to enact workers' compensation laws holding employers responsible for most workplace injuries. Large businesses already subject to compensation arrangements in union contracts were happy to endorse this bargain, to replace much of the unwieldy and expensive tort-law apparatus.

Even as courts expanded the rules allowing plaintiffs to recover for injuries, they also changed the rules about how trials were conducted—giving birth to the modern adjudicatory trial. The common-law prohibition against either plaintiffs or defendants testifying in a civil action was in place throughout the United States and England when Simon Greenleaf published his first treatise on evidence in 1842—the definitive nineteenth-century treatment of the subject. This rule mattered little for contract cases, which depended on the words in documents, and criminal trials had workarounds when a defendant wanted to tell his story. But the limitation on plaintiff and defendant testimony proved fatal to many a tort dispute, in which the injured party and the party accused of causing the injury often had the only stories to tell. In 1848, Connecticut was the first state to abolish the rule prohibiting plaintiffs and defendants from testifying in their own cases, and most other states soon followed.

• • •

That same year, the New York legislature enacted a new code of civil procedure that had been developed by the lawyer David Dudley Field, the brother of a future U.S. Supreme Court justice. Many other states adopted the same rules, or close variants, in subsequent years, as did the federal courts. Beyond loosening the old writs to ease the bringing of lawsuits alleging injury, Field's new rules also codified a change that had emerged in the early years of the Republic somewhat by accident: the end of statutory schedules of attorney fees. This change, deemed inconsequential at the time, would lead American law in a completely new direction, as lawyering-for-profit encouraged litigation.

Since the early sixteenth century, British courts had had a rule that the loser in litigation paid the costs of the other side. Such a rule made intuitive sense. If a court determined that someone was unlawfully injured, it would hardly seem fair that the injured party not be wholly compensated; far fairer that the party judged to have caused the harm cover the costs of bringing the legal action. Similarly, if someone has to pay lawyers for a court defense but is deemed not to have caused any harm, by what rationale should he lose a lot of money in legal expenses—effectively punished merely for being *accused*?

Of course, the rule that one party would pay the other party's fees after trial had unintended consequences, as people sought to game the system. So the British courts developed rules to deter parties from playing games. Limiting legal costs to the level of damages discouraged parties from turning to courts for minor injuries. Requiring courts to approve fees prevented lawyers from overcharging the losing side.

Eventually, British courts and their American descendants published fee schedules listing customary charges for lawyering that led to court. Such fee schedules typically applied to what lawyers could charge their own clients as well as to what they could recover from the other side when they prevailed at trial. For the incentives to work out, the pay schedules had to be equal.

But in the new American republic, litigants began to seek to pay "above schedule" fees to top lawyers to gain an edge. Not all lawyers are created equal, and early American courts bristled at letting government courts dictate private lawyers' pay. So courts began to rubber-stamp such practices. But in doing so, a gulf opened up between what lawyers charged their own clients and what winning parties could recover from the other side in court. As early as 1792, a bar association in Massachusetts set *minimum* fees for lawyers at double the level scheduled for recovery by the prevailing side. Before long, the fees recoverable by the losing party in a lawsuit were but a small fraction of the fees paid by one's own client.

When New York enacted the Field Code (developed by David Dudley Field) in 1848, it paid lip service to loser-pays principles: "The losing party, ought however, as a general rule, to pay the expense of the litigation. He has caused a loss to his adversary unjustly, and should indemnify him for it." But the legislature scheduled the recoverable fees so low that they little mattered. The American Rule was effectively born. And prospective defendants like Kathie Reece-McNeill would thereafter be in jeopardy of financial ruin for fighting back against a threatened lawsuit, regardless of whether they won their case in court.

• • •

Soon after courts permitted lawyers to charge their clients fees according to private agreement rather than court-approved fee schedules, they also began to permit them to be paid not by hourly rates but through a percentage of prospective winnings from a lawsuit. Such "contingent fee" arrangements are the norm for the plaintiff side in almost all modern American tort litigation. But they were wholly illegal under the old rules. Since at least 1275 in England, a contingent fee would be strictly forbidden as "champerty." The old English rule was predicated upon a view of litigation as "a vice" and "a threat to the king's peace."

Even someone with a more sanguine view of litigation itself might worry about how giving a lawyer a cut of his client's winnings could encourage unsavory practices. As my former colleague Walter Olson observed in his seminal book *The Litigation Explosion*, there's a reason why professions like accounting don't allow practitioners to retain a percentage of clients' tax savings; and a reason why Roman tax collectors, allowed to keep a portion of their bounty, were despised—often lumped in with sinners in the New Testament. As we saw in Chapter 2, the practice of paying government officials in the nineteenth-century New York Customs House a portion of their levies nurtured substantial corruption. Lawyers filing suit are, in essence, a form of tax or duty collector—with monies usually flowing to private rather than government coffers, but only through access to government courts and the implicit threat of government force. There's good reason to worry about the corrupting influence of giving suing lawyers a piece of the action, too.

Some nineteenth-century American courts began to take a very different view. In 1855, in the case of *Major's Executor v. Gibson*, the Virginia Special Court of Appeals upheld an 1848 contract for a fee arrangement that would pay a plaintiffs' lawyer a share of the proceeds in a contract dispute in the event of successful recovery—even though a statutory code prohibiting champerty was still on the books. Justice Lucas Thompson rejected the argument that the contingent fee would give "an undue stimulus to the zeal and to the selfish passions of the counsel" so as to "corrupt and obstruct the pure administration of justice." Brushing aside the old rules "borrowed from the Roman law...or from the ancient common law...as inapposite or inappropriate," Thompson instead extolled the new arrangement as consistent with "the genius of this practical and utilitarian age, and the exigencies of society."

Perhaps Thompson should have been less dismissive of the ancient wisdom. But the contingent fee does have its advantages. Most obviously, such fees permit those without money to get a lawyer to sue over an injury. Under a loser-pays system like the one America originally inherited—the type that is still the rule in Britain and almost all other developed countries—an injured individual without means can still get a lawyer for a case that courts are likely to compensate. The lawyer knows that he will get reimbursed when he wins. Insurance companies write policies—called "after the event" insurance—to cover fees in the event of an unexpected legal loss. Legal aid societies fill in the gaps. But under the American Rule, where each side pays its own way, win or lose, the *only* way a poor client gets money for a plaintiffs' lawyer is from a successful case. In some sense, then, the American decision to get rid of fee shifting made the contingent fee a practical necessity.

Beyond opening up the courts to poor plaintiffs, the contingent fee helps to fix some problems that economists call "information asymmetries." Clients are typically unable to assess the value of a prospective lawsuit. But with payment conditioned on recovery, plaintiffs' lawyers have a strong incentive to take only those cases with a reasonable chance of paying off. Similarly, clients are typically unable to know what legal work is truly necessary, so a lawyer working by the hour can bilk his client—at least in an American Rule system in which each party pays its own way, win or lose. But a lawyer whose payment is a fixed portion of recovered proceeds has an incentive not to spend time and money unrelated to winning the case.

Still, that's not the end of the story. Those information asymmetries cut both ways. Precisely because a lawyer knows a lot more about the value of a case than his plaintiff, the plaintiff cannot really bargain over what percentage of the ultimate winnings make sense in a given case. In many a modern case, a plaintiffs' lawyer may have to do very little work to net his client a recovery under an insurance contract, at the contract's specified "policy limit." Any plaintiffs' lawyer could get the same amount with a simple form letter—and the lawyer knows this. But the plaintiff, unaware, signs away one-third of the proceeds.

In addition to enabling plaintiffs' lawyers to exploit some plaintiffs, the contingent fee—in combination with the American Rule making each party responsible for its own costs—gives plaintiffs' lawyers strong incentives to exploit defendants like Kathy Reece-McNeill. Knowing that the defendant will incur significant costs in a lawsuit, win or lose, plaintiffs' lawyers can engage in a game of chicken. Of course, the defendant also knows that the plaintiffs' lawyer has to spend time and money bringing a case. Sophisticated and well-funded defendants—like big companies—can fight back. Even if the defendant spends more money defending a case than it could have paid to settle, it pays to fight sometimes to keep the lawyers at bay.

But plaintiffs' lawyers can make those calculations, too—and they do. By pursuing the occasional claim that may pay off less than it costs to litigate— like the suit against Reece-McNeill—a plaintiffs' lawyer makes the game of chicken credible against other defendants. Small-business owners simply don't have the money to launch a successful defense the way a big corporation can.

What my former colleague Marie Gryphon Newhouse calls "nuisance suits" tend to have relatively low settlement values—$18,000 was the offer given to Reece-McNeill. Yet $18,000 a pop from hundreds of defendants who get identical shakedown letters adds up to a very healthy profit for a lawyer who pockets a percentage of the take. Thomas Frankovich, a lawyer in California, earned notoriety—and judicial reproach—for generating disability-law-related judicial demand letters of the sort given to Reece McNeill: a state court judge accused him of "a pattern of unethical behavior designed ultimately to extort money from businesses and their insurers." But Frankovich built a multimillion-dollar practice, in offices decorated with pricey collectors' art and antiques, and acquired multiple homes domestic and abroad, including a ranch with a herd of some 140 bison.

• • •

By the turn of the twentieth century, more and more lawyers were specializing in personal injury suits, and these specialists pursued their personal injury cases exclusively with contingent-fee contracts. Justice Thompson had questioned the claim that contingent fees would corrupt the "pure" administration of justice by stimulating lawyers' "zeal" and "selfish passions." But personal injury lawyers in the early twentieth century developed strategies to drum up business by sidestepping legal ethics rules prohibiting the direct solicitation of clients. Contract "runners" for the plaintiffs' bar scoured for business in hospitals and police stations. A 1928 report of the Law Association of Philadelphia compared the "rapacity" of these agents to "the descent of vultures on an expiring carcass" and estimated that 15 percent of total payouts in personal injury litigation went to underwrite these third-party "solicitors."

American tort law had been transformed. Initially a legal backwater, the expanded tort law flooded court dockets. By making it easier to file and litigate claims, loosening the standards for finding defendants liable for various classes of injury, and changing the way lawyers were compensated so they had powerful new incentives to drum up business, the courts had begun making the United States a litigation nation.

The next wave of civil-procedure reforms would make it easier still to bring lawsuits. Plaintiffs' lawyers would soon be able to file lawsuits without proof and force defendants to spend extraordinary amounts of time and money to help them make their case. Lawyers would be able to construct cases that merged hundreds or thousands of disparate claims into single causes of action, thus expanding the scope of shakedown opportunities. New theories of liability would give juries vast powers to second-guess product designs and warning labels, thereby serving as bottom-up regulators and turning manufacturers into de facto insurers of their customers.

None of these changes would be voted on by Congress or state legislatures. That's the story of the next two chapters.

CHAPTER 8

Lawyers Without Clients

The Subway fast-food chain built a brand reputation through an advertising campaign that included a catchy jingle promoting the restaurant's "five-dollar footlong" sandwich. But in 2013, an Australian teenager posted a picture on Facebook of a Subway footlong sandwich that measured only eleven inches!

For most people, the Subway sub's failure to measure up provided light amusement. But American class action lawyers smelled profit. In June 2013, nine different class action lawsuits were consolidated into a single cause of action in a federal court in Milwaukee, Wisconsin.

Class action lawsuits are legal vehicles that allow individuals who have suffered small injuries from a common source to adjudicate their claims in a single cause of action. But the common truth about class action lawsuits is that they, more than any other type of litigation, are conceived by and for the benefit of attorneys. Bill Lerach, who at one time was arguably America's most successful securities class action attorney, boasted to *Forbes* magazine: "I have the greatest practice of law in the world. I have no clients." Lerach's statement is ironic—he ultimately went to federal prison after being charged with bribing individuals to be his clients—but is also essentially an apt description of how class action litigation functions. Once a plaintiff class is defined by an attorney and certified by a court, any individual falling under the definition is automatically a plaintiff unless he affirmatively opts out. Thus, people are commonly plaintiffs in class action lawsuits they know nothing about.

Three in ten class action lawsuits involve consumer fraud—the theory underlying the Subway suit. Nobody is going to file an individual lawsuit over a too-short sandwich. (Anyone truly offended is free to take his business to Blimpie or another hero-sandwich competitor.) But if you string together a class action lawsuit on behalf of *every* consumer who has purchased a Subway sandwich, you're talking real money—even if payouts amount to pennies on the hoagie.

In February 2015, Subway and the class action attorneys announced that they had reached a settlement. The ten "named" plaintiffs—those listed on the lawsuit—would divide among themselves $500. (That's ten footlongs apiece, for the mathematically challenged.) The restaurant chain promised to instruct its franchisees to keep a ruler or tape measure handy. And the lawyers would be paid $520,000 in legal fees.

If you think this settlement appears to be much more about the lawyers than the customers, you aren't alone. The Center for Class Action Fairness, a nonprofit public-interest firm, challenged the terms of the settlement in federal court. In August 2017, the Seventh Circuit U.S. Court of Appeals in Chicago threw the settlement out. Writing for the three-judge panel, Judge Diane Sykes was unsparing: "A class action that seeks only worthless benefits for the class and yields only fees for class counsel is no better than a racket and should be dismissed out of hand."

Unfortunately, most cases are lower-profile than Subway's, and small non-profits like the Center for Class Action Fairness have insufficient resources to challenge every "racket." According to a 2015 survey of businesses of varying sizes, 54 percent faced a class action lawsuit that year. More than one in three of these companies faced multiple lawsuits. The average among all companies surveyed was five class action lawsuits at the time; clearly some faced a great many more than that.

•   •   •

As described in the previous chapter, the American personal injury bar emerged after courts made it easier to file lawsuits, expanded the scope of liability, and changed the ways that lawyers are compensated, giving them powerful incentives to sue for profit. Still, most of tort law's modern regulatory sweep was yet unknown at the onset of the Great Depression. Soon, however, both the procedural rules governing the litigation process and the substantive laws of recovery would shift, setting off America's second great litigation explosion. In both instances, law professors would be much more involved in driving these changes than elected legislators.

The procedural changes came first—beginning, as with much of America's multifaceted system of regulation by the unelected, during the New Deal era. Although the emergent tort law developed in the states—drawing from colonial and Crown law—the tectonic shift in procedure happened at the federal level.

Early America, like Britain, had different courts for different types of litigation. The two main types of court, courts of law and courts of equity, each had different rules and different histories. Courts of law—such as those that heard criminal trials and tort lawsuits—used lay juries. In civil cases, law courts were empowered solely to pay money damages to winning parties. Such courts had strict pleading requirements for private parties who wanted to get their cases to trial, and narrow procedural rules, such as the limitations on witnesses. In contrast, courts of equity, such as those governing trusts and estates, eschewed juries—and in the early days oral public trials as well. The "chancellors" who oversaw such courts made it much easier to plead cases, join different cases together, and interrogate witnesses. Equity courts also fashioned injunctions and other remedies that went beyond money damages.

When Congress established the federal courts, it kept the distinction between law and equity intact. The Supreme Court defined the procedural rules in equity cases, under a grant of authority by Congress, but it ordered the federal courts to follow state rules in cases of law. This made federal legal practice a maddeningly complex endeavor: the federal rules of the game shifted not only between law and equity but also from state to state. By the late nineteenth century, the American Bar Association had formed a Committee on Uniformity of Procedure and Comparative Law to explore and ultimately advocate for uniform federal rules of civil procedure. Among those speaking in favor of the idea in 1888 was none other than David Dudley Field, who had revolutionized New York's civil procedure forty years before.

In the early twentieth century, President William Howard Taft—a former judge and future chief justice of the United States—threw his considerable weight behind reform and began advocating for new rules that consolidated law and equity. Nevertheless, reform efforts languished for decades and seemed destined to fail early in Franklin Roosevelt's administration when the president tapped as his first attorney general Senator Thomas J. Walsh of

Montana, the fiercest congressional opponent of the long-debated procedural consolidation. But as fate would have it, Walsh died before assuming the position. In his place, Roosevelt appointed as attorney general his convention floor manager, Homer Cummings, a graduate of Yale Law School. Cummings would push for a sweeping federal procedural rewrite as part of the early New Deal reforms. In June 1934, Congress passed the Rules Enabling Act, which gave the Supreme Court broad powers to draft new Federal Rules of Civil Procedure. Under the terms of the legislation, the Court could propose its rules, and unless Congress took action in a short period of time to stop the rules from going into effect, they would have legal force.

• • •

The following year, 1935, the Supreme Court appointed a rules advisory committee composed of leading lawyers, principally from prestigious New York and Boston firms, and five law professors from elite schools. The "reporter" of the committee and its driving force was Charles E. Clark, who served as dean and taught civil procedure at Yale Law School.

The legal academy was still relatively new, having been fashioned in its modern form at Harvard in the late nineteenth century. Yale was the epicenter of the "legal realist" school, which disdained the "formalisms" of the law and sought a data-based, outcome-driven jurisprudence consistent with Progressive and New Deal principles. According to one of the leading scholars of the era:

> Clark was impressed with the observation that one could not define what was a fact [or] evidence...in a scientific way, and that such terms were best seen as a continuum, without logical cutoff points. The deductive reasoning of the common law was flawed, and set, defined legal categories were suspect. Balancing tests replaced attempts at categorization and definition.

In a 1935 law review article, Clark had written that the federal equity rules should "furnish the substantial model for the new Federal procedure of the future." Along those lines, the advisory committee imported equity procedures such as loose pleading standards to initiate a case, ample opportunities to amend legal claims, and easy mechanisms for joining cases together. The strict common-law rules—which served in no small part to narrow disputes for lay jurors' consideration—were essentially thrown out the window.

Perhaps the most consequential change wrought by the rules advisory committee was drafted by Edson Sunderland, a professor of civil procedure at the University of Michigan. Sunderland had long advocated for broadening the "discovery" techniques available to attorneys to obtain information from opposing parties before trial—which he viewed as essential to ferreting out the "true nature of the controversy." Up to that point, legal rights of discovery were extremely limited in American courts, in both law and equity. (They remain quite limited outside the United States.) The pretrial oral "deposition" of a party of interest was not unknown but generally restricted to cases in which an important witness was unavailable for trial. Sunderland's approach was completely unprecedented, as he freely admitted. In essence, if a court somewhere in the United States had come up with some major device permitting "discovery" by the plaintiffs to a lawsuit, Sunderland threw it into the mix. He also added in his own new, untested ideas. All of these made it into the final draft of the new rules. And the final draft even dispensed with some of the constraints that Sunderland had put in early drafts and that the advisory committee had considered in their deliberations.

Sunderland's new discovery rules contained broad rights to depose witnesses and inspect the other party's documents. It did not matter if the evidence that lawyers sought to discover would "be inadmissible at trial" so long as "the testimony sought appears reasonably calculated to lead to the discovery of admissible evidence." In other words, a party to a lawsuit could force the other party to give over any evidence that might lead to more evidence.

George Wickersham, a committee member who had served as attorney general under President Taft, worried openly about "fishing expeditions," but he passed away before the committee had completed its work. The American Bar Association supported the reforms, which after all generated a lot of new work for lawyers. The final federal rules were presented by the Supreme Court to Congress in 1938 and went into effect later the same year. State after state began to adopt close variants of the federal rules or at least incorporate their core principles.

• • •

The new federal rules revolutionized the practice of law in America. The rules loosened pleading standards so that a party merely needed to give "notice" to the other party with a "plain statement" of the alleged facts of the case and theory of injury. This is called "notice pleading." At this early stage of the case, the court would have to accept as true the facts as presented by the plaintiff. Then, before trial, the suing party could build its case by interviewing the defendant—including multiple related parties who might supply a link to new evidence—and by poring over documents it could freely demand from the other side, regardless of their admissibility in court. These new rules combined to make it next to impossible to toss a theoretically viable case before the discovery process, and it made legal costs escalate long before trial. This was particularly problematic in light of the American Rule on fee shifting that meant a defendant in litigation had to bear its own costs, win or lose.

The personal injury bar that had been so energized by the contingent fee came to realize that it could exploit the new system. *Almost any* legal filing could trigger an expensive discovery process under the new rules—meaning that a defendant like Kathie Reece-McNeill had an incentive to settle for a tidy sum rather than resist. And if a defendant decided to go through the process, the fishing expedition might uncover something else to sue over, even if the original theory of the case got no bites.

Discovery in modern litigation is frightfully expensive. Some studies estimate it constitutes as much as 90 percent of all litigation expenses; essentially every study finds it constitutes a majority. In the electronic age, the volume of documents produced in lawsuits can approach the absurd. In one case involving the semiconductor manufacturer Intel, the electronic documents produced would, if printed on paper, have amounted to a pile 137 miles high.

In the last couple of decades, the U.S. Supreme Court has belatedly made an effort to rein in out-of-control notice pleading and discovery. In its 2007 decision in *Bell Atlantic v. Twombly*, the Court rejected a plaintiff's pleading as insufficient and insisted that the pleading had to allege enough facts "to raise a reasonable expectation that discovery will reveal evidence" to build a case. In 2015, the Supreme Court accepted revisions to the discovery rules developed by its advisory committee established under the still-in-force Rules Enabling Act.

But these tweaks operate only on the margins. They have merely curtailed fishing expeditions in the deepest of waters. The core architecture erected by Professors Clark and Sunderland continues to permit plaintiffs' lawyers to file suits without evidence and build their cases at defendants' expense.

• • •

The particular legal device that enabled the Subway lawsuits—the ones that Judge Sykes labeled a "racket"—emerged later. The rules advisory committee run by Professor Clark was not a one-time project; a standing advisory committee on the federal rules exists to the present day. In the 1960s, a federal rules advisory committee led by law professors developed the "opt out" class action lawsuit for damages. Their new rule, like Sunderland's approach to discovery, was unprecedented. And they had little idea that their innovation would have such a far-reaching impact on American law.

As mentioned, equity courts had a long history of merging cases together. The English chancery court began joining "necessary" parties to legal disputes in the late seventeenth century. In estate, bankruptcy, and similar proceedings that involved multiple claimants on a defendant's limited resources, equity-court judges sought to bring in competing parties with a financial interest in the litigation. On occasion—when the number of competing claimants was large and their interests very similar—courts would consider the interests of absent parties that were not formally joined to the case. In addition, through a mechanism known as the "bill of peace," equity courts had long issued injunctive actions—forbidding a certain practice but not requiring payment of money damages—that were binding on a "multitude" of parties not literally before the court.

American courts of equity imported the British practice. In 1842, the U.S. Supreme Court adopted Equity Rule 48, which authorized courts to proceed in cases when necessary parties were not present if the parties "on either side are very numerous, and can not, without manifest inconvenience and oppressive delays in the suit be all brought before it." The rule applied only to equity cases—not tort lawsuits for damages—and the absent parties could not be bound by the judgment.

When Professor Clark's advisory committee crafted the new Federal Rules of Civil Procedure in the 1930s, they imported something like the equity rule for all litigation. Class action lawsuits involving the interests of absent parties were possible when those parties were "so numerous as to make it impracticable to bring them all before the court." The new Rule 23 governing class actions was drafted by the "chief research assistant" on Clark's staff, a newly minted lawyer named James William Moore. (Moore would go on to be a longtime professor of law at Yale and author of a thirty-four-volume treatise on federal legal practice.)

Unfortunately, Moore's class action rule proved confusing to courts. The rule set up three categories of class action lawsuit. These came to be called "true," "hybrid," and "spurious" class actions. In the first two, the parties in the class were already legally joined in some fashion. Spurious class actions involved lawsuits seeking "a common relief" for disparate parties when "there is a common question of law or fact." Critically, however, parties that were not actually joined in the litigation before the court retained all their legal rights, even when those suing in their name lost in court. This allowed those with an interest in the case to sit on the sidelines and see what happened.

In 1961, the Union Carbide & Carbon Corporation lost an antitrust case. It was structured as a "spurious" class action lawsuit, with absent parties not formally joined in the legal action. The U.S. Court of Appeals for the Tenth Circuit nevertheless permitted absent plaintiffs to recover damages, without having to relitigate their claim. The court viewed its decision as economical: why go through another trial on liability when the absent plaintiffs' case involved identical facts? But this created a "one way" problem: had Union Carbide won its case, it could not have blocked the absent plaintiffs from suing it again on the identical theory, since the class action rule retained all their legal rights. The Tenth Circuit's holding was the minority rule— other courts had decided the issue the other way—but the rules advisory committee wanted to clear things up. They also sought to clarify the class action rules because judges were struggling to apply them in emergent civil rights litigation.

The reporter for the rules advisory committee that amended federal class action rules in the 1960s was Benjamin Kaplan, a Harvard professor who specialized in copyright law. The committee separated out class action suits seeking injunctions from those seeking money damages. The damages lawsuits were defined in the new Rule 23(b)(3). A young law professor named Arthur Miller hammered out the new rule on a manual typewriter in the back seat of Professor Kaplan's car, as they took a ferry to Kaplan's summer home in Martha's Vineyard. Miller would go on to be a leading academic scholar of federal civil procedure who coauthored his own treatise on the subject, in more than thirty volumes. Currently at the NYU School of Law, Professor Miller has also in recent years served as "special counsel" to Milberg LLP, one of the nation's largest class action plaintiffs' law firms. (Milberg once employed Bill Lerach, the highly successful securities class action attorney who boasted that he had "no clients.")

The rule that Miller and Kaplan crafted would, for the first time in American legal history, permit broad actions for damages in court on behalf of absent plaintiffs. The class of plaintiffs would be defined at the outset; the court would direct some form of notice to class members; and all class members would be included in the action unless they affirmatively opted out of the litigation.

• • •

In a 1967 article summarizing the committee's work for the *Harvard Law Review*, Professor Kaplan said that the group's objective in crafting the new class action lawsuit for damages binding on absent parties was "to get at the cases where a class action promises important advantages of economy of effort and uniformity of result without undue dilution of procedural safeguards for members of the class or for the opposing party." The committee intended for judges to take "a close look at the case before it is accepted as a class action." The notice and opt-out provisions would allow "individual preference…to operate" and "democratize the procedure for members of the class." Kaplan admitted the new procedure was "somewhat novel."

Some critics of the proposed rule suggested that the committee limit the class action device to cases seeking injunctions, not the lawsuits for money damages established by Rule 23(b)(3). Professor Kaplan saw such a "timid course" as "unthinkable." He similarly brushed aside concerns that the new device might unfairly eliminate the legal rights of absent parties looped into the lawsuit, especially if notice to those parties "may turn out to be inadequate." Kaplan argued that requiring individuals to opt into the lawsuit upon receiving notice, rather than assuming their consent absent their opting out, ran the risk of "freezing out the claims of people—especially small claims held by small people—who for one reason or another, ignorance, timidity, unfamiliarity with business or legal matters, will simply not take the affirmative step."

The advisory committee that drafted the new class action rule gave little thought to how it might be applied, as Professor Miller later freely admitted. Professor Kaplan's law review article posited only two types of cases as "likely, although not by any means sure candidates for class treatment under subdivision (b)(3)": antitrust cases, like *Union Carbide & Carbon Corp. v. Nisley* (1961), and certain cases involving fraudulent misrepresentation in the sale of securities, such as the Supreme Court case of *Guaranty Trust Co. v. York* (1944).

• • •

All fifty states except Mississippi adopted close variants of Miller and Kaplan's class action rule, and its application has proved far different from Kaplan's prediction. The most common type of class action lawsuit today involves not antitrust or securities claims but consumer-fraud actions like the lawsuit against Subway's eleven-inch footlong. Among the thirty-eight states that allow for class action consumer-fraud lawsuits, eleven permit plaintiffs to recover minimum "statutory" damages without any showing of injury. In recent years, lawsuits on these theories have become especially common; one study found that the number of court decisions involving fraud actions filed under state consumer-protection acts increased 119 percent from 2000 to 2007.

Even without the class action mechanism, these consumer-fraud lawsuits with minimum statutory damages can encourage legal mischief. In 2005, a dissatisfied customer sued a dry cleaner in Washington, D.C., for $67 million—for allegedly losing his pants. The case was predicated on consumer fraud, given the establishment's signs promising "Same Day Service" and "Satisfaction Guaranteed." The plaintiff, at the time an administrative law judge, added up per-day statutory damages, given his lack of satisfaction, and topped those off with claims of mental anguish. He rejected multiple settlement offers that eventually rose to $12,000. (The customer ultimately lost his case, but not before the Korean immigrants running the business closed up shop. Like Kathie Reece-McNeill, they found that in the American legal system, even when you win, you lose.)

Such consumer-fraud statutes become particularly dangerous when combined with the class action device. Regulation-by-litigation lawsuits have frequently targeted the producers of common processed foods—such as Pop-Tarts, Froot Loops, and Fruit Roll-Ups—for deceptively implying that the products are "healthy" because their packaging uses the word "fruit." On a single day in October 2016, a Missouri law firm filed nine class action lawsuits against the manufacturers of movie-theater and Halloween candy favorites, including Skittles, Reese's Pieces, and Junior Mints. The lawsuits claimed that the candy makers were engaged in deceptive marketing because their boxes weren't filled to the brim with candy—notwithstanding that content weights clearly appeared on the packaging. (Incredibly, Missouri courts have ruled that a consumer-fraud action is not precluded by accurate package labeling.) Consumer-fraud lawsuits of this sort rarely have giant paydays; but by combining the claims of thousands or millions of consumers who buy everyday products, lawyers can drive big companies to settle.

Other types of class action lawsuits can be very costly to large corporate defendants. More than a quarter of class action lawsuits today involve labor issues—the most frequently filed type of class action litigation after consumer fraud. Pension-related lawsuits alone netted $1.3 billion in settlement money in 2014. And those securities lawsuits that Kaplan's rules advisory committee contemplated? They typically pay out more than $1 billion annually in fees to plaintiffs' securities class action lawyers, based on published federal securities settlements.

Why have the volume and value of securities and other class action lawsuits exploded? In no small part, the boom in class action litigation is a function of courts shifting legal rules and developing new legal theories, even when the statutes written by elected legislatures say nothing about them. When Congress enacted the Securities Act of 1933 and the Securities and Exchange Act of 1934 in the early days of the New Deal, it said nothing about private lawsuits. But federal courts saw "implied" rights to sue in the statutes.

Kaplan's rules advisory committee had anticipated that some securities lawsuits might be suitable for their new class action device, but they did not foresee how courts would create a new industry for such lawsuits based on ordinary company statements unrelated to the public offering of a stock or bond. Some federal courts determined that owners of publicly traded shares could sue a company over alleged misstatements that made them pay too much money for shares of stock from other shareowners in the marketplace. And courts deemed it possible to bring a class action lawsuit even though most members of the class did not rely on the company's alleged misrepresentation, because the alleged falsehood would be reflected in the company's market price. In 1988, the U.S. Supreme Court agreed.

Whatever the theoretical niceties of this "fraud on the market" theory, it encouraged a massive new line of business for plaintiffs' lawyers.

• • •

Courts have developed new theories allowing class action lawsuits for damages to proceed even when the plaintiffs in the class receive no compensation whatsoever. A longstanding feature of the Anglo-American law of charitable trusts, with roots going back to the legal code of the sixth-century Byzantine emperor Justinian, is the *cy pres* doctrine. Derived from the medieval French expression *cy pres comme possible* ("as near as possible"), the doctrine enables charitable trustees to alter a trust's terms if a change in law or circumstances has made fulfilling the original terms of the trust impossible. For example, in 1867 the Massachusetts Supreme Judicial Court permitted trustees to revise a trust created to fight for the abolition of slavery, allowing the trust to fund efforts to fight poverty among freed slaves.

What does all this have to do with class action lawsuits? Well, nothing, if we're talking about any statute enacted by Congress or even the rules adopted by the Supreme Court under the advice of its advisory committee. But in 1971—six years after opt-out class action lawsuits were established under federal rules—a law student at the University of Chicago, in a student-edited law review, suggested importing the *cy pres* doctrine to class action settlements. The student observed that class action payouts were typically small and that the new rules made no provision for what to do when very few of the plaintiffs in the class signed up to get their small settlement awards. As a remedy, the student proposed allowing class action attorneys to distribute their clients' cash to charities that would benefit the plaintiffs' interests.

Congress enacted no law—and federal courts adopted no rule—that allowed plaintiffs' proceeds to be distributed to charities in this way. Nevertheless, shortly after the student law review note was published, judges began rubber-stamping class action settlements that distributed proceeds to charities rather than to plaintiffs. Because lawyers' contingent fees are a function of overall settlement size, these *cy pres* awards have allowed lawyers to bump up their own fees by inflating settlement levels. The average *cy pres* award has totaled more than $5.8 million. Some plaintiffs' firms have specialized in the practice—turning themselves into major philanthropists repurposing class proceeds. The Ohio plaintiffs' firm Dworken & Bernstein has a charitable arm, Ohio Lawyers Give Back, which it boasts "has been responsible for the distribution of over $37 million to many deserving communal organizations since 2003."

• • •

Under the rules developed by Professors Kaplan and Miller, judges are supposed to review class action settlements, and to reject settlements that are not "fair, reasonable, and adequate." But judges are ill-equipped to do so, and have little incentive to second-guess a settlement when attorneys on both sides support it.

Why wouldn't defendants object? They have already decided that they are better off agreeing to settle. Class action litigation, by stringing so many causes of action together, involves very high potential payouts. Surveyed companies reported that in 2014, more than 16 percent of class action lawsuits were high-risk, "bet the company" cases. Defendants can hardly be expected to worry about whether the other side's lawyers have structured a settlement to benefit themselves and their preferred charities, rather than the plaintiff class.

In theory, members of the class can object to a settlement, as the Center for Class Action Fairness did, successfully, in the Subway sandwich case. But with the stakes for each member of a class so small, nobody really has an incentive to do so—which is why the Center for Class Action Fairness is a small outfit, structured as a nonprofit reliant on charitable donations. (There are some individuals who have profited as professional class action objectors, but they do little to change the process, as they usually accept money from the parties to walk away, with minimal adjustments to the settlement's terms.)

The U.S. Supreme Court has placed some modest boundaries on class action litigation. In 2011, it threw out a massive class action employment lawsuit that used statistical models to allege that all female employees at Wal-Mart had been the victims of discrimination. The Court determined that the individual situations of all Wal-Mart employees were too different to constitute a common class. But most courts remain quite willing to "certify" class action claims, and appellate courts over time have become somewhat less likely to review such decisions made by trial court judges.

Another 2011 Supreme Court decision, *AT&T Mobility v. Concepcion*, proved more significant. In that case, the Court interpreted an old law, the 1925 Federal Arbitration Act, to permit companies to use contractual language that called for private arbitration instead of litigation to resolve customer complaints—even if that meant it foreclosed class action lawsuits. Because arbitration is a significantly cheaper and faster mechanism for resolving small consumer claims than class action litigation, some companies began adopting more such provisions. There's some evidence that the savings from avoiding class action litigation were passed on to consumers.

The plaintiffs' bar predictably howled. Sympathetic news outlets presented horror stories in which aggrieved parties claimed they had been ripped off by private arbitrators, and complained about the unfairness of limiting consumers' legal rights in boilerplate contracts that nobody reads. None of the stories raised the question of how many class members typically read class action notices about settlements that similarly compromise their right to sue.

Today, scaling back companies' ability to foreclose class action lawsuits with arbitration contracts is atop the legislative wish list for the organized plaintiffs' bar. The lawyers had some success in doing so through administrative agency actions during Barack Obama's presidency—though most of these successes were promptly reversed by the Trump administration or rescinded by Congress.

Still, despite decades of business-sponsored reform efforts, Congress has done very little to rein in class action lawsuit abuse, even though it never wrote legislation to create the problem. A 1995 bill, enacted over President Bill Clinton's veto, placed somewhat tighter controls on securities lawsuits, requiring slightly heightened pleading rules that made law firms articulate with somewhat greater specificity the allegedly fraudulent misstatements. A 2005 bill made it possible for defendant companies to get nationwide class actions into federal court. (The tort system's role in allowing localities and states to impose national standards is the subject of Chapter 11.) But the basic class action architecture remains in place.

CHAPTER 9

Bottom-Up Regulators

$\mathbf{I}$f you mention "lawsuit abuse" or "tort reform" to most Americans over the age of thirty-five, they are likely to think of the McDonald's coffee case. A jury in Albuquerque, New Mexico, awarded $2.86 million in damages to Stella Liebeck in a product liability lawsuit in 1994. She had suffered burns after spilling hot McDonald's coffee on her lap.

The verdict quickly circulated on the press wires. ABC News called the Liebeck case "the poster child of excessive lawsuits." The popular television show *Seinfeld* spoofed the case in 1995. In the *Seinfeld* version, the clumsy character Cosmo Kramer attempts to sneak a cup of coffee into a movie theater and spills it on himself. He contracts with a flamboyant plaintiffs' lawyer who promises him "millions." Terrified executives of the gourmet coffee store that sold him his joe quickly offer a settlement.

On *Seinfeld*, Kramer's burn is minor, and he heals the wound with a Chinese balm before he and his lawyer go to negotiate. But the real McDonald's coffee victim actually suffered serious injuries. Stella Liebeck, who was seventy-nine years old, had spilled an entire cup of coffee on her lap as she opened the lid to add cream and sugar. Her cotton pants absorbed the liquid, holding it against her skin. She then remained seated for ninety seconds in the passenger seat of her grandson's car. Her burns were so severe that she spent eight days in the hospital, had to undergo skin grafts, and lost some twenty pounds.

It's not hard to see how a jury might want to help a plaintiff suffering from such severe injuries. To be sure, coffee is *supposed* to be hot, as Seinfeld remarks to Kramer in the television version of the case. But just how hot? Liebeck's coffee, when spilled, was somewhere between 165° and 175° F—having cooled off somewhat from the 180–190° F that McDonald's prescribed for its franchises in operations manuals. A Texas attorney, Reed Morgan, showed that evidence to the jury, along with evidence gathered by his own investigators from various restaurants around Albuquerque purportedly showing that other restaurants served coffee some 20 degrees cooler than the McDonald's standard. Morgan argued that coffee should be served no hotter than 140°, at which temperature human skin could easily withstand sustained contact with a hot liquid. He also showed the jury evidence that McDonald's had received more than seven hundred complaints in the preceding decade about burns from hot coffee, and had paid out more than $500,000 to settle claims. Thus, Morgan argued, McDonald's coffee was "unreasonably dangerous" and "defectively manufactured."

With these facts before it, the jury decided to punish the fast-food restaurant. Morgan had told the jury that McDonald's earned some $1.35 million daily from coffee revenues. The jury settled on twice that amount as a "punitive" damage award.

But Morgan had spun a fable for the Liebeck jury. Whatever the merits of his investigation of restaurants around Albuquerque, McDonald's served coffee consistent with guidelines from the National Coffee Association. To this day, the industry group prescribes "a water temperature between 195–205 degrees Fahrenheit for optimal extraction" and counsels that coffee's "temperature should be maintained at 180–185 degrees Fahrenheit" if it will be served within minutes. After the Liebeck verdict came down, the *Los Angeles Times* did its own investigation and found that Burger King and Starbucks served coffee at higher temperatures than McDonald's.

• • •

For most of American history, bringing a lawsuit against a manufacturer—or a restaurant—alleging an injury from its product would have been impossible. Tort law involved accidents. Buying and selling products was a matter of contract. The class of cases in which "a contract may be turned into a tort" was narrowly limited to those involving a "public duty."

Throughout the nineteenth century, American courts followed the English-law rule concerning contract and liability, as illustrated by a case from 1840. A horse-drawn mail coach in Chester County, England, had collapsed on its route. The driver sued the individuals who had contracted with the British postmaster general to maintain the coach. The British courts said that the mail-coach driver was not "privy to the contract" between the postmaster general and the individuals maintaining the coach, so he was out of luck in the courts.

As the products manufactured in the emerging industrial economy became increasingly complex, American courts began to see the old limitations on liability as unreasonable. They carved out exceptions. A plaintiff whose injury was attributable to a "latent defect" in a product could sue for damages, but the plaintiff had to establish that the manufacturer had knowledge of the defect.

In 1916, the New York Court of Appeals threw out the old rules altogether. *MacPherson v. Buick* involved the successor to the mail coach—the automobile. The 1909 Buick Runabout had wooden wheels. In 1911, a wheel on a Runabout driven by Donald MacPherson collapsed. When the case reached the Empire State's highest court, Judge Benjamin Cardozo—a future New Deal–era justice on the U.S. Supreme Court—announced a new rule. The manufacturer of a product "reasonably certain to place life and limb in peril when negligently made" was liable for injuries caused by such negligence "irrespective of contract." A plaintiff did not have to show that a manufacturer had knowledge of a product defect—only that the danger was reasonably foreseeable and that the manufacturer had been negligent in failing to foresee it.

Not requiring a plaintiff to show a manufacturer's actual knowledge of a product defect certainly made theoretical sense, at least in the early twentieth century. Before the open-ended discovery rules were written into the Federal Rules of Civil Procedure by Professors Edson Sunderland and Charles E. Clark in 1938, it was nigh impossible for a plaintiff to obtain evidence showing manufacturer knowledge, absent an unlikely admission on the witness stand. But whether a "defect" actually exists in the first place can be a tricky question of fact—as the McDonald's coffee case would later show.

Just as Stella Liebeck's attorney, Reed Morgan, had presented a misleading picture to the jury, Judge Cardozo fudged the facts in his *MacPherson v. Buick* opinion. Cardozo credited MacPherson's word that he had been driving only eight miles per hour. But every eyewitness at the trial had testified that MacPherson's car had been going more than thirty miles per hour—a high speed for a wooden-wheeled car made in the early twentieth century. Moreover, an expert witness had testified that the Buick would have stalled in a high gear at eight miles per hour on a gravel road—making MacPherson's self-serving claim a logical impossibility. No competing expert contradicted that testimony. If a learned judge could play fast and loose with the facts to reach the outcome he wanted, it's little wonder that a jury might do the same when faced with a sympathetic plaintiff like an elderly woman who suffered severe burn injuries.

Of course, we now know that automobile tires are best made from substances other than wood. Plaintiffs' lawyers tend to claim credit for product improvements spurred by the threat of their lawsuits. While these claims are not wholly fantastical, they are not broadly supported by the record. The B.F. Goodrich Company figured out how to add carbon to the rubber in 1910. The Hardman Tire & Rubber Company marketed the first commercially successful air-filled rubber tire in 1911. These innovations came after Buick's 1909 model—but years before Cardozo's court opinion. When Professor George Priest of Yale Law School studied accident rates and product liability law over time, he reached a surprising conclusion. The rate at which products sold in the marketplace caused consumer injuries continued to decrease throughout the twentieth century. But following the explosion in product liability litigation, the rate at which product safety improved actually fell.

• • •

Fifty years before Liebeck's case made national headlines, another case involving a beverage ushered in the era of modern product liability law. In 1944, a California jury held Coca-Cola responsible for severe hand injuries suffered by a waitress, Gladys Escola. According to Escola's account, a Coca-Cola bottle exploded when she was putting it into a refrigerator. The bottle's pieces were subsequently discarded, and the jury was presented with no evidence of error in Coca-Cola's manufacturing process. Escola's lawyer, Melvin Belli, called as a witness a Coca-Cola delivery driver who said he had seen some of the company's bottles explode. The California Supreme Court affirmed a verdict for Escola under the doctrine of *res ipsa loquitur*—the Latin phrase meaning "the thing speaks for itself"—under which courts had long permitted juries to infer negligence from circumstantial evidence.

The *Escola* case was not particularly notable for its ruling. Holding manufacturers liable for negligence in product manufacturing had been established decades before in *MacPherson*, and the *res ipsa loquitur* doctrine traced back to the nineteenth century. Assuming that a soda bottle exploded under normal conditions, it is hardly unreasonable to hold the bottle's manufacturer responsible for any foreseeable injuries that resulted.

Yet thirty years later, Belli remarked, "If there is one legal decision upon which Ralph Nader built, this was it." (Nader was a prominent advocate for the plaintiffs' bar in the 1960s before becoming a well-known consumer advocate.) Why did Belli say that? Aside from ordinary trial-lawyer bravado, he was referring to *Escola*'s concurring opinion, written by Justice Roger Traynor. Traynor argued that the court should dispense with negligence altogether in assessing manufacturers' liability for injuries traced to their products. He pushed instead for a doctrine of "absolute liability" whenever a manufacturer's product has a "defect that causes injury to human beings." Nineteen years later, Traynor would win over enough of his colleagues to enshrine his notion of "strict liability" in California law. According to a poll of the membership of the Association of Trial Lawyers of America conducted in 1996, the case adopting Traynor's legal theory, *Greenman v. Yuba Power Products* (1963), was the most significant change made to tort law in the previous fifty years.

. . .

The strict-liability rule had long been on law professors' wish list. William Prosser, at the University of Minnesota, had argued for strict product liability in his 1941 torts treatise—three years before Justice Traynor wrote his opinion in *Escola*. (Prosser would later become dean of the Boalt Hall School of Law at the University of California at Berkeley, where Belli studied, and where Traynor taught tax law.) Two years after *Yuba Power*, the American Law Institute (ALI) would adopt Traynor's strict-liability rule in its influential Second Restatement of Torts.

The American Law Institute was founded in 1923 by "the cream of the American legal establishment." In that era, before computers were available to aid in legal research, lawyers and judges were finding the accumulation of legal precedents "unmanageable." The ALI sought to help practitioners by drafting "codes" that would "minimize, if not dispense with" the need to look through the mass of earlier legal opinions.

The ALI lacked the legal authority that the Supreme Court would later give to the rules advisory efforts headed by Charles Clark and Benjamin Kaplan. Its clout rested on its members' prestige and skills of persuasion. But like the advisory committees, law professors would play an outsized role in the ALI's work. Professors were the "reporters" who drafted each "restatement" of the law. William Draper Lewis, dean of the law school at the University of Pennsylvania, would serve for twenty years as the ALI's first executive director.

Before long, the professors began to advocate that the ALI's restatements of the law not merely characterize the law as it was, but state what the professors thought the law should be. Among those taking this view was Professor Clark. A legal realist, the Yale Law dean found the ALI's "general purposes of clarification and simplification" to be "fallacious." Clark argued that the ALI should reject a "simple" law in favor of one that would "keep abreast of business and social life." Responding to such criticisms, the ALI commissioned a series of "Second Restatements" that purported to update the earlier committees' work—and in fact significantly changed it. As reporter for the Second Restatement of Torts, the ALI selected none other than William Prosser.

• • •

When Prosser wrote strict liability for product manufacturers into Section 402A of the Second Restatement, he had in mind cases like Coca-Cola's exploding bottle, not the hot coffee that McDonald's served to Stella Liebeck. In comments to the general strict-liability rule, Prosser's restatement observed that some products "cannot possibly" be made "entirely safe" for consumption. A product should be deemed "unreasonably dangerous" only if "the ordinary consumer who purchases it" would not contemplate the product's risk. The comment explained: "Good butter is not unreasonably dangerous merely because, if such be the case, it deposits cholesterol in the arteries and leads to heart attacks; but bad butter, contaminated with poisonous fish oil, is unreasonably dangerous."

As Liebeck's case shows, however, a skilled lawyer can make bad butter out of good. Dubious evidence—like the claim that McDonald's was serving its coffee at temperatures exceeding industry norms—can encourage jurors to accept the notion that the coffee was "unreasonably" hot. Notwithstanding the Second Restatement's commentary, Prosser's strict-liability rule ushered in a new wave of "design defect" lawsuits asking juries to play scientist and engineer. Would an alternative product design have reduced or avoided injuries?

The Liebeck jury was aware that McDonald's had received hundreds of prior complaints about hot-coffee burns. (It and other restaurant chains continue to get complaints, and the occasional lawsuit, to this day.) But it does not follow from these complaints that McDonald's needed to lower its coffee's serving temperature. The hundreds of complaints need to be weighed against the number of cups of coffee sold daily. McDonald's has long touted its "billions and billions served." The percentage of McDonald's coffee drinkers complaining about hot-coffee burns is lower than the percentage of Americans killed annually by lightning. And most of those complaints involve burns significantly less severe than Liebeck's.

Defenders of the Liebeck verdict often observe that McDonald's rejected her lawyers' early offer to settle the case for $20,000—a bit more than double her medical bills. In hindsight, that was doubtless a strategic error. But it's also hard to see why a restaurant chain serving billions would offer to be a general insurer for its customers against product-related injuries when its product conforms to industry guidelines and consumer risks are self-evident. Why not hold the car manufacturer liable, since the 1989 Ford Probe, in which Liebeck was seated, had no cup holders? Or how about the manufacturers of Liebeck's pants, which could have mitigated her injuries if made of a different fabric? McDonald's had indeed settled some earlier cases involving hot-coffee spills, but those typically involved coffee spilled by McDonald's employees, for whose negligence the restaurant *was* responsible. Before the Liebeck decision, a dozen juries had faced cases involving coffee spills by restaurant customers, and none had found the restaurant legally responsible.

The Liebeck case caught the public's attention precisely because it involved an everyday product causing injuries that any adult could reasonably have foreseen. As the Second Restatement itself suggested, sometimes customers simply like products that involve some risk. Ted Frank, a lawyer who is critical of the Liebeck verdict, points out that between 2002 and 2010, 17,616 men went to the emergency room for genital injuries related to pants zippers—a risk sufficiently common that it was lampooned in the 1998 Farrelly brothers film *There's Something About Mary*. A manufacturer of men's pants clearly could alter its designs to mitigate or eliminate this risk. Indeed, not all pants have zippers. But clearly, some customers prefer those that do.

Similarly, McDonald's could decide only to serve its coffee iced. But its customers prefer otherwise. Were McDonald's to serve its coffee *too* hot, it would doubtless lose customers over time. But so too would it lose customers by cutting its temperatures so low that one's cup of coffee was lukewarm when consumed. McDonald's franchises continue to serve coffee today in the same temperature range as in 1992.

• • •

McDonald's has made one change to its coffee since 1992. It has added a slightly larger warning label. But even at the time when it served Liebeck her notorious brew, McDonald's had used coffee cups that featured the prominent warning: "Caution: Contents Hot."

Such warning labels are a peculiarly American phenomenon. One Canadian company had fun at Americans' expense by making coffee cups that read, "If this was another country, we'd have to tell you that this coffee may be hot. Good thing this is Canada!"

These silly warning labels also have their roots in Professor Prosser's Second Restatement of Torts. In comment (j) to the strict-liability rule, Prosser's ALI committee clarified that "directions or warnings" would "prevent" a product "from being unreasonably dangerous." The warning exception was consistent with the committee's view that manufacturers should not be held liable for known risks like the artery-clogging properties of butter. By making a safety hazard known, a manufacturer could insulate itself from harm. And the manufacturer need not worry if a consumer had *actually* read the label; in the committee's formulation, "Where warning is given, the seller may reasonably assume that it will be read and heeded."

In practice, just as the committee's sensible distinctions between good and bad butter did not prevent lawyers from making jurors experts on coffee production, the warning rule did not really establish a safe harbor from lawsuits. Like design-defect cases, "failure to warn" lawsuits asking juries to assess products' warning labels have proliferated since the Second Restatement. Is a warning label really clear? Perhaps it might have been placed differently, or used a bigger or bolder font? As long as judges leave such questions to juries, they might look to a deep-pocketed defendant to cover a sympathetic victim's costs. McDonald's had a clear warning label on its coffee. Like many companies before and since, it found the warning insufficient insulation against liability.

That hasn't stopped companies from trying to make their labels bulletproof. The results inspired Bob Dorigo Jones, a Michigan tort-reform advocate, to start an annual "wacky warning labels" contest in 1997, to focus consumers' attention on the issue. Among some of his greatest hits were an iron that warned, "Do not iron while wearing shirt"; a flushable toilet brush that warned, "Do not use for personal hygiene"; and a can of self-defense pepper spray that warned, "May irritate eyes." In 2007, Jones compiled his favorite warning labels in a book, *Remove Child Before Folding: The 101 Stupidest, Silliest, and Wackiest Warning Labels Ever.* The drafters of the Second Restatement of Torts wanted to encourage sellers in the marketplace to warn consumers of product risks. In that, they succeeded.

• • •

There's little question that the Liebeck verdict became a national story not only because hot coffee can self-evidently be harmful when spilled but also because of the verdict's size. Yes, Liebeck was seriously injured—though some members of the public may have been under the misimpression that her injuries, like the fictional Cosmo Kramer's, were minor. But *$2.9 million*?

Even those sympathetic to the idea that McDonald's should have paid her medical bills might have deemed such a figure unreasonably large. Particularly if they understood that those medical bills totaled $10,500. The judge in Liebeck's case ultimately lowered the jury's initial punitive award to "only" $480,000, triple the award it deemed appropriate to compensate her for her injuries. But that figure still implies compensatory damages of $160,000—more than an order of magnitude larger than Liebeck's medical bills. (The jury actually determined that $200,000 was the appropriate compensatory award—ten times Liebeck's original damage demand—but reduced that total by 20 percent, owing to negligence it attributed to her.)

Eye-popping damages like Liebeck's would have been unthinkable, even adjusting for inflation, before the mid-twentieth century. One man is chiefly responsible for the growth in modern damage awards: Melvin Belli, the San Francisco personal injury lawyer who was Gladys Escola's attorney.

Belli was "a man of scarlet silk-lined suits, of multicolored Rolls-Royces, of courtroom theatrics and Hollywood hijinks." His celebrity clients included the Rolling Stones, Jack Ruby (Lee Harvey Oswald's killer), and the Hollywood stars Mae West and Errol Flynn. In 1954, *Life* magazine dubbed Belli the "King of Torts."

That same year, Belli published a three-volume treatise, *Modern Trials.* It earned him more than $1 million in royalties. Other lawyers had reason to buy Belli's book, which explained the tactics he had used to revolutionize the world of tort law. Beyond his win in *Escola*, Belli launched modern pharmaceutical litigation in the 1950s with his successful case against a manufacturer of polio vaccines—the forerunner of lawsuits that almost eliminated the vaccine industry entirely in the 1980s. (We'll cover that litigation in more detail in the next chapter.)

Belli aggressively argued for substantially increasing tort awards. In court, and through a seminal law review article, he successfully made the case for compensating "intangible" injuries like pain and suffering. Such awards, unlike medical bills or lost wages, would be hard for judges to second-guess—and would permit juries to throw real dollars behind their sympathies.

To play upon jurors' heartstrings and put them in a more generous mood, Belli pioneered the use of "demonstrative evidence." With photographs and props, he depicted and dramatized his clients' suffering. Some of Belli's theatrics seem bold even today. In one case, he arranged for the hoisting of a 680-pound client through a courthouse window. In another, he shocked a 1940s jury "by having a client bare her chest to show scars from an injury. She then shed tears that landed right on her scars."

• • •

As a matter of theory, Belli's notion that damages in a tort lawsuit shouldn't be limited to those that are easily quantifiable has appeal. His client's scars may not have caused much financial injury, but they left her body disfigured, exacting a serious emotional toll. In practice, however, the explosion of damages unlinked to knowable facts—and essentially unreviewable by judges—also comes at a cost.

To an individual jury facing a perceived injustice—whether that injustice is rightly or wrongly perceived—hitting a company with a big verdict can seem more than appropriate. If McDonald's is indeed flouting industry standards by serving unreasonably hot coffee to its customers, and if we don't think the restaurant's need to continue selling coffee is sufficient to encourage more "reasonable" behavior, why not punish the company with two days' worth of total coffee sales?

Well, here's one problem: nothing is stopping the next jury from punishing McDonald's the same way. And the jury after that. Is the right punishment to deter McDonald's from serving hot coffee $2 million? $4 million? $40 million? There's no real check on how high the damages might rise; no cost-benefit analysis of the sort a federal administrative agency might employ in its rulemaking. Agency rulemaking is certainly not without its flaws, but at least the agency can assess the numbers and make a decision—and that decision can be reviewed by judges.

To defenders of regulation-by-litigation—typically administrative-law skeptics such as late-life Roscoe Pound and more than a few conservative and libertarian analysts today—the risk of jury error is still better than entrusting regulatory decisions to administrative agencies. It's fallacious to think of tort litigation as a private market, since defendants aren't willing customers or suppliers; but maybe random people making decisions in a series of jury trials might get it right more often than agency experts. Maybe we should embrace tort litigation's "bottom-up" regulatory regime. After all, William F. Buckley, the founder of *National Review*, famously quipped that he'd "rather be governed by the first two thousand people in the Boston telephone directory" than by the Harvard faculty. If we're worried about rule by the unelected, what's more democratic than rule by civil juries?

There are two big problems with that view. First, we don't face an either-or choice. There *are* situations in which litigation after the fact is indeed preferable to agency rulemaking up front. But tort lawsuits haven't stopped administrative rulemaking. Nor does administrative rulemaking generally preclude tort lawsuits, as we'll find out in Chapter 11. We have the administrative state—and we have tort lawsuits, too.

What's more: large possible verdicts untethered to actual damages can lead to a paradoxical result, in which the jury that gets it *wrong* decides the regulatory rule. Remember that Stella Liebeck wasn't the first person to spill hot coffee on herself and sue McDonald's, and that the first dozen juries to hear a case like hers *rejected* the plaintiff's claim. But those dozen jury wins for the company are far outweighed by the one jury loss with a payout that dwarfs the $20,000 initially sought in settlement by Liebeck's attorneys. Even after the trial judge reduced the damages awarded by the jury, Liebeck received double the sum that twelve such settlements would have cost McDonald's. On the margin, the bottom-up regulation by juries created pressures for the company to follow the course that twelve of thirteen juries thought made less sense.

McDonald's has not adjusted its coffee serving temperature; so presumably, McDonald's management thinks the risk of future Liebeck-type verdicts is outweighed by the cost of losing too many coffee sales to competitors. But not all products offer such clear customer feedback as fast-food coffee, and very few cases generate the kind of public attention we saw with Liebeck's. In the ordinary case, the bottom-up system of regulation by jury verdict has a problem: the outlier jury, by assessing outsized damages, is the jury that gets to decide. It's a regulatory race to the bottom.

In recent years, the U.S. Supreme Court has tried to rein in outlier punitive-damage awards, such as the $2.9 million initially imposed by Liebeck's jury, in part on this rationale. In 1996, the Court considered *BMW v. Gore*, a case in which an automobile dealer sold a previously damaged vehicle to a customer. The damage had been minor, but the dealer did not disclose it. The jury's finding that the undisclosed damage had lowered the value of the car was unexceptional. So was its award of $4,000 in ordinary damages as compensation. But the jury also levied $4 million in punitive damages, fully a thousand times its compensatory award.

In *Gore* and a later case, *State Farm v. Campbell*, the Supreme Court ruled that a punitive damage verdict ten or more times an underlying compensatory damages award was constitutionally suspect. But the Court's willingness to police outlier punitive damage verdicts is in some doubt. Four of the five justices that formed the *Gore* and *Campbell* majorities are no longer on the Court. The leader of the Court's conservative wing, Justice Clarence Thomas, has opposed the decisions' holdings as unsupported by the text of the Constitution. The leader of the progressive wing, Justice Ruth Bader Ginsburg, also opposed the holdings, much as she has opposed essentially every Supreme Court decision limiting the reach of civil litigation. In 2009, the Supreme Court let stand a $79.5 million punitive judgment against Philip Morris, the cigarette manufacturer. The award was ninety-seven times the jury's compensatory damages award.

In any event, rather than treat the Liebeck verdict as an unfortunate outlier, trial-lawyer advocates continue to defend it. In 2011, Susan Saladoff, a medical malpractice plaintiffs' lawyer, released a one-sided documentary, *Hot Coffee*, which premiered at the Sundance Film Festival and aired on HBO. Saladoff pushed the narrative that the public reaction to the Liebeck case was merely a function of a corporate misinformation campaign—even though the widespread press reaction to the case appears to have been organic and it was the *plaintiffs' lobby* that quickly held a press conference defending the verdict. Those lobbying efforts have won over many reporters and law professors. We'll turn to that lobby, and its emergence, in the next chapter.

CHAPTER 10

The Lawsuit Industry

A federal judge in Corpus Christi, Texas, held hearings in 2004 to get to the bottom of a flood of lawsuits coming into her courtroom. The cases involved silica, or silicon dioxide. Silica is found in nature as quartz and makes up most of sand. It's also commonly used to make glass, fiberglass, paints, and ceramics. It's safe for those of us who use silica-containing products, but it can be dangerous for mining or metal foundry workers who make those products possible: silica dust, when repeatedly inhaled, can cause permanent lung scarring, or silicosis, which makes it difficult to breathe.

Lawyers for the defendant company in the Texas lawsuits, U.S. Silica, were reviewing the list of plaintiffs when they kept getting computer-error messages. They brought in technical experts, who discovered that the computer program they were using to organize their case was objecting to plaintiffs that were already in the attorneys' database. These lawyers had regularly handled cases for defendant companies being sued over injuries allegedly caused by another product linked to lung ailments—asbestos. It seemed that many of the plaintiffs seeking to collect payments for lung injury from U.S. Silica had already collected from other companies for alleged injuries from other products, under alternative theories. They were attempting to "double-dip."

The district judge in charge of the case, Janis Graham Jack, had been a nurse before Bill Clinton appointed her to the federal bench. After reviewing the evidence, she discovered that fully 60 percent of the patients that doctors had certified as having silica-related lung injuries in the litigation in front of her had previously been plaintiffs for the same law firms in suits attributing their impairments to asbestos exposure.

For years, rumors abounded about how law firms handling large numbers of claims related to products like silica and asbestos generated their client lists. Judge Jack documented it, in all its sordid detail. The head of the screening company that had "diagnosed" 6,500 plaintiffs was a junior college dropout who taught himself how to run an X-ray machine and take medical histories. One Texas doctor admitted that he had "diagnosed more than 800 patients during a 72-hour period," and that he "spent no more than a few minutes reviewing X-rays and writing a report for each patient." Another doctor admitted that he never interviewed, examined, or checked the work records of some 2,700 claimants—people who received diagnosis letters stamped with his signature. A Mississippi doctor revealed that his equipment was owned by a Century 21 real estate agent and that his office was a van in a Sizzler restaurant parking lot.

• • •

The lawsuits against U.S. Silica were not class actions, like those described in Chapter 8. For lawyers to bring class action suits, the plaintiffs' cases have to be "similarly situated." Most lawsuits alleging a defective product design or an inadequate warning—the sorts of claims that followed in the wake of the Second Restatement of Torts—are not similarly situated, or at least not sufficiently similar to bring a class action claim. Such lawsuits involve physical injuries, and the individual cases differ according to the plaintiffs' varying health characteristics and product usage. For this reason, some defendant companies face a flood of individual cases that are similar but must be litigated separately. This is generally called "mass tort" litigation.

Perhaps more than any other kind of litigation, mass torts typify the modern lawsuit industry. Mass tort lawsuits have generated fabulous wealth for attorneys ranging from Peter Angelos, an asbestos lawyer and owner of the Baltimore Orioles, to Mark Lanier, a Texas superlawyer who tried the first case against the pharmaceutical company Merck over its now-recalled medicine Vioxx. Mass tort stories are a familiar theme in the popular culture, from John Grisham's novel *The King of Torts* to Hollywood movies like *Erin Brockovich* and *A Civil Action*.

By attracting large numbers of clients suing a common defendant under a common theory, plaintiffs' lawyers essentially guarantee themselves a healthy return. Remember that under the American Rule, each party must pay its own legal bills, win or lose. Present a defendant with enough lawsuits that need separate trials, and the expected legal bills can be crippling—even if a defendant were to win every single case.

Generating lots of similar cases also facilitates mischief. Even if there is a clear scientific basis for a particular allegation of harm—such as the association between asbestos exposure and lung disease—there is nothing to ensure that *every* plaintiff has an ailment caused by a defendant's product.

That's what Judge Jack discovered in her review of silica lawsuits. And although the details she uncovered shocked the public, they are rather typical of mass tort litigation. Law firms specializing in asbestos litigation have long run "screening" operations to organize their mass tort client pool. These screening clinics have typically been run by people with little or no medical training. High school students or clerical workers have regularly taken patient histories, conducted breathing tests, and taken X-rays that were later analyzed by medical specialists known as "B readers." After the B readers have checked off a diagnosis form, screening companies prepare a diagnosis letter for a signing physician. These letters appear to be individualized, but they are signed with a rubber stamp.

The B readers hired by the law firms' screeners have often found positive results with suspicious frequency. How suspicious? In 2004, Johns Hopkins radiologists looked at a sample of 492 X-rays from asbestos screening clinics. The lawyers' B readers had identified lung abnormalities almost 96 percent of the time. But the independent readers hired by the Hopkins researchers found abnormalities in less than 5 percent of the identical pool of cases.

However dubious a diagnosis may be, litigation-industry attorneys with a doctor's note in hand have tended to leave little to chance in preparing for a possible trial. The giant asbestos plaintiffs' firm then known as Baron & Budd prepared a memorandum, eventually discovered by defense attorneys, that coached plaintiffs on their testimony. Among other things, the memo urged plaintiffs "to maintain that you NEVER saw any labels on asbestos products that said WARNING or DANGER."

Little wonder that defendants almost always settle asbestos cases: less than 1 percent have traditionally gone to a jury verdict. Of course, the defendant companies and their employees and shareholders lose from this game. But at least in the case of asbestos and silica exposure, so too do many plaintiffs who have been genuinely harmed and may have legitimate claims. Companies that liquidate into bankruptcy trusts have a limited pool of money to distribute, and every dollar shelled out for a bogus claim is one that might have gone to a legitimate claimant. And with bundles of clients and lax ethical oversight, lawyers have tended to pitch their own plaintiffs' futures like used cars, offering 40 percent off for immediate settlements.

• • •

Asbestos is a powerful flame retardant. And it was once ubiquitous. Asbestos insulation fireproofed the nation's fleet in World War II. Asbestos ceiling and floor tiles protected millions of American schoolchildren from fire. Exhibits at the 1939 World's Fair in New York touted asbestos as the "magic mineral." Millions of Americans would be employed in asbestos-related industries— which helps to explain the size of the ultimate "mass tort" litigation related to asbestos exposure.

Health concerns about asbestos had been raised long before it was dubbed a magic substance. In 1918, the U.S. Department of Labor declared an "urgent need for more qualified extensive investigation" into the health effects of asbestos. In the *British Medical Journal* in 1924, Dr. W. E. Cooke attributed a lung-related death to asbestos exposure, and he named the disease *asbestosis*. But the evidence was long viewed as inconclusive. In 1938, the U.S. Public Health Service established a tentative standard for acceptable asbestos exposure "until better data are available." The standard would last for the next three decades.

A more definitive answer to the question came in 1964. Dr. Irving Selikoff, of Mount Sinai Hospital in New York, established links between asbestos exposure and high cancer and asbestosis rates among insulation installers. The imminent adoption of the Second Restatement of Torts in 1965, with its strict product liability, soon precipitated an avalanche of lawsuits.

In 1973, in *Borel v. Fibreboard Paper Products*, the U.S. Court of Appeals for the Fifth Circuit held that asbestos manufacturers were strictly liable for asbestos-related injuries. Over the next decade, 25,000 asbestos cases were filed. By 1981, more than two hundred companies and insurers had been sued. By 1982, defendants' costs had topped $1 billion. Lawsuits soon drove most companies involved in manufacturing asbestos into bankruptcy. Today, the remnants of these companies exist only as special trusts to pay asbestos claimants.

And yet the lawsuits kept piling on. In 1983, fewer than 5,000 plaintiffs filed asbestos-related lawsuits annually. That number grew to 15,000 in 1986, and 59,000 in 1989. By 1992, 100,000 asbestos claims had been resolved, 100,000 new ones had been filed, and "two to three new claims" were emerging "for each claim resolved." By 2005, an estimated 322,000 claims were pending in state and federal courts. Some analysts estimate that the ultimate cost of asbestos litigation may hit $265 billion—more than double the cost of the whole Superfund program established in 1980 to clean up toxic waste at thousands of sites around the nation.

And who was paying for the asbestos claims? Nothing but shells remained of the original asbestos companies, so remote defendants with little connection to the product—those who may have included some asbestos-containing part in a much larger manufacturing operation—have been hit by the new onslaught of claims.

• • •

Recruiting all these asbestos plaintiffs is itself a big business. Advertisements seeking victims of mesothelioma, the deadly cancer linked to asbestos exposure, fill late-night and daytime television spots—as well as many a public subway car. The most expensive Google Ads search term today is often "mesothelioma treatment options." Lester Brickman, former Cardozo law professor, a legal ethics expert and the nation's foremost authority on asbestos litigation, calls the setup "the most extensive recruitment process since World War II, when Uncle Sam wanted you."

If the Second Restatement of Torts and the *Borel* decision jump-started modern mass tort litigation, the U.S. Supreme Court's 1977 decision in *Bates v. State Bar of Arizona* accelerated and sustains it. In that decision, the Court overturned timeworn state-bar ethics rules that prohibited attorney advertising. The Court determined that such advertising amounted to speech protected by the First Amendment to the U.S. Constitution.

Lawyers recruiting plaintiffs had long been deemed anathema. As a young attorney, Abraham Lincoln implored his fellow lawyers: "Never stir up litigation. A worse man can scarcely be found than one who does this." Legal ethics rules have long barred attorneys from directly soliciting clients—what's called "ambulance chasing." That's why the leadership of the Law Association of Philadelphia had been so distraught by the prevalence of "runners" trawling for clients in hospital waiting rooms in the 1920s.

Directly soliciting clients remains verboten. But with attorney advertising afforded constitutional sanction, lawyers today spend $1 billion annually on television ads. Typically avoiding national broadcasts, law firms tend to buy up inexpensive local spots in hours likely to reach the unemployed. In 2015, mass tort law firms were five of the top six legal advertisers on television. (The other was LegalZoom.)

The firms that appear on TV are not necessarily the ones that try to negotiate a settlement or that take cases to trial. Many advertising law firms mostly offload the plaintiffs they sign up to other plaintiffs' firms. The new firm controls the case; the referring firm shares in any contingent fee or settlement that may result.

Beyond television advertising, the Internet has afforded lawyers the ability to look for clients in far more targeted ways. Nine of the top ten and twenty-three of the top twenty-five most expensive keywords purchased from Google to attract Web searchers are tied to potential legal claims. Such advertising tactics allow law firms and their marketing agents to seek out plaintiffs with precision, in the wired-world version of the old hospital-room runners.

· · ·

At least some asbestos and silica plaintiffs have a serious injury that is actually linked to exposure to a defendant company's product. Far too often, however, a real scientific link between a lawsuit and a plaintiff's ailment simply doesn't exist. Over the years, a large volume of mass tort litigation has been predicated upon "junk science": assertions presented as scientific fact but in reality more like astrology than astronomy, more like alchemy than chemistry, and more like numerology than mathematics. By exploiting loose evidentiary requirements, clever lawyers have been able to use junk-science testimony to dupe unsophisticated juries into believing their farfetched claims.

In 1995, for example, 400,000 women registered for a $4.25 billion fund established to compensate them for injuries—breast cancer or connective tissue diseases—allegedly caused by silicone breast implants. Dow Corning had lost a $7 million verdict in 1991 to a woman claiming her illness had been caused by the breast implants that the company manufactured. From 1992 to 1994, some 20,000 women sued Dow. The company lost tens of millions of dollars in jury verdicts, in trial and on appeal.

But there was no scientific basis for the lawsuits' claims. Two 1992 studies had actually shown that "breast implants were associated with a reduced rate of breast cancer." And, just after the settlement that established the $4.25 billion compensatory fund was announced, an epidemiological study published in the *New England Journal of Medicine* found "no association between implants and the connective tissue diseases and other disorders that were studied." Notwithstanding the science, Dow Corning filed for bankruptcy.

Breast-implant litigation may strike some as trivial, since the device's typical purpose is cosmetic. But other drugs and devices with genuine lifesaving and life-enhancing effects have also been driven off the market by the litigation industry's junk-science lawsuits.

Take, for instance, the morning-sickness drug Bendectin. By 1980, it was used by as many as one in four of all expectant mothers. Then trial lawyers generated a national panic over the claim that the drug was associated with birth defects. Many women who had been taking the drug actually aborted their unborn children. By 1983, the drug's manufacturer, Merrell Dow Pharmaceuticals, faced $18 million in annual legal bills against only $20 million in total sales.

But the lawyers' claim was bunk. More than thirty subsequently published studies examining over 130,000 patients failed to find a link between the drug and birth defects.

In 1993, ongoing Bendectin litigation prompted the U.S. Supreme Court to reinterpret the Federal Rules of Evidence. In *Daubert v. Merrell Dow Pharmaceuticals*, the Court rejected "general admissibility" of expert evidence—the standard that a litigant could produce any witness with an academic degree to hypothesize a scientific theory. At least in federal courts, judges are now required to reject expert testimony unless "the reasoning or methodology underlying the testimony is scientifically valid." But not all states have adopted the federal rule, and claims without good scientific underpinnings remain legion in American courts.

By the time *Daubert* was decided, Bendectin had already been off the market for a decade. The product's exit had real health effects. The percentage of pregnant women hospitalized each year for morning sickness doubled. The incidence of birth defects did not change. Finally, after thirty years, Bendectin was reintroduced to the U.S. market, by a different manufacturer, in 2013. The drug had remained on the European market throughout the intervening decades.

• • •

In the 1980s, Congress stepped in to stop one line of mass tort litigation that was creating a major threat to public health: lawsuits over injuries caused by vaccines. Vaccines are among the greatest accomplishments of modern medicine. They have virtually eliminated the widespread scourge of killer diseases like diphtheria, polio, and smallpox. Each year, millions of American children are vaccinated against many such infectious diseases, an essential precaution for the broader public health. The Covid-19 pandemic of 2020 underscores the pressing importance of vaccine research, development, and distribution. But in the 1980s, tort litigation almost killed the private vaccine industry in the United States.

Unfortunately, a very small percentage of vaccinated children can develop side effects, or even die. The Second Restatement of Torts opined that drug and vaccine manufacturers could not be held strictly liable for selling unavoidably dangerous products. Such products were deemed "useful and desirable" and their risks "known but apparently reasonable."

In the 1960s and 1970s, however, courts loosened these restrictions. First, they allowed lawsuits against the Sabin live-virus polio vaccine under a "failure to warn" theory. As the courts continued to apply novel liability theories, vaccine manufacturers were flooded with lawsuits. The manufacturer of the diphtheria, pertussis, and tetanus (DPT) vaccine faced just one lawsuit in 1979, but 255 in 1986.

In 1984, juries slapped vaccine makers with huge verdicts over two individual claims. The first, against a manufacturer of the DPT vaccine, was for over $1 million. The second, against a manufacturer of the Sabin polio vaccine, was for $10 million, including $8 million in punitive damages. Each case was predicated on the theory that alternative vaccines were available or could have been developed. Although the latter verdict was subsequently overturned, the damage had been done. Claims multiplied: the vaccine maker Lederle estimated that total sales of its 1983 polio vaccine were only one-twelfth the value of claims filed against it, and in 1983 its DPT vaccine sales were dwarfed by claims 200 to 1.

Vaccine manufacturers responded predictably. First, they exited the market. Of the twenty-six vaccine manufacturers in business in 1967, only fifteen still existed in the early 1980s. The number plummeted to three by the middle of the decade. Second, the remaining manufacturers raised prices commensurate with their increased costs. The DPT vaccine cost 10,000 percent more in 1986 than it did in 1980. The few remaining suppliers reported that they were having trouble finding liability insurance at all, and the Centers for Disease Control, fearing a shortage, asked doctors to delay giving children DPT booster shots.

Responding to the crisis, Congress in 1986 established the Vaccine Injury Compensation Program, which bars all tort claims until parents of children allegedly injured by a vaccine have exhausted an administrative no-fault remedy. In essence, the system makes the federal government an insurer for vaccine-related injuries. Payouts come from a fund supported by a small vaccine surtax. Claimants appear before a "special master" (an administrative judge). To collect, a claimant must establish injury, according to a "vaccine injury table." The Department of Justice has the option of contesting a finding and overturning it if the injury is shown not to have been caused by the vaccine.

The program established by Congress largely stemmed the tide of vaccine lawsuits. In general, the program effectively compensates those who actually are injured. The average award under the program has been high—$824,463—for the minority of claims that have been compensated. Administrative costs are only 9 percent of payouts to claimants. In contrast, as we've seen, the greater part of payments in the ordinary tort system goes to lawyers and administration.

With the liability climate more stable and predictable, research into new vaccines began to proliferate. Safer "whole cell" DPT vaccines replaced older versions. Several new vaccines were widely adopted. The vaccine industry was now attracting new entrants researching new drugs, among them biotechnology firms.

• • •

The success of the congressional reform that saved the vaccine industry has not been widely replicated. The plaintiffs' bar has developed unrivaled expertise in playing the political influence game in Washington and state capitals alike. It has thus blocked many efforts to reform legal rules in ways that would undercut its profitability.

The politically organized trial bar emerged shortly after World War II. In 1946, two attorneys who handled workers' compensation claims for employees injured on the job formed the National Association of Claimants' Compensation Attorneys. The two were Sam Marcus, a Detroit lawyer who represented the Congress of Industrial Organizations, and Sam Horovitz, a Boston attorney who represented the American Federation of Labor. Initial membership was eleven. Marcus was the group's first president.

Three years later, the group began to take on its modern shape when Melvin Belli, the "King of Torts," persuaded the group to admit all tort lawyers rather than merely those representing injured workers. As chronicled by John Witt, a legal historian at Yale, Horovitz "took his family on a three-month, 10,800-mile tour across the South and Southwest in a silver aluminum Airstream trailer to establish local branches and chapters" of the new lawyers' group. Horovitz's "Silver Bullet Tour" brought hundreds and then thousands of new recruits to the lawyer-lobby cause.

Reflecting its new focus beyond employee-injury claims, the group in 1964 renamed itself the American Trial Lawyers Association. In 2006, it rebranded again, opting for the innocuous-sounding American Association for Justice. (The Justice League of America was already taken by a group of DC Comics superheroes.)

Whatever it calls itself, the trial lawyers' political and lobbying arm is among the most powerful interest groups in Washington and the states. Campaign finance rules that limit individual contributions to political candidates to a few thousand dollars per candidate leave campaigns hungry for cash. Trial lawyers have become a major source of cash for these campaigns by "bundling" individual donations. In every campaign cycle this century, lawyers have given more to congressional campaigns than any other interest group has given. Three of the top five campaign contributors to Senator Dick Durbin of Illinois—the Democratic minority whip and a senior member of the Judiciary Committee—are plaintiffs' law firms.

In addition to legislators, trial lawyers heavily fund the campaigns of state attorneys general and other state officials who have the power to hire them. In states that elect their judges, the plaintiffs' bar heavily funds judicial campaigns; and in those with judicial-selection committees, they work hard to make sure such committees are filled with their members.

The trial bar has typically concentrated its money mostly on Democratic candidates, but not exclusively. Particularly at the state level, the plaintiffs' bar has worked to maintain its influence in Republican-leaning states by supporting religious conservative candidates who are favorable to plaintiffs' lawyers.

• • •

The litigation industry supplements its political lobbying with a strong web of ties to the academy, media, and various "consumer" groups. By encouraging law review articles and amicus briefs; news stories, movies, and television programs; and studies and statements from purportedly independent nonprofit organizations, the trial bar works to reinforce its mythical identity—and thus head off and disarm popular opposition.

As the organized plaintiffs' bar developed, its leader, Melvin Belli, befriended Roscoe Pound, the former dean of Harvard Law School—whom we first met in Chapter 3, which described how he led the American Bar Association's efforts to redefine administrative rulemaking. Pound had been an early critic of common-law torts. But in his later years—he was in his seventies when befriended by Belli—Pound became a leading advocate for the plaintiffs' bar. In part, that's because he viewed tort lawsuits as preferable to administrative rulemaking. He penned a glowing introduction to Belli's book *Modern Trials*, and overall gave the nascent plaintiffs' bar an air of academic legitimacy. In 1956, a group of plaintiffs' lawyers founded the Pound Civil Justice Institute, a think tank that publishes pro-litigation papers and conducts seminars, including some for judges.

The tort bar continues to cultivate relationships with academics who are willing to speak on its behalf. Drawing upon their institutions' lofty reputations for seriousness and their own for independence, many professors profit handsomely from their ties to the trial bar. Law professors regularly serve as expert witnesses in civil trials—giving an academic seal of approval to mass-litigation settlements, dodgy fee arrangements, and questionable theories of injury. They tend to be very well paid for this outside work.

To further cultivate an air of legitimacy, trial lawyers rely on a network of allied "consumer" groups that promote a pro-lawsuit agenda to the press and the general public. Many of these groups trace, directly or indirectly, to the Harvard-trained lawyer Ralph Nader.

Nader rose to fame in 1965, at the age of thirty-one, when he published *Unsafe at Any Speed*, a book attacking the automobile industry and its products. Nader focused his criticism on the Chevrolet Corvair, an economy car that drew upon design features of European car models and thus differed from its American competitors. Although some of his safety criticisms doubtless had merit, the National Highway Traffic Safety Administration—founded by Congress in 1966, partially in response to Nader's book—ultimately determined that "the 1960–63 Corvair compares favorably with contemporary vehicles" tested.

Unfortunately, however, lay juries are unable to engage in the sort of comparative and cost-benefit analysis employed by the federal regulatory body. So Nader's attacks on the auto industry helped generate waves of automobile "design defect" cases. Many of these, like Nader's attacks on the Corvair, were unwarranted. Some were predicated on phantom risks like "sudden acceleration."

A plethora of Naderite consumer groups—Public Citizen, the Public Interest Research Group, the Center for the Study of Responsive Law, and Citizens for Justice and Democracy—push pro-trial-lawyer talking points in the guise of the public interest. It's little secret who cuts many of the checks bankrolling these efforts. In 1986, plaintiffs' lawyers set up their own charitable trust, the Civil Justice Foundation, to support consumer groups furthering the trial bar's interests. Herb Hafif, a prominent California plaintiffs' attorney, said that the trial bar supported Nader "overtly, covertly, in every way possible," and the late Texas tort king Pat Maloney noted that the litigation industry supported Nader's efforts "for decades," contributing "a huge percentage of what he raises."

In 2015, Nader opened the American Museum of Tort Law in his hometown of Winsted, Connecticut. Its list of founders reads like a who's who of the U.S. plaintiffs' bar. It prominently features a red 1963 Corvair.

Trial lawyers also court the media directly. To gin up interest in potential new cases, trial lawyers regularly funnel victim stories to news reporters. John Stossel, a news analyst who won nineteen Emmy Awards as a consumer reporter, notes that trial lawyers are the reporter's "perfect source." According to Stossel, trial lawyers are hard for TV news reporters to resist:

> [The lawyers] do most of the work for us. We don't need to make phone calls to search for victims; the lawyers identify the most telegenic of them, the people whose stories make you cry, and they'll bring them right to our office. Then they identify the "bad guy" for us. We don't need to do much original investigating…we're following the lawyers' script.

That script even makes its way to Hollywood. Trial-lawyer mythology permeates the books and movies written by John Grisham and the television shows produced by David E. Kelly: the little-guy-against-corporate-evildoer makes for good theater. Grisham is himself a former plaintiffs' lawyer who makes no secret of his friendship with Richard "Dickie" Scruggs, a fellow

Mississippian and an asbestos lawyer who scored north of $1 billion in legal fees by suing tobacco companies on behalf of state governments.

• • •

Samuel Tilden, the twenty-fifth governor of New York, was the Democrats' nominee for president in 1876. Before that, he was a legal reformer in his home state. In 1870, he admonished the Association of the Bar of the City of New York: "If the Bar is to become merely a method of making money...then the Bar is degraded. If the Bar is to be merely an institution that seeks to win causes and to win them by back-door access to the judiciary, then it is not only degraded, but corrupt."

Unfortunately, Tilden's worst fears have come to pass. Trial lawyers' modern business model resembles that of many other industries. The plaintiffs' bar employs sophisticated Madison Avenue–style marketing tactics. It has developed assembly-line-style plaintiff processing. Its lobbying efforts are unrivaled.

But unlike other industries, the trial bar isn't selling a product to willing consumers. It is exploiting its unique access to the courts to extract money from unwilling defendants. Far too often, it has done so by peddling junk-science theories, such as the claims that Bendectin causes birth defects or that silicone breast implants cause cancer. Even when science is on the lawyers' side—asbestos and silica dust are clearly linked to lung impairments—it has manufactured bum claims to capture illicit profits, while shortchanging genuinely injured clients in the process.

And these lawyers exert enormous regulatory powers, although nobody elected them. Perfectly safe products get pulled from the market. As a result, American expectant mothers for decades went to the hospital with extreme morning sickness, while mothers across the Atlantic could avoid it.

The harmful effects of unelected trial lawyers' regulatory power go far beyond the removal of existing products from the market. Countless other potentially useful drugs sit in petri dishes because companies hesitate to spend hundreds of millions of dollars on products that could land them in court, costing hundreds of millions more.

For decades, following on the heels of successful lawsuits against the manufacturers of IUDs, contraceptive research virtually stopped. Lawyers managed to kill off other contraceptives such as Norplant, a long-term reversible contraceptive that was used by a million women in the United States and that is still used by millions in other countries. U.S. companies spend twenty times more on cosmetics research than on developing new contraceptives.

On one notable occasion, Congress stepped in to save the vaccine industry. But lawyers' regulatory power can often exceed—and effectively override—the already awesome powers of the administrative state. Lawyers can kill cars deemed perfectly safe by the National Highway Traffic Safety Administration. They can pummel the manufacturers of drugs and consumer products deemed safe by the Food and Drug Administration. How this absurd backward regulation came about and how it works is the subject of our next chapter.

CHAPTER 11

Magic Jurisdictions

Most Americans today were reared with baby powder on their rears. In 1894, an eight-year-old surgical supply company, Johnson & Johnson, introduced a powder product made from talc, a naturally occurring mineral composed of magnesium, silicon, and oxygen. For more than 120 years, the product was a staple in hospitals and nurseries alike. But no more: on May 19, 2020, Johnson & Johnson announced it was pulling the product from the shelves. In the United States and Canada, anyway: J&J's talcum-based product will still be available overseas. The product's demise in North America owes to the loose scientific standards governing U.S. tort litigation as well as our peculiar system that enables plaintiffs' lawyers to ship claims to lowest-common-denominator jurisdictions.

About a decade ago, plaintiffs' lawyers began filing suits alleging that talcum powder caused ovarian cancer, which afflicts more than 20,000 American women annually. Some studies had found that women with ovarian cancer remembered using baby powder slightly more often than those who did not. But such "case cohort" studies are necessarily prone to bias in recollection; and "prospective cohort" studies—which follow actual usage over time—have failed to find any similar associated risk. In January 2020, doctors from major cancer-research institutes published a prospective-cohort study in the *Journal of the American Medical Association* that had tracked more than 250,000

American women for eleven years; they found no ovarian cancer risk associated with use of talcum powder.

The new *JAMA* study comports with federal regulators' assessments. The Centers for Disease Control do not list talc as an ovarian-cancer risk. The FDA has consistently found insufficient evidence to mandate an ovarian-cancer warning label on talcum powder.

But determinations by federal regulators that a product is not dangerous do not stop jurors from deciding it is. As we've seen, many courts apply lax evidentiary rules that permit plaintiffs' lawyers to put their preferred experts in front of juries. The lawyers' paid experts aren't always that persuasive: most juries that have heard J&J baby-powder cases have not found that the product was carcinogenic. But as was the case with suits against McDonald's over coffee spills, one big verdict for a plaintiff can override many verdicts for a corporate defendant—and in this case, given the FDA's position, a big jury verdict can effectively override the regulator's judgment, as well.

And some of the verdicts that were levied against Johnson & Johnson were big indeed. In 2016 and 2017, four different juries hearing four different cases handed down Johnson & Johnson baby-powder verdicts totaling an eye-popping $307 million. What's remarkable about these verdicts, beyond their size, is that all four emanated from courtrooms in St. Louis, Missouri, half a country away from Johnson & Johnson's headquarters in New Brunswick, New Jersey. The plaintiffs in the four cases were not locals but hailed from Alabama, California, South Dakota, and Virginia.

It may seem strange that a court in St. Louis could adjudicate a lawsuit against an out-of-state company by out-of-state plaintiffs, but that's the way tort litigation in America has evolved (though the Supreme Court has recently tried to put some brakes on the process). The baby-powder cases fit a well-worn litigation "business model": develop a theory, recruit plaintiffs, do some "forum shopping," and then funnel cases from around the country to the most favorable jurisdiction possible. And pummel that jurisdiction with advertisements, which not only recruit clients but also influence the jury pool. In one survey around the time of the aforementioned trials, the average person in the St. Louis area remembered recently seeing nine television commercials involving Johnson & Johnson baby-powder lawsuits; a majority remembered seeing one within the past two days.

By the summer of 2016, among the 2,100 lawsuits nationwide alleging that talcum powder caused ovarian cancer, two-thirds were situated in the City of St. Louis Circuit Court. The plaintiffs' bar has since moved on to several other venues—in part because Missouri appellate courts knocked out the four big St. Louis verdicts with out-of-state plaintiffs. But the cases, and the verdicts, kept coming.

Eventually, some of the baby-powder suits became asbestos suits. Asbestos appears in trace amounts in naturally occurring talc. Despite longstanding efforts by Johnson & Johnson and other manufacturers to eliminate asbestos entirely from consumer products, a small number of tests over the past five decades have detected some asbestos in talcum-powder samples. These readings may have been false positives, as they were not replicated by additional testing. And even if a trace of asbestos showed up in some batch of talcum powder, it's extraordinarily unlikely to have caused an individual plaintiff's mesothelioma. But talcum-based baby powder has been used near universally, mesothelioma still exists, the plaintiffs' bar has a time-proven asbestos-litigation business model, and Johnson & Johnson—unlike asbestos manufacturers—is solvent. So it's hardly surprising that the company decided to pull its product from American shelves.

• • •

As discussed in Chapter 8, the legal system largely imported from England to the United States at the time of the American founding had separate courts of "law" and "equity," utilizing different rules for different types of cases. The constitutional framers extended the federal courts' judicial power "to all Cases, in Law and Equity" that arose under the U.S. Constitution, federal law, or treaties. But they also allowed federal courts to resolve "controversies" in which state courts might be deemed non-neutral arbiters: lawsuits involving the federal government, lawsuits involving foreign states or subjects, lawsuits between two states, lawsuits between a state and a citizen of another state, and lawsuits between citizens of two different states.

When the First Congress passed the enabling legislation to set up the federal courts, it preserved separate courts of law and equity. In the case of "law" courts, Congress deferred to the existing body of state court rules governing trial procedures (as discussed in Chapter 1). In the specific language of the Judiciary Act of 1789, "the laws of the several states, except where the constitution, treaties or statutes of the United States shall otherwise require or provide, shall be regarded as rules of decision, in trials at common law, in the courts of the United States, in cases where they apply."

In 1842, the Supreme Court interpreted this provision in *Swift v. Tyson*. At issue was a legal dispute over payment of a promissory note by citizens of two different states, New York and Maine. The contract was entered into in New York. The New York courts had a legal doctrine on a question essential to determining whether the contract would be enforceable. The Supreme Court found that the New York courts' doctrine was "fully settled"—but not founded "upon any local statute or positive, fixed or ancient local usage." In a unanimous decision authored by Justice Joseph Story, the Supreme Court decided that the New York courts' doctrine did not amount to "laws" under the federal statute:

> In the ordinary use of language, it will hardly be contended that the decisions of courts constitute laws. They are, at most, only evidence of what the laws are, and are not, of themselves, laws. They are often re-examined, reversed and qualified by the courts themselves whenever they are found to be either defective or ill-founded or otherwise incorrect. The laws of a state are more usually understood to mean the rules and enactments promulgated by the legislative authority thereof, or long-established local customs having the force of laws....
>
> [W]e have not now the slightest difficulty in holding that this section, upon its true intendment and construction, is strictly limited to local statutes and local usages of the character before stated, and does not extend to contracts and other instruments of a commercial nature, the true interpretation and effect whereof are to be sought not in the decisions of the local tribunals, but in the general principles and doctrines of commercial jurisprudence. Undoubtedly the decisions of the local tribunals upon such subjects are entitled to, and will receive, the most deliberate attention and respect of this court, but they cannot furnish positive rules or conclusive authority by which our own judgments are to be bound up and governed.

The Court thus relied on its own prior cases interpreting contracts, as well as principles of commercial law across U.S. state jurisdictions, some dating back to English and even Roman law.

By the twentieth century, many legal intellectuals had grown skeptical of the notion that there existed a body of general, discernible legal principles. Justice Oliver Wendell Holmes lampooned *Swift* as invoking "a transcendental body of law outside of any particular State but obligatory within it unless and until changed by statute." By the New Deal era, Holmes's views were ascendant among those in the legal realist school, such as Charles Clark, the Yale Law dean who crafted the new Federal Rules of Civil Procedure in the 1930s. In the realists' view, judges did not "find" law; they *made* it, just like legislators.

In 1938, the same year those new civil-procedure rules were adopted, the Supreme Court heard *Erie v. Tompkins*, a case that involved the burgeoning field of tort law. Harry Tompkins had been out for a walk in his home state of Pennsylvania when he was struck by something sticking out of a passing train car. He fell, and the train's wheels crushed one of his arms. The train belonged to Erie Railroad, a New York corporation. Tompkins sued in federal court in Pennsylvania and won a jury verdict.

But the jury had been instructed in the *federal* negligence standard, not the Pennsylvania standard, which for this class of accident was stricter. In a split decision authored by the progressive champion Louis Brandeis, the Supreme Court decided that the Pennsylvania standard should instead apply. Brandeis wrote that, *contra Swift*, "There is no federal general common law." Nor did he reach this conclusion merely as a statutory interpretation, as Story had done in *Swift*; Brandeis and the other justices in the majority decided that Congress had no power whatsoever "to declare substantive rules of common law applicable in a State," and that "no clause in the Constitution purports to confer such a power upon the federal courts." The Court's new view was that the federal courts' common law—including tort liability—was "reserved by the Constitution to the several States." After ninety-six years, the Court had overturned *Swift v. Tyson*. The federal common law was no more.

Before turning to its constitutional analysis, Justice Brandeis's decision criticized the *Swift* doctrine on policy grounds—assailing it for its "defects, political and social." He observed that having a federal legal standard distinct from the state standard had resulted in what is now commonly called forum shopping: parties to a lawsuit would strategically opt for federal rather than state jurisdiction when they thought it could benefit their case. Indeed, that's what Tompkins had apparently done (and understandably so). And in a case ten years earlier where Brandeis had been in the dissenting group calling for *Swift*'s reversal—before a change in personnel shifted the Court's position—a corporation had actually changed states, filing new incorporation documents in another state, to create "diversity" of citizenship in the litigation and avail itself of the federal rule.

Brandeis was clearly correct that under the *Swift* standard, parties to litigation were strategically trying to maximize their position by opting for federal or state court depending on which offered a more favorable legal standard. But he was wrong when he assumed that deferring to underlying state law would end forum shopping. State judges can often differ in disposition or quality from those on the federal bench. Moreover, the new *procedural* rules under the Federal Rules of Civil Procedure often differ from those in the state—as do, for instance, the Federal Rules of Evidence. And before long, another rule revision by the Supreme Court would make it easier for plaintiffs seeking a favorable court to do yet another type of forum shopping: from one state to another.

• • •

Historically, a state's courts had limited power to enforce judgments against nonresidents. In the colonial era, a British court would have had great difficulty enforcing its judgment against a resident of France, and the same principle tended to apply between states in the new American republic. A state's courts could generally enforce a judgment only against a party within its territory.

There were ways around the limitation. For instance, an out-of-state party might enter into a contract that gave consent to be subject to a state's jurisdiction. And if the dispute involved property within the state's territory, the lawsuit could attach to the property (*in rem* jurisdiction) rather than a person (*in personem* jurisdiction). But as the Supreme Court decided in 1878 in *Pennoyer v. Neff*, the suit had to be in the right form. If filed against the person, not the property, then the person being sued had to be served notice of the suit while physically present within the state for a state court to assert power over the individual.

In 1945, seven years after it decided *Erie*, the Supreme Court created a more relaxed jurisdictional standard, in *International Shoe Company v. State of Washington*. Headquartered in Missouri and incorporated under the laws of Delaware, the International Shoe Company had no facilities in the state of Washington, but it did have about a dozen salesmen there who brought in a bit more than $30,000 in revenue annually. Washington sought to tax the company. The Supreme Court agreed—and established a new standard that allowed a state court to exercise jurisdiction over an out-of-state defendant that had "sufficient minimum contacts" in the state. Companies that introduced products into the stream of commerce, like International Shoe, fit the bill.

The holding in *International Shoe* is unexceptional: it's hardly a strange rule to allow a state to collect taxes on a company doing business there, even if headquartered elsewhere. But by allowing state courts to assert broad jurisdiction over out-of-state defendants, the new rules enabled plaintiffs' lawyers to shop their cases to favorable jurisdictions: as long as a state court would allow them a forum, a lawyer could sue a business there. And if lawyers are able to shop their case to the most favorable of fifty states, the forum is likely to be favorable indeed.

Judges and plaintiffs alike, in moments of candor, have acknowledged as much. At a 2002 investor conference at Prudential Securities, the Mississippi mass tort lawyer Dickie Scruggs was honest about how some jurisdictions were uniquely plaintiff-friendly:

> [W]hat I call the "magic jurisdiction," . . . [is] where the judiciary is elected with verdict money. The trial lawyers have established relationships with the judges that are elected; they're state court judges; they're popul[ists]. They've got large populations of voters who are in on the deal, they're getting their [piece] in many cases. And so, it's a political force in their jurisdiction, and it's almost impossible to get a fair trial if you're a defendant in some of these places. The plaintiff lawyer walks in there and writes the number on the blackboard, and the first juror meets the last one coming out the door with that amount of money. . . . The cases are not won in the courtroom. They're won on the back roads long before the case goes to trial. Any lawyer fresh out of law school can walk in there and win the case, so it doesn't matter what the evidence or the law is.

One of those elected, populist state court judges, Richard Neely—former justice of the Supreme Court of Appeals of West Virginia—openly admitted to preferring cases brought by in-state plaintiffs' lawyers against out-of-state defendant companies:

> As long as I am allowed to redistribute wealth from out-of-state companies to injured in-state plaintiffs, I shall continue to do so. Not only is my sleep enhanced when I give someone else's money away, but so is my job security, because the in-state plaintiffs, their families, and their friends will reelect me.

To test this effect, the economists Alex Tabarrok and Eric Helland ran a statistical analysis examining the behavior of state judges. They were able to compare federal judges with their state counterparts, both elected and appointed. Their experiment was quite well controlled: because of *Erie*, federal and state judges applied the same body of laws (albeit with some procedural and evidentiary differences). And Tabarrok and Helland's results comported with Scruggs's and Neely's claims: plaintiffs tended to win higher tort awards in lawsuits against out-of-state companies, before elected (not appointed) state judges, relative to the norms in the federal system.

To be sure, a business might try to remove a case to federal court rather than face a "magic jurisdiction" judge—there's at least some greater likelihood of fairness with a life-appointed federal judge than an elected state court hack hoping to curry favor with voters by redistributing out-of-state companies' wealth. But clever plaintiffs' lawyers have developed ingenious ways to game the system. Among these is what's commonly called "fraudulent joinder": adding a nonessential defendant to the case to defeat the requirements for federal jurisdiction. Federal courts, unlike state courts, have limited jurisdiction. If there's no issue of federal law raised in a lawsuit, federal courts can hear the case only if there is "complete" diversity: none of the plaintiffs can come from the same state as any of the defendants. This means that "joining" a local defendant to the lawsuit can prevent a defendant the lawsuit is really targeting from removing a case to federal court—and out of a magic jurisdiction.

That's what happened in Jefferson County, Mississippi, which had emerged as a hotbed for mass tort lawsuits against pharmaceutical companies in the late 1990s. The poor, rural county had fewer than 10,000 people. It had twenty-two retail shops. And it only had one civil judge, Lamar Pickard. But Judge Pickard made decisions favorable to trial lawyers, so Jefferson County was a magic jurisdiction and "ground zero for the largest legal attack on the pharmaceutical industry." In 2000, a total of 3,322 plaintiffs joined seventy-three mass-joinder legal actions against out-of-state defendants in Pickard's court. To keep defendant drug manufacturers from removing their cases to federal court, plaintiffs' lawyers also sued the county's one local pharmacy. In Senate testimony, the proprietor, Hilda Bankston, described what happened to her:

> No small business should have to endure the nightmares I have experienced....I've searched record after record and made copy after copy for use against me. I've had to hire personnel to watch the store while I was

dragged into court on numerous occasions to testify. I have endured the whispers and questions of my customers and neighbors wondering what we did to end up in court so often. And, I have spent many sleepless nights wondering if my business would survive the tidal wave of lawsuits cresting over it.

No Jefferson County jury ever found Bankston's store liable. Meanwhile, the flood of lawyers rolling into town to sue in the magic jurisdiction enriched many other businesses.

• • •

Besides subjecting innocent parties like Hilda Bankston to legal nightmares, the essential supremacy of state tort law turns ordinary federalism on its head. In general, federalism is one of the linchpins of America's constitutional genius, enabling robust but limited government by dividing power vertically with the states. The key virtue of federalism is that it allows people and firms to "vote with their feet," choosing the set of rules that best allows them to pursue a livelihood or build a thriving business. Federalism thus tends to encourage a "race to the top" among competing state polities.

Federalism in tort law sometimes works this way, at least to some degree. It happens when the effects of lawsuits are mostly localized. As noted earlier, a state with excessively loose laws concerning recovery for workplace accidents will lose employers over time. Likewise, a state that permits excessive recoveries in medical malpractice claims will lose doctors and see higher health-care costs. But in other cases—those that most affect national commerce—there is little incentive for states to rein in abusive lawsuits. Under *International Shoe*, a company making a product in one state can generally be sued for alleged product defects in another state, so a business gains little by moving between states. And the states have little incentive to make their own legal regime more hospitable when out-of-state defendants are lawsuits' target.

Federalism stops working when it becomes such a "race to the bottom"—when one state can dictate the terms of national commerce. We saw in Chapter 9 how tort litigation can serve as a "bottom-up" regulator: a hundred juries might reject a claim, but the next one accepts it, levies a hefty punitive verdict, and sets a new regulatory standard. This bottom-up regulation is somewhat random—the bad luck of the draw. The inverted federalism that allows plaintiffs' lawyers to shop for their preferred jurisdiction is a stacked deck.

State tort lawsuits can interfere with other states' regulatory choices. East St. Louis, Illinois—across the Mississippi River from its Missouri sister that attracted so much talcum-powder litigation—has long been a favorite jurisdiction of the plaintiffs' bar. In 2003, it handed out eye-popping verdicts like a more than $10 billion award against Philip Morris, the cigarette manufacturer, for allegedly "misbranding" its "light" cigarettes by misleading customers to think they were safer than heavier-tar alternatives. (Appeals courts later threw out the award.) Never mind that the out-of-state company's package labeling was heavily controlled by both a federal regulatory scheme and a 1990s-era settlement with state plaintiffs (which we'll come to in the next chapter).

Class action lawsuits in East St. Louis exploded at the turn of the twenty-first century. Four in five involved out-of-state defendants. One that targeted an Illinois defendant, the State Farm insurance company, demonstrates how sometimes even a lawsuit against an in-state company can override the preferences of *other* states' elected legislatures. State Farm had authorized the use of "generic" auto parts in vehicle repairs under its policies, as opposed to only "original equipment manufacturer" parts from the damaged car's manufacturer. A lawsuit claimed that this was "fraudulent" under the state's consumer-fraud law. In November 1999, an Illinois judge in the East St. Louis area awarded a national class of plaintiffs $1.2 billion in a lawsuit against State Farm. Because it was a national class of plaintiffs, the verdict necessarily included individuals in other states, not subject to Illinois law. Using generic auto parts in car repairs was not deemed fraudulent in all those states; to the contrary, some state legislatures actually *required* it, if less expensive, as a way to keep auto insurance rates down.

In the wake of the State Farm verdict, the Jefferson County story, and similar stories of a few plaintiff-friendly state courts attracting the lion's share of national cases, Congress finally stepped in. The 2005 Class Action Fairness Act (CAFA) allows class action lawsuits and certain "mass action" joined lawsuits to be removed to federal court if they involve a national class of plaintiffs and a sufficiently high dollar amount. CAFA doesn't prevent plaintiffs from opting for their preferred *substantive* law—which depends on state law, under *Erie*. But it does at least prevent the most national of cases from being heard before populist judges in magic jurisdictions. At his White House signing ceremony, President George W. Bush gave one of the pens to Hilda Bankston.

• • •

Although the Class Action Fairness Act did fix some of the most egregious examples of inverted federalism in tort litigation, plaintiff-friendly states still have the ability to create de facto national regulatory standards through product liability lawsuits, particularly those involving mass tort claims. And in the general case, state tort law can even override *federal* regulatory choices.

Consider *Wyeth v. Levine*, a 2009 case in which a divided Supreme Court upheld a Vermont jury's "failure to warn" tort-law verdict against the pharmaceutical company Wyeth. Wyeth manufactured Phenergan, an antihistamine, which had been approved by the FDA in 1955. Phenergan had been commonly used for decades to treat migraine headaches and severe nausea. Medical professionals administered the drug intravenously. Phenergan did have a very serious side effect if injected into an artery rather than a vein: it could lead to gangrene. But the FDA had long been aware of this risk and nevertheless deemed the benefit worth the risk. It worked with the company to compose the proper warning label—and trusted medical professionals to heed the warning when administering the drug.

Tragically, a physician's assistant had failed to heed the warning when she administered Phenergan to Diana Levine, and injected the drug into an artery. The error caused the arm to gangrene. Levine, a professional guitarist, had to have her arm amputated below the elbow.

Given Levine's gruesome injury, it's not surprising that a Vermont jury found Wyeth liable. But the warnings about the risk of gangrene from arterial exposure were there, prominently, in four places on Phenergan's labeling. In two places, the label bore a direct, bold, uppercase warning: "INTRA-ARTERIAL INJECTION CAN RESULT IN GANGRENE OF THE AFFECTED EXTREMITY." The physician's assistant had simply missed it.

The jury presumably thought that some other label might have been better or harder to miss. And a majority of the Supreme Court agreed that the jury could adopt that view, notwithstanding the fact that Wyeth had worked with the FDA on the warning labels for more than two decades, from 1973 to 1997.

Defenders of this regulatory regime say that's a feature, not a bug: state tort law fills in the "gaps" that the FDA can't fully police. But safety isn't unidirectional: drugs that vastly improve and save lives can have severe and even deadly side effects. There is a very real risk of overwarning, which discourages doctors and patients from using medications that improve health or save lives.

And too many superfluous warnings can distract medical professionals from the ones that really matter—like those warning of gangrene when you hit an artery instead of a vein.

Superimposing state tort law on top of federal regulation doesn't merely undercut federal regulators' decision making; it's an obvious one-way ratchet toward heavier regulation. And the implicit tax imposed on a manufacturer can be levied by a single state—even if ill-founded, even if contrary to federal regulators' judgment, and even if the other forty-nine states disagree.

CHAPTER 12

Act Locally, Sue Globally

In January 2018, Mayor Bill de Blasio announced that New York City was suing five multinational oil companies: BP, Chevron, ConocoPhillips, ExxonMobil, and Royal Dutch Shell. On Twitter, he exclaimed, "We are fighting for our lives and we will not wait for anyone else to do it for us." Announcing the litigation, the mayor brashly asserted his prerogative to set national policy terms for combatting climate change. "We never make the mistake of waiting on our national government to act when it's unwilling to. This city is acting. We want other cities to act. We want other states to act."

De Blasio is hardly alone among state and local officials in flexing his muscles in this most global of policy disputes—trying to push the regulation of carbon emissions more aggressively than the federal government has yet been willing to do. His lawsuit followed similar litigation initiated by the cities of Oakland and San Francisco in September 2017. And as far back as 2004, New York City and eight states filed suit against five electric power companies over their alleged contributions to climate change; the lawsuits claimed that the companies' carbon emissions constituted a "public nuisance" under state common law.

These various climate-change lawsuits typically ask energy companies for money. The premise behind such lawsuits is that climate change imposes costs on states—e.g., to prepare for higher sea levels caused by rising global temperatures.

To date, the climate suits have largely failed. The 2004 "public nuisance" suit, for instance, was rebuffed in 2011, in an opinion by Ruth Bader Ginsburg for a unanimous Supreme Court.

Yet in other policy areas, state and local governments' efforts to regulate national and multinational companies through litigation have had profound effects. The model for large-scale state and local litigation against big business-es is the 1990s-era suits by state governments against tobacco companies—which ended up netting state governments hundreds of billions of dollars. Since the Big Tobacco payout, state officials and trial lawyers have regularly joined forces to sue a host of private businesses, from firearms manufacturers to pharmaceutical companies to financial institutions.

Beyond the monies sometimes collected from the suits, there are regula-tory objectives. The tobacco settlement led to significant regulation of tobacco markets—against a backdrop of Congress declining to grant regulatory authority over cigarettes to the FDA. Lawsuits against gunmakers have come from state and local officials who want stricter gun control nationwide. Litiga-tion against pharmaceutical manufacturers and financial companies has often piggybacked on federal regulatory and enforcement actions—upping penalties agreed to by national adjudicators—or sought to achieve new quasi-regulatory schemes similar to those implemented against Big Tobacco.

To be sure, political debates over climate change and gun control and financial regulation are fierce. But when state and local officials are supersed-ing Congress, they're inverting normal federalism. State and local officials are filing local lawsuits designed to address global problems—and they're often seeking regulatory goals that *conflict with* federal law and threaten to override the policy judgments of elected national officials. Environmental activists have long invoked the slogan, "Think Globally, Act Locally." But now, local actors are seeking to direct national or even global policy.

I've dubbed these state and local actors who seek national regulatory pow-ers the *new antifederalists*—the natural heirs to the opponents of the federal constitutional project. To achieve their goals, they've exploited the inverted federalism of our modern tort law and sweeping state prosecutorial powers, as well as the investment clout of massive (if underfunded) state pension plans.

• • •

Before New York City officials and other state and local government leaders commenced litigation aimed at regulating greenhouse gas emissions, the hard-charging New York attorney general Eliot Spitzer used his enforcement powers to overhaul huge swathes of the financial sector. Seeking publicity—and eventually higher office—the self-styled "Sheriff of Wall Street" brought threats down upon the national investment banking, mutual fund, and insurance industries, refashioning them to his will.

Spitzer's principal tool was New York's Martin Act, a 1921 state law that gives the attorney general extremely broad powers to investigate, subpoena, sue, and prosecute companies and individuals. The Martin Act does not require any showing of intentional wrongdoing to establish criminal liability. And a Martin Act violation need not show any actual injury or a fraud material to investors—or various other conditions that would apply under the Securities and Exchange Commission's federal regulatory plan.

The Martin Act's loose standards and broad prosecutorial authority enable a single elected state official to pursue regulatory ends with national implications. And because state attorneys general have broad plenary enforcement powers, they can do so even if their preferred ends conflict with the judgment of federal officials enforcing federal law.

On October 14, 2004, Spitzer filed a civil suit against Marsh & McLennan, the world's largest insurance broker. He also announced a settlement with employees at two insurance companies: ACE, a property-casualty insurer, and AIG, an industry giant.

Beyond the companies themselves, the targets in Spitzer's crosshairs were a father and his sons. AIG had been built over decades by its longtime chairman and CEO, Maurice "Hank" Greenberg. His two eldest sons, Jeffrey and Evan, had trained under his watch before heading out on their own; Jeffrey was the CEO of Marsh, and Evan ran ACE.

At the heart of Spitzer's complaint was alleged bid-rigging and efforts to inflate corporate reserves artificially. But no less significant than the charges were the extraordinary remedies sought by the aggressive Sheriff of Wall Street. Jeffrey was forced out at Marsh, and the attorney general set his sights on the elder Greenberg—going after him as zealously as Ahab hunted the white whale. Spitzer warned the board of AIG that he would pursue criminal charges against the company unless it ousted Greenberg. Facing a bet-the-company legal tussle, the board was forced to comply.

What happened next would prove calamitous. Hank Greenberg had watched like a hawk the company's "financial products group," a division he started and its greatest default risk. Among the products the division sold were contracts with creditors who worried about a supplier or customer going broke and being unable to pay up—so-called credit-default swaps. But with Greenberg out the door and new management focused on placating Spitzer and other swarming regulators, the company leadership took its eye off the ball. In the seven months following Greenberg's departure, AIG issued as many credit-default swaps as it had in the prior seven years. In fall 2008, those swap contracts came due. The financial company faced a liquidity crisis. And the federal government pumped $185 billion into the embattled insurer, essentially assuming control of the company and wiping out most of its shareholders' wealth.

• • •

Not all the new antifederalists hail from New York. Bill de Blasio and Eliot Spitzer had a predecessor who hailed from the South: Mississippi's Mike Moore. As the attorney general of the Magnolia State in the early 1990s, Moore was approached by a fellow native of the Gulf Coast town of Pascagoula: Richard "Dickie" Scruggs, the asbestos lawyer. Scruggs suggested that the state might sue tobacco companies for damages—and hire him to handle the case. Scruggs had given substantial sums to Moore's campaign. And Moore happily accepted the proposal.

Up to that point, smokers who had developed lung cancer—and their estates—had found little success in suing tobacco companies. Tort claimants generally cannot seek compensation for injuries caused by inherently dangerous products. The Second Restatement of Torts from 1965, which generally birthed design-defect and failure-to-warn product liability litigation, expressly listed tobacco along with whiskey and butter as "inherently dangerous" products not amenable to tort lawsuits. Besides, federally mandated warning labels had been prominently placed on every pack of cigarettes since the 1960s. In 1992, the U.S. Supreme Court held that legislation formalizing those labels, the Public Health Cigarette Smoking Act of 1969, preempted state-law failure-to-warn claims against cigarette manufacturers.

The Court left open other potential avenues for filing suits, but tobacco companies fiercely defended themselves against product liability actions. Filing individual smoking lawsuits was an expensive and risky proposition. And lawyers could not combine smoking lawsuits into class actions: since every person's health profile and smoking history is individual, smokers lack the "commonality" that members of class actions must have under Federal Rule of Civil Procedure 23.

Scruggs had an idea to open up the litigation spigot. *States* might sue tobacco companies over costs to their health systems from handling smoking-related ailments. States as plaintiffs would have massive potential harms, given their role in delivering Medicaid. And states as plaintiffs would not have to comply with class action commonality rules.

The logic was not without its problems. States had no contractual relationship with tobacco companies. State excise taxes on cigarettes exceeded the cost of treating smoking-related illnesses, according to the Congressional Research Service. And there was that 1969 federal law that preempted state regulation in this area.

But Scruggs knew that evidence had begun to emerge that the companies had known about the dangers and addictiveness of smoking a good bit earlier than they'd let on. Tobacco companies couldn't afford to roll the dice with a jury, given the potential size of damages an entire state might be able to show. Scruggs thus rightly assumed that his gambit would bring tobacco companies to the settlement table.

Scruggs's theory of harm was not his only innovation. Rather than Mississippi paying him an hourly rate, as states had typically done when they needed to bring in extra manpower or expertise, Scruggs offered to litigate the case for the state for "free"—but with a hefty contingent fee should the suits recover money.

Scruggs had a winning offer. State officials could score political points by taking on a reviled industry—and refill government coffers at the same time. And owing to the contingent-fee structure, there was essentially no downside risk, at least in terms of fiscal resources. After initial settlements reached by Mississippi, Florida, Texas, and Minnesota, all forty-six remaining states entered into a master settlement agreement with cigarette manufacturers. Some state attorneys general went so far as to lobby their legislators to change existing law so that they and their states could get in on the deal.

The tobacco master settlement agreement imposed new limitations on cigarette advertising, beyond those already present in the federal regulatory scheme. It appropriated large sums of money to fund nonprofit entities designed to warn the public about tobacco's harms. On their face, these terms made some sense: advertising may have induced people, especially youth, to take up smoking, and public-interest ads about the dangers of smoking might deter folks from picking up the habit. But these terms were the very sort of regulation that Congress in its 1969 law had prohibited state legislatures from mandating directly.

In addition to appropriating funds, the settlement essentially levied a new tax on cigarette sales. Payouts were not an estimate of static damages but were specifically linked to future sales volume. To maintain sales volume, the agreement essentially froze existing market share. New companies could enter the market, but they had to pay into an escrow fund purportedly to cover future liabilities. Perversely, the settlement gave states every incentive to protect Big Tobacco. The states were set to receive more than $200 billion from the cigarette industry over the next quarter century, with multibillion-dollar payouts promised in perpetuity, and they became fiscally dependent on this gargantuan cash flow.

The litigation also made a billionaire out of Scruggs, and made many of his fellow lawyers extraordinarily wealthy. The attorneys representing Florida were paid, on average, $233 million each. Lawyers representing states that joined the action late—such as Illinois, Michigan, and Ohio—scored huge payouts for very little work. The legal fees paid out of those three states' settlements totaled $836 million. The lawyers handling the case for Illinois took no depositions and never submitted a reckoning of their hours. Overall, plaintiffs' lawyers took home some $30 billion of states' settlement sums. The effective hourly rates for the lawyers, when hours were accounted for, typically exceeded $10,000 per hour.

Unsurprisingly, some of the money that flowed to private lawyers found its way back into the campaign chests of the state attorneys general who had hired them. Scruggs emerged as Moore's largest campaign contributor, and flew the attorney general to campaign stops in his private jet. The attorney general of Kansas at the time, Carla Stovall, hired her former firm, Entz & Chanay, as "local counsel" in the settlement negotiations—and later received sizable campaign donations from her local colleagues. In one extreme case, a former Texas attorney general, Dan Morales, was indicted on federal corruption charges for allegedly converting campaign contributions to personal use. He pleaded guilty. Scruggs himself subsequently pleaded guilty to federal corruption charges, for allegedly bribing a judge in an unrelated case.

• • •

The tobacco litigation was sold by its proponents as a "unique" affair that would not be replicated against other industries that might implicate the public health. But after the tobacco-suit bonanza, the strategy of outside lawyers suing companies on behalf of states, on contingent-fee contracts, emerged as a template for hosts of new actions.

In October 1998, the ink was barely dry on the tobacco settlements reached with Mississippi and the other early-suing states; the lawyers' take wouldn't be announced for another month, and the master settlement agreement was still a month away, too. But the City of New Orleans saw an opportunity and announced it was hiring private lawyers to sue gun manufacturers. The lawyers leading the litigation included Wendell Gauthier, Elizabeth Cabraser, Stanley Chesley, and Joan Coale—who had previously scored big paydays in the tobacco litigation. In fact, they called themselves the Castano Litigation Group after Peter Castano, a smoker who had died of lung cancer in 1993.

Chicago filed its own gun lawsuit two weeks later. Twenty-seven more municipal governments joined in over the next year. Among the forty entities targeted were not only gun manufacturers but also trade associations such as the National Shooting Sports Foundation.

What was the basis for the cities' claim? Like a cigarette, a gun is not a good target for a product liability lawsuit: it's obviously an "inherently dangerous" product. A defectively designed gun—say, one that backfired or blew up on the shooter—would obviously be subject to a product liability claim, just like an exploding Coca-Cola bottle. But to a significant extent the *point* of a firearm is to be deadly—and the risks are well known to any purchaser. The New Orleans suit claimed that guns were nevertheless "unreasonably dangerous" and should have had various safety features added. Chicago advanced a novel theory that gunmakers had "negligently marketed" their product and sold too many, thus creating a "public nuisance" and undue safety risks.

The public-nuisance theory had been developed in 1996 by David Kairys, a professor at Philadelphia's Temple University who specialized in civil rights law. The longstanding "nuisance" tort, dating to twelfth-century England, was originally a criminal cause of action. As discussed in Chapter 6, the king of England could initiate a nuisance suit to police infringements on public roads or waterways. In early America, public-nuisance law was also adopted as a mechanism for policing establishments perceived as a threat to public morals—from taverns to gambling establishments to "houses of ill repute."

But the use of the public-nuisance tort had waned with the rise of the regulatory state, as specific statutes targeted "public" offenses and supplanted ad hoc judicial remedies. By the time of the New Deal, public nuisance had become a mere "footnote" in the law of tort, unmentioned in the American Law Institute's 1939 version of the Restatement of Torts.

The city-plaintiffs were strange advocates for the public-nuisance theory, given that most of them regularly sold old guns from their own police departments to private dealers to generate revenue. But the point wasn't to win in court so much as to force settlements out of gun manufacturers, which had far lower cash flows than tobacco companies. New York State's attorney general told gun companies they would face bankruptcy if they didn't settle the case. Andrew Cuomo, then the secretary of housing and urban development, promised that gunmakers would suffer "death by a thousand cuts."

The cities and their private lawyers attempted to develop a comprehensive gun-regulation scheme. Chicago's suit, for instance, sought to ban sales to any individual who had bought a firearm within the past thirty days, and to outlaw all sales of "firearms that by their design are unreasonably attractive to criminals." Initially, the suits against gunmakers had some success. Smith & Wesson agreed to a settlement brokered by President Bill Clinton in 2000.

But most gunmakers fought back, and the cities' public-nuisance theory was rejected by most courts that considered the claims. In 2005, Congress stepped in and enacted the Protection of Lawful Commerce in Arms Act, which preempted most lawsuits over the sale of guns used to commit crimes. When the families of children killed in the massacre at Sandy Hook Elementary School in 2012 filed a lawsuit against the Remington firearms company, the Connecticut state judge handling the case dismissed it, ruling that the lawsuit fell "squarely within" the congressional statute's "broad immunity." On March 14, 2019, the Connecticut Supreme Court disagreed and resuscitated the case. Remington had filed for bankruptcy protection one year earlier.

• • •

Apart from the gun lawsuits, cities and states contracted out other litigation based on a public-nuisance rationale. Among these were suits against paint manufacturers for decades-old sales of products containing lead, and the ill-fated suits against energy companies construing carbon emissions as a public nuisance. Other lawyers developed claims expressly premised on the tobacco suits' Medicaid-reimbursement model. Dickie Scruggs led state-backed lawsuits against health-management organizations. Other attorneys led state suits against pharmaceutical manufacturers.

The State of Alabama, among others, filed a suit alleging that pharmaceutical companies had been "price gouging" the state by recommending average wholesale prices to pharmacists who prescribed drugs covered by Medicaid. When Alabama's attorney general Troy King, a Republican, filed this suit against seventy-three pharmaceutical companies, he farmed it out to the Montgomery personal injury firm Beasley Allen. (The firm's founder, Jere Beasley, has long been one of America's most prominent plaintiffs' lawyers; he previously served as the state's attorney general under Governor George Wallace.)

According to a report by the American Tort Reform Association, Beasley Allen played a big role in bankrolling King. The firm and its lawyers donated over $760,000 to eight separate political action committees from 2006 through 2010; these same PACs in turn gave $240,000 to support King's campaigns.

This largesse paid back handsomely to Beasley Allen. The firm took in more than $20 million of over $120 million paid to the state in 2008 and 2009 settlements. Those payouts came notwithstanding the shakiness of the case's legal theory. Three companies—AstraZeneca, GlaxoSmithKline, and Novartis—had decided to roll the dice and take the state to trial. In reversing jury verdicts against each company in 2010, the Alabama Supreme Court observed that the state had provided no evidence that the companies had made any misrepresentations, and noted that nothing was preventing Alabama from negotiating its own pricing with the companies. But the earlier jury verdicts against the three companies, before the supreme court's judgment, totaled almost $340 million—which shows why so many other companies had been willing to settle.

Many of these state-led pharmaceutical cases, like King and Beasley's "price gouging" case, are simple shakedowns designed to funnel money to states and private lawyers alike. But other cases have regulatory goals, like those reached in the tobacco settlement. Some 24,000 American municipalities are seeking to negotiate a master settlement with drug manufacturers in a federal court in Cleveland. At issue is the prescription of legal but addictive opioid drugs. In parallel litigation, Purdue Pharma, the maker of Oxycontin, agreed to pay out $270 million to the State of Oklahoma in April 2019; some thirty-five additional state lawsuits are pending.

Like tobacco, opioid drugs such as Oxycontin have real social costs when abused. An estimated 400,000 Americans have suffered opioid-related deaths in the last two decades. Studies place the total social cost of opioid abuse as high as $1 trillion. The dramatic increase in opioid addiction cries out for policy action. But state- and local-led litigation is a strange way to approach a national public-health issue. Particularly when private plaintiffs' attorneys stand to take a sizable fraction of the proceeds that may come from payout schemes or bankruptcy trusts on the asbestos and tobacco models.

State lawsuits led by private counsel over opioid prescriptions are nothing new. One of the earliest state lawsuits filed by private attorneys against pharmaceutical companies was filed in 2001 by West Virginia against Purdue Pharma—for allegedly "aggressive" marketing tactics that understated Oxycontin's risks. The lawsuit did little to curb opioid abuse, but it did win the state a $10 million settlement, which the state attorney general, Darrell McGraw, allocated to various charitable causes of his choosing. Of that sum, $3 million went to four plaintiffs' law firms that had contributed $47,500 to McGraw's campaigns.

• • •

State and local officials also regularly outsource to private lawyers class action litigation premised on "securities fraud." They're able to sue over alleged securities violations because states and municipalities hold more than $3 trillion in financial assets to help cover their pension obligations to public employees. (We'll turn to these pensions in more detail in the next chapter.) Securities class action litigation, discussed briefly in Chapter 8, has brought in more than $100 billion in settlements since 1996. In many years, state and municipal pension funds have led nearly half of all such lawsuits.

Securities class action lawsuits trace to a pair of federal laws enacted in 1933 and 1934 in the wake of the great stock market crash of 1929. In 1942, the agency tasked with the new regulatory effort, the Securities and Exchange Commission, promulgated Rule 10b-5. This rule forbade frauds and false statements connected to the sale of nationally traded securities.

As mentioned previously, a "private" enforcement mechanism enabling plaintiffs to sue alleged violators was notably absent from both Congress's statute and the SEC's rule. Indeed, neither the congressional debates nor the SEC commentary at the time show any evidence that the legislators or the commissioners were contemplating private-enforcement lawsuits. Nevertheless, in 1946, a federal district court in Pennsylvania "found" an "implied" right to sue for civil enforcement under the law and the SEC rule. Other federal courts followed. By the time the Supreme Court got around to a case involving a 10b-5 claim in 1971, the justices tersely noted in a footnote that private lawsuits under the rule were "now established."

Although the courts had created a new class of lawsuit under the federal securities laws, they also adopted various rules—many imported from long-existing state common-law doctrines—that made spurious lawsuits somewhat less likely. A plaintiff suing for fraud under Rule 10b-5 had to be an actual purchaser or seller of a security, the alleged fraud had to be intentional, and it had to matter enough to affect the security's price. Also, critically, the plaintiff had to "rely" on the misrepresentation in buying or selling the security.

The "reliance" test made it next to impossible to create a class action lawsuit out of a securities-fraud case. How would one prove that every investor in a class of plaintiffs actually relied on a false statement? In 1988, the Supreme Court had an answer: you basically didn't have to. In *Basic v. Levinson*, the Court decided that it was possible to *infer* reliance based on the "fraud on the market" theory: even if an individual shareholder did not personally rely on a fraud, the fraud was presumably reflected in a security's market price, since some other investor in the market was using the misinformation. The modern securities class action suit was born.

In short order, plaintiffs' law firms developed securities class action practices in which they monitored stocks for abrupt price movements. A sharp drop in price would trigger a lawsuit alleging that some fraud had caused the stock to move—with the details to come later. Because defending against securities class action lawsuits involves expensive document production and the risk of unfavorable verdicts in the millions or even billions of dollars, these suits are almost always settled. The new lawsuits essentially redistribute wealth from one class of shareholders to another: investors who bought securities in a certain period are paid out of the general company coffers (i.e., all remaining shareholders' money). Of course, the lawyers take a sizable cut.

Critics soon dubbed these suits "legal extortion." A Florida judge compared securities class action lawyers to "'squeegee boys' who...run up to a stopped car, splash soapy water on its perfectly clean windshield and expect payment for the uninvited service of wiping it off."

In 1995, Congress took action and passed the Private Securities Litigation Reform Act. This law did not override the court-created securities class action lawsuit, but it did raise the threshold for pleading an initial case. It also ordered judges to choose the "lead plaintiff" in a securities class action rather than simply rely on who had filed suit first—a practice commonly derided as the "race to the courthouse door." Among the key criteria that Congress selected for choosing a lead plaintiff was the investor claiming the most losses. An unintended side effect of the rule was that it empowered state and local pension funds to take control of the securities class action business.

Many did. Securities cases with public pension funds as lead plaintiffs rose steadily from four in 1996 to fifty-six in 2002. In the first eight years under the new law, the Teachers' Retirement System of Louisiana was involved in sixty different class action suits. In 2004, an Ohio judge chastised the fund as a "professional plaintiff" and found that it had wastefully sought to appoint four different firms as counsel for a case.

It isn't hard to figure out why public-employee pension funds would be enthusiastic about hiring law firms to sue companies in class action securities suits, at least if they were controlled by elected officials. In his 2002 campaign for New York State comptroller, Alan Hevesi received $100,000 in donations from Milberg Weiss, then the largest plaintiffs' securities class action law firm, as well as more than $25,000 in contributions from senior partners at the firm. After winning election, Hevesi—the sole fiduciary of the New York State Common Retirement Fund, the nation's third-largest state pension— hired the Milberg Weiss firm to lead a securities class action suit against Bayer. He hired two other firms, Bernstein Litowitz and Barrack Rodos, to lead a securities class action suit against Citigroup. The firms, and their attorneys, had given $121,800 in donations to Hevesi's campaign.

At least the attorneys in those New York firms had a plausible excuse for giving money to Hevesi. Perhaps they were simply public-interested Empire State citizens? But securities class action firms in New York and California have also donated hundreds of thousands of dollars to the political campaigns of officials in *other* states.

Sometimes, the timing of these gifts left little to the imagination. In mid-February 2006, five Bernstein Litowitz partners gave a combined $25,000 to the reelection campaign of Jim Hood, Mike Moore's successor as Mississippi attorney general. Mere days later, between February 21 and March 14, Hood entered into signed contracts hiring Bernstein Litowitz on a contingent-fee basis to lead securities-fraud lawsuits on behalf of Mississippi against three different out-of-state defendant companies. He hired the firm to lead another securities class action case on May 17. The following year, Bernstein Litowitz partners donated thousands of dollars more to Hood's campaign.

Bernstein Litowitz and another New York firm specializing in securities class action suits, Kaplan Fox & Kilsheimer, also contributed a combined $445,000 to the Ohio Democratic Party in 2007 and 2008, among a total of $830,000 given by out-of-state firms. The largesse went principally to benefit Richard Cordray's candidacy for attorney general. Cordray won his election, and then hired private law firms to lead multiple securities class action suits on behalf of state pension funds. He would later be tapped by Barack Obama as the first head of the federal Consumer Financial Protection Bureau.

• • •

Some twenty-five years after Dickie Scruggs approached Mike Moore to hire him on behalf of Mississippi to sue tobacco companies, such lawsuits have become a staple of state and local efforts to extract monies from national and international companies. These lawsuits effectively levy taxes—and often appropriate funds—without state legislatures' consent. Along with state enforcement actions like Eliot Spitzer's Martin Act machinations, they steer national regulation from state capitals and city halls.

Beyond enforcement actions and private litigation, state and local officials are working to regulate national commerce and effect interstate regulation without Congress by leveraging their workers' retirement assets. At the same press conference at which Mayor de Blasio announced his lawsuit, he also promised to divest New York City's pension fund of its holdings in oil companies, due to concerns about climate change. The accumulation of such investment assets has given the new antifederalists another opportunity to flex their regulatory muscles—which is the story of the next chapter.

CHAPTER 13

Stock Market Politics

Who's the most important investor in the American stock market? Anyone who regularly tunes in to CNBC might point to Carl Icahn or Nelson Peltz, the hedge fund titans. Or maybe to younger activist investors like Dan Loeb or Bill Ackman. To be sure, these shareholders send corporate executives scrambling to curry favor when they come calling.

But so too does a nondescript New York City politician, Scott M. Stringer. After graduating from the John Jay College of Criminal Justice, Stringer has spent his entire adult life in the political arena—as a legislative assistant, state assemblyman, or local elected official. In November 2013 he was elected comptroller of New York City, a position that gave him power in the stock market. The comptroller oversees five pension funds for New York City employees. Collectively, those funds constitute the fourth-largest public pension plan in the United States, with more than $200 billion in assets.

One year after his election, Stringer announced the launch of what he called the Boardroom Accountability Project. The express purpose of the project was to influence corporate behavior by leveraging the power of the pension funds' shares.

Stringer's initial idea was to grant large corporate shareholders the power to nominate board directors on the company's proxy statement. In terms of shareholder voting results, his effort was quite successful: a majority of shareholders at most of the targeted companies supported his shareholder proposal. By Stringer's own count, some 270 publicly traded U.S. companies have now adopted a version of his preferred "proxy access" rule. So perhaps the rule makes sense, from shareholders' perspective.

But Stringer's ultimate aims were more political than economic. Stringer did not target companies based on lagging share prices, nor lapses in corporate governance structure. Rather, he focused on "climate change" and "board diversity," which subsequently became the principal focus of his efforts to "ratchet up the pressure on some of the biggest companies in the world."

Corporate boards of directors hold fiduciary powers over companies' affairs. Essentially, they're the bosses of chief executive officers. So, who sits on the boards makes a lot of difference.

And lots of evidence suggests that diversity matters. A board has to consider strategy, finance, accounting, marketing, research and development, and a host of other factors. But it's far from clear that a political push to "diversify" corporate boards based on race, sex, sexual orientation, and gender identity—the focal points of Stringer's campaign—makes sense for shareholders. To the contrary, empirical scholarship suggests that government-mandated gender quotas for corporate boards in other countries have tended to drive down shareholder value.

Nor is it likely that the public employees in Stringer's New York City offices have any specialized grasp of how climate change affects corporate share valuation. Studies have shown that "green" investing portfolios tend to underperform their fossil-fuel-laden brethren. But maybe those past returns won't hold true in the future. Stringer and other New York City officials are hoping so: as previously noted, they announced in 2018 that the Big Apple would divest its pension plans of energy companies focusing on fossil fuel by 2022.

It's the type of bet we've seen before—and it's unlikely to pay off. In 2001, California decided that its Public Employees' Retirement System should divest of tobacco stocks. In 2016, a report by an outside consultant calculated that the fund's boneheaded decision had cost the pension system more than $3 billion in lost investment gains. Of course, oil isn't tobacco. But if anything, New York City's decision makes even less sense: oil stocks constitute a much larger share of the market, and because energy price shocks tend to send overall markets reeling, energy-company stocks are often an effective hedge against market downturns.

In any event, if Stringer's climate-divestment bet backfires, the city will suffer—which matters for New Yorkers but not really for anyone else. But like the state attorneys general and the local district attorneys we saw earlier, Stringer aims to *pressure* companies as a way of influencing *national* policy. And although he won local elections in the nation's largest city, he hardly speaks for everyone else. Nobody in Alabama or Utah or Wisconsin voted for him. Nobody in Kentucky or Montana or New Hampshire signed off on his social-investing activism. His efforts thus embody the new antifederalism.

Politicians like Stringer, running public pension funds, are not the only players in the new antifederalist shareholder-activism game. The Securities and Exchange Commission—one of those "independent" federal agencies that operate under broad congressional grants of power, without presidential oversight—has empowered numerous unelected actors to push publicly traded corporations toward political ends. Among these actors are labor unions, religious and policy groups, and investing funds with a "social" purpose apart from maximizing returns for investors. Their agendas often work to the detriment of most shareholders, and subvert the central purposes of stock markets.

• • •

The roots of stock markets and shareholder-owned corporations go back to medieval Europe. Banks in twelfth-century France hired *courtiers de change*, forerunners of stock brokers, to manage agricultural debts. In the fourteenth century, bankers in Venice began to trade in government debt instruments. Around the same time, in Flanders, agricultural contracts came to be traded in common marketplaces. Today's stock exchanges in continental Europe (and Philadelphia) derive their name, *Bourse*, from the Antwerp trading house of the Van der Beurze family during that era.

Stock ownership akin to what we see in most large commercial enterprises today emerged in the Netherlands in the seventeenth century. The world's first corporate enterprise to be listed on a public stock exchange was the Dutch East India Company, which the Dutch government created by combining several rival trading companies. It was chartered in 1602 and granted a twenty-one-year monopoly on the spice trade with the East. The new monopoly issued bonds (debt interests) and permanent joint stock (shares in the company's residual earnings). Its corporate "securities"—the financial instruments distributed to members of the general public—were commonly traded in bourses. The British East India Company, which had received its royal charter in 1600, eventually followed the Dutch model and issued its own shares in 1657.

Dutch traders soon developed option contracts, futures contracts, and other derivative instruments—so called because they were *derived* from the value of an underlying financial security. Traders "speculated" on the value of these instruments. In 1637, the price of futures contracts on certain tulip bulbs skyrocketed to more than ten times the average worker's annual wages, before plummeting down to earth. This "tulip mania" is generally regarded as the first "speculative" financial market bubble. The first notable "stock market" bubble came in 1720, when the British South Sea Company, recently granted a monopoly to do business in South America, ballooned in price before deflating back to its original value. Economists still debate the causes of these and other financial market bubbles—including the twenty-first-century market bubbles that roiled the American economy, involving "dot-com" stocks and real estate.

The South Sea bubble cut off the growth of stock corporations for a time, as Parliament passed the Bubble Act of 1720 and limited stock issuance to firms granted a royal charter. At the time of the American Revolution, corporate charters remained rare. William Blackstone's definitive 1765 treatise, *Commentaries on the Laws of England*, gave little attention to corporate law, and did not even mention limited liability, the principle under which an investor who puts his money in an outside enterprise will not be on the hook personally for the business's losses if it goes belly-up. Adam Smith, in his 1776 magnum opus, *The Wealth of Nations*, was skeptical that the corporate form would expand beyond its limited early role.

But expand it did—in the newly independent colonies across the Atlantic. Before the Revolutionary War, only a handful of corporate charters had been granted by colonial governments. But the issuing of such charters exploded after the war, with hundreds granted by state governments in the first decade under the U.S. Constitution.

As industrialization took off in the new nation, states began relaxing corporate charter requirements. Most enacted statutes allowing incorporation without special legislation. In 1869, the U.S. Supreme Court ruled that a state could not prevent companies chartered by other states from doing business there—essentially destroying the old royal and colonial powers to limit the corporate form.

New Jersey liberalized its corporation laws in 1875, and before too long, most large businesses in the country incorporated in the Garden State—wherever they did most of their business. Delaware followed suit in 1899, and most businesses moved their corporate charters to that state after New Jersey's governor, Woodrow Wilson, sought to exploit his state's dominant position in corporate charters to pursue a Progressive antitrust agenda. Two-thirds of large corporations in America today are chartered in Delaware.

• • •

When shareholder-owned corporations emerged as the generally preferred organizational structure for large businesses, they weren't without their growing pains. The annals of early capitalism in post–Civil War America are replete with examples of canny financiers duping unsuspecting investors.

In the cattle business, traders often bloated their cows with water before putting them up at auction, since the extra weight would command a higher price. Daniel Drew, a former cattle drover who made a fortune in the steamboat business, brought a similar practice to the burgeoning stock market on Wall Street as a speculator in the mid-nineteenth century. Unscrupulous traders would acquire control of a company and "water" its stock by surreptitiously issuing new shares, and then pull in funds from unsuspecting investors. In the late 1860s, Drew and his allies James Fisk and Jay Gould used the tactic to bilk no less than Cornelius Vanderbilt, then the nation's wealthiest man, while blocking him from seizing control of the Erie Railroad.

Such stock-manipulation games were risky. In 1864, Drew had lost $500,000 taking on Vanderbilt in a railroad-stock challenge. And by 1876, setbacks had cost Drew so much that the onetime multimillionaire declared bankruptcy.

But Drew's cautionary tale did not deter others from trying to make a fortune through stock market deceptions. In 1910, the banking commissioner of Kansas, Joseph Norman Dolley, prevailed upon his state's legislature to address the problem. Dolley declared that some fraudsters were offering stocks backed by nothing but the "blue sky" of Kansas. One year later, the state enacted the nation's first "blue sky" law, designed to curtail such fraud.

Other states followed suit. In 1917, the U.S. Supreme Court affirmed states' power to enact such securities laws "to stop the sale of stock in fly-by-night concerns, visionary oil wells, distant gold mines and other like fraudulent exploitations." By 1933, every state but Nevada had enacted some version of the Kansas statute.

That's when the federal government entered the securities-regulation business. The original rationale for federal oversight of the stock markets (as mentioned earlier) was the Great Crash of 1929, which destroyed fortunes and triggered the Great Depression. Shortly after his inauguration as president in 1933, Franklin Roosevelt signed into law the Securities Act, as part of his "new deal for the American people." This law regulated the offering or sale of securities using the "means and instrumentalities of interstate commerce." One year later, Congress enacted the Securities Exchange Act, which extended the scope of regulation to trades of securities in secondary markets, rather than merely when initially issued. To enforce the new regulations, the 1934 act established the Securities and Exchange Commission.

Notwithstanding the populism of Roosevelt's New Deal, the new securities laws were broadly market-friendly. They did not displace the corporate laws of Delaware and other states, which allocated the rights of shareholders and directors. Nor did they displace the state blue-sky laws. The central premise of the new federal regulatory regime was to facilitate *disclosure* so that investors would be able to assess the risks of securities they purchased on a national exchange. Professor Roberta Romano of Yale Law School has called this the "genius" of American corporate law. Federal rules ensure that information is readily available and comparable on national markets, but because the *substantive* allocation of power between shareholders and directors remains with the states, corporate-law rules tend to be efficient: if a state adopts a package of rules inimical to investors' interests, as New Jersey did under Woodrow Wilson, business enterprises seeking to minimize their capital costs can reincorporate in a different state.

Overall, the new regime worked exceedingly well. At Roosevelt's inauguration, the Dow Jones Industrial Average was below where it had stood at the turn of the twentieth century. Eighty-six years later, it had grown more than 38,000 percent—amounting to an annual return of more than 7 percent, even ignoring the value of corporate dividends. While the American share of the global economy has shrunk since World War II, our stock markets remain the most robust in the world: about 43 percent of world stock market valuation is in the United States.

The competitive capital markets have efficiently reallocated investment dollars to nurture new enterprises and remake American society. In 1933, the Dow Jones average included companies like Nash Motors, a carmaker; International Harvester, an agricultural supply company; the American Can Company, a maker of tin cans; Borden, a milk distributor; F. W. Woolworth, a retailer; and Johns-Manville, an asbestos manufacturer. Fifty years ago, Apple and Microsoft did not exist. Amazon, Facebook, and Google did not exist twenty-five years ago. Today those are the five most valuable companies in the world.

• • •

Although the federal regime regulating the trade in financial securities has generally worked well, this does not mean that regulators have not sought powers beyond those clearly in the law enacted by Congress. In the congressional design, the federal regulatory role was to promote the disclosure of investment information to shareholders. It was not to dictate the powers of shareholders or the duties of directors, which remained a matter of *state* law. But the line between disclosure and substantive allocation of powers can sometimes be blurry.

Such is the case with the "shareholder proposal rule," first introduced by the SEC in 1942. Following from its disclosure power, the agency requires companies to distribute "proxy statements" to shareholders, in parallel with other required documents such as offering memoranda and quarterly and annual reports. Proxy statements give information to shareholders desiring to cast ballots in corporate annual meetings without attending in person. But the agency decided to allow corporate shareholders to introduce ballot items for a vote—a provision that Scott Stringer would later exploit as comptroller of New York City.

When the SEC first introduced the shareholder-proposal rule, the SEC chairman at the time, Ganson Purcell, argued that it was justified because the size of modern corporations precluded shareholders from addressing a meeting. Because there were so many shareholders in publicly traded companies regulated by the SEC, a stockholder could express his judgment only "at the time when he considers the execution of the proxy form." By allowing shareholders to introduce a proposal on the proxy, the SEC's new rule would make "the proxy a real instrument for the exercise of...fair corporate suffrage."

But "fair corporate suffrage" appears nowhere in the statutory text of the Securities Exchange Act of 1934. It was only mentioned briefly by a single House representative in congressional debates when the act was under consideration. The section of the statute upon which the shareholder-proposal rule is based was meant to ensure corporate disclosures to investors and prevent deception.

Whether or not the shareholder-proposal rule was warranted under the law enacted by Congress, the SEC was initially careful to limit its scope. The director of the agency's division of corporate finance emphasized that shareholder proposals had to involve the "proper subjects of stockholders' action under the laws of the state under which it was organized." Specifically, the rule would not "permit stockholders to obtain the consensus of other stockholders with respect to matters which are of a general political, social or economic nature."

Various shareholders tested the SEC's position, particularly with regard to companies doing business in the segregated American South. But the agency continued to tell companies that they need not include shareholder proposals on their proxy statements if they involved general social or economic concerns, rather than appropriate business matters. (The SEC did this through a series of "no-action letters" somewhat akin to the guidance letters discussed in Chapter 4: essentially, the agency told companies that it would not pursue enforcement actions if they excluded a shareholder proposal from their proxy ballots.)

But the SEC's position shifted in the 1970s, ultimately flipping upside down. During the Vietnam War, a shareholder of Dow Chemical sought to include on the corporate proxy ballot a proposal asking that the company cease manufacturing napalm, the controversial war product. The SEC staff issued a letter to Dow stating that the agency would take no action against the company were it to exclude the proposal from the ballot. The shareholder sued, and the D.C. Circuit Court of Appeals sent the case back to the agency for further fact finding.

Although the judges did not *overturn* the SEC's longstanding position on permitting companies to exclude from proxy statements any shareholder proposal with a general social or policy purpose, they did express skepticism of the agency's viewpoint. The SEC chose not to relitigate the point. Instead, the agency issued an "interpretive release" in 1976 stating that companies could exclude shareholder proposals related to the "ordinary business" of the corporation—but only if they "involve business matters that are mundane in nature and do not involve any substantial policy or other considerations." Essentially, the SEC inverted its previous rule, and the modern era of social and political agitation through the proxy process was born.

• • •

The SEC's rule enabling virtually any shareholder to force his way into company boardrooms has given implicit national regulatory powers to a strange coterie of political agitators. Consider the People for the Ethical Treatment of Animals (PETA), which in 2019 announced it was acquiring shares in Levi Strauss in order to propose shareholder resolutions involving the use of leather patches. The jeans manufacturer had filed the paperwork to become a publicly traded corporation only one month before. PETA said it would buy only the minimum number of shares required to reach the SEC's $2,000 threshold for filing a proposal.

The agency has recently proposed a modified rule that allows a shareholder with such a limited holding to introduce a proposal only if it has held shares for a minimum of three years. If an investor has owned a company's shares for only one year, it must hold at least $25,000 in stock to get on the proxy ballot. Still, this is a laughably small holding for a large publicly traded company. At a company as valuable as Apple, it's the functional equivalent of allowing any American and five of his friends to get a referendum item on the national political ballot.

With such a loose standard, it's little surprise that a significant number of social activists have exploited the SEC rule in an effort at backdoor corporate regulation. In recent years, between 43 percent and 56 percent of all shareholder proposals on corporate proxy ballots have involved social or policy concerns with only an attenuated connection, if any, to share value.

For example, in 2019, Amazon faced twelve shareholder proposals, on such far-flung topics as workplace diversity, sexual harassment, hate speech, facial-recognition software, food waste, and climate change. Sponsors included social-investing funds like Zevin Asset Management, special-interest groups like the Amazon Employees for Climate Justice, and religious groups like the Sisters of St. Joseph of Brentwood.

Similarly, when McDonald's shareholders gathered for the company's annual meeting in May 2017, they had to vote on seven shareholder proposals. One concerned the company's use of antibiotics in its meat supply and was sponsored by the Benedictine Sisters of Boerne, Texas. At the time, the Catholic order owned 52 shares in McDonald's, among 816,753,115 outstanding. Another proposal was sponsored by Holy Land Principles, a nonprofit group that wanted the company to modify its employment practices in Israel. The organization owned 47 shares. None of the sponsoring shareholders owned more than 0.0001 percent of the company's stock.

Labor unions with their own pension funds and other investment vehicles—such as the American Federation of Labor and Congress of Industrial Organizations (AFL-CIO) and the American Federation of State, County, and

Municipal Employees AFSCME—have also frequently introduced shareholder proposals on company proxy ballots. The Office of the Inspector General of the U.S. Department of Labor found that labor pension funds may be using "plan assets to support or pursue proxy proposals for personal, social, legislative, regulatory, or public policy agendas"—and that was in 2011, during the generally labor-friendly Obama administration. Confirming this suspicion, empirical evidence shows that labor-affiliated investors are selective in their shareholder-proposal filings, and regularly gang up on companies that are the targets of union-organizing campaigns or that give disproportionately to Republican political candidates through their corporate political action committees.

The SEC's permissive shareholder-proposal rule has also allowed very small individual shareholders to exercise a large voice in the boardroom—and sometimes to profit off the exercise. The late Evelyn Davis spent decades introducing shareholder proposals, and company executives showered her with largesse to stay in her good graces. According to one report in the 1990s, executives of all three major American car companies offered to deliver any car she wanted to her door. Lee Iacocca reportedly said that he would do so in person. As a cottage industry, she published a yearly investor newsletter, *Highlights and Lowlights.* The pamphlet ran some twenty pages but earned her an estimated $600,000 annual income, as she "cajoled the nation's business titans into subscribing...with a minimum order of two copies"—at $495 a pop.

Shareholders like Evelyn Davis amount to little more than a corporate nuisance: among the more than 150 shareholder proposals Ms. Davis introduced in the last decade of her activism, only one received the support of a majority of shareholders over board opposition. But in many cases, corporate boards have changed practices based on social-interest shareholder activism—even when most of the company's shareholders rejected a proposal. In recent years, the largest publicly traded companies in America have faced hundreds of proposals asking them to change how they disclose or engage in political activity and lobbying. Only one of these received majority shareholder support over board opposition. But the Center for Political Accountability, the group coordinating the shareholder-proposal push on that subject, claims that 292 companies have changed their approach to politics as a result of its efforts. The organization's president, Bruce Freed, was a congressional staffer for the late Senator Ted Kennedy.

• • •

Beyond empowering political operatives like Freed, private labor unions, and activist groups like PETA, the SEC's shareholder-proposal rule has transferred de facto regulatory power to state and local officials overseeing public pension funds.

New York City was the first government entity in the United States to offer lifetime pensions for its employees—in 1878, three years after American Express offered pensions for its workers. In 1894, Manhattan teachers were given their own pension plan. In the early twentieth century, during the Progressive Era, these innovations spread. Massachusetts was the first state to offer all state employees a pension, in 1911. In 1920, Congress passed the Civil Service Retirement Act, which created a pension plan for all federal civil workers.

Today, pension obligations have multiplied across all levels of government in the United States. Unlike the Social Security program, in which retirees are paid out of current government receipts, these public-employee pension plans are backed by actual funds. Crucial to their viability, at least without imposing significant new costs on the public, are the decisions to put away adequate resources to meet future promised obligations. They've fallen woefully short in recent years. The $3 trillion in assets that state and municipal pension funds have invested are covering approximately $4 trillion in obligations. This shortfall is squeezing state and local budgets, leading to cuts in public services as well as increased taxes. Still, $3 trillion is a lot of money for state and local officials who oversee such funds to play around with.

And play around with it they have. In recent years, pension funds for state and municipal workers have introduced hundreds of shareholder resolutions at publicly traded companies under the SEC's shareholder-proposal rule. Many of these have had express policy purposes, concerning issues such as companies' political spending and lobbying, their human rights policies, their gender pay gaps, their policies on sexual orientation and gender identity, their policies on climate change and other environmental issues, and a host of labor concerns. Through such proposals, state and local politicians attempt to effect national regulatory decisions.

The pension funds for New York City, headed by Scott Stringer, have been the most active among state and municipal investors involved in regulation by shareholder activism. The next most active is the fund for the employees of

New York State. (New York's state fund is headed by the elected comptroller, Thomas DiNapoli, a former state legislator with no prior investment experience; he was selected by his political allies for the job after his predecessor, Alan Hevesi, whom we met in the last chapter, was indicted on a corruption scandal.) Other state and local governments seeking to effect national policy through their public-employee pension funds have included Connecticut, Minnesota, and North Carolina, as well as Kansas City, Miami, and Philadelphia.

The elected leaders guiding these public pension funds' shareholder activism invariably defend their social-investing agendas as consistent with an emphasis on "long-term share value." But the evidence suggests anything but. A 2015 Manhattan Institute study by Tracie Woidtke of the University of Tennessee found that social-investing activism on the part of public pension funds was significantly associated with *lower* share values. That means lower investment returns, and it's a drag on already underfunded state pension systems. But it also hurts the ordinary investor whose retirement savings depend on stock portfolios. In total, "social investing" costs shareholders hundreds of billions of dollars annually.

Beyond its financial price tag, this kind of shareholder activism is yet another example of state and local elected officials working for policy changes outside their borders, to shift the national policy direction. To be sure, the national government has enabled this to happen—albeit through rules developed by an independent agency without any clear directive from elected legislators. No enactment of Congress gives PETA authority over the manufacture of Levi's jeans, or small Catholic orders authority over McDonald's supply chains. No enactment of Congress gives the AFL-CIO boardroom authority. No enactment of Congress gives quirky investors like Evelyn Davis the power to coopt corporate annual meetings. And no enactment of Congress gives the career politicians overseeing public pension funds in New York the authority to serve as a meta-regulator of America's biggest companies.

CHAPTER 14

Restoring the Republic

It's impossible to know how America's constitutional framers would view the modern republic. Doubtless, many of them would be proud of their work's endurance—and of how the government they fashioned helped enable the young nation to grow beyond measure and to shape world history. Some of them might be troubled by certain actions taken by the government in the course of those events. Many would certainly be proud that their nation abolished the odious practice of slavery, if saddened that it took a bloody civil war to do it. (Benjamin Franklin and Alexander Hamilton were among those Founding Fathers who led early abolition movements. Others of course resisted such efforts, and some were themselves slaveholders, unwilling to make the personal and political sacrifices required to end the practice, whatever their own internal conflicts and misgivings might have been.)

What we can say for sure is that the Founding Fathers would hardly *recognize* much of what modern American government has become. The government's size and scope have expanded by many orders of magnitude: the appropriations allocated by the First Congress, $639,000, would amount to scarcely more than $10 million in today's dollars, while the federal budget for 2019 spent $4.4 trillion, a good chunk of it borrowed. (Spending in 2020, with unprecedented trillions borrowed to mitigate the effects of an economically devastating pandemic, will blow through that record level.)

But beyond the government's growth—and intertwined with it—there has been a withering of the government's accountability to the public, in a wide departure from the original constitutional design.

The Framers viewed the legislative branch as paramount, and set it out first in the Constitution for a reason. But the legislature has now delegated much of its power to the executive, which the Framers feared. And in more than a few cases, it has given its powers to executive officials who, unlike the elected president, are not accountable to the people. The judicial branch has left these broad delegations of power largely unchecked. Thus, the carefully delineated powers allocated among legislative, executive, and judicial functions have been collapsed into a single locus of power. The modern executive regularly serves as lawmaker, prosecutor, judge, and jury.

Many of the Framers, like many modern politicians, were trained in the law. And they would doubtless be shocked by the changes in the legal system that have made the originally unimportant field of "tort law" the domain of a mass engine of private lawyers who directly shift around 2 percent of the nation's economic output—and are an implicit, unelected regulator shaping the American economy, alongside the administrative state. It's hard to imagine that many of our eighteenth-century political leaders, committed to representative rule, would not be taken aback by the way fundamental changes to the legal system were crafted out of thin air by law professors at universities.

And even the most ardent Antifederalists of the founding era would likely be troubled by some of the tactics of the new antifederalists. While the original Antifederalists feared a larger central government and desired some measure of autonomy for state governments, that hardly means allowing state officials to co-opt policy choices in *other* states.

· · ·

That the rule of the unelected is a radical departure from America's founding principles is hard to deny. But many a modern American progressive might retort: "Why should we listen to dead white men who lived more than two hundred years ago—many of them slaveholders?" Whatever the merits of looking to the original understanding of the American constitutional design as a *legal interpretive tool*, it would be circular to say, "We ought to follow the original plan because it was original." And we know that the Founding Fathers got some things very, very wrong.

That said, their concerns about the dangers of overreaching government have proved prescient in many ways. For one, a bigger government encourages corruption—enabling the use of state power for personal benefit. In spending money raised by taxation, and with the law-enforcement power to say "no" to private activity, governments have long been able to create opportunities for private gain at public expense. In the nineteenth century, the job of running the New York Customs House was a prized sinecure: being able to control the flow of imported goods into the country, and taxation on those goods, offered unique possibilities for personal enrichment. When the government role was cabined, such opportunities were few, but the potential for mischief grew as the government reached into more and more areas of life.

Although some form of the overt government-enabled graft of the sort we saw in nineteenth-century customs enforcement still exists, the modern mischief under expanded government is generally somewhat different. Government actions that benefit the public across the board are relatively rare; there are usually clear winners and losers. Big government thus creates a host of opportunities for constituencies to jostle for government largesse. When government takes in and spends a lot, those who earn salaries on the government payroll or receive government transfer payments emerge as powerful political constituencies, seeking to defend and expand such pay and benefits.

The need to raise taxes to fund it all offers some check on government expansion, but the check is limited, at least in the short run, as long as individuals can be taxed at different rates and some not at all. Which has been the case in the United States since 1913, with the ratification of the Sixteenth Amendment permitting the taxation of income. (The amendment reversed the Constitution's original prohibition on "direct taxes" unless apportioned among states by population. Even with that limitation, the first century-plus under the Constitution demonstrates that any tax not apportioned by population causes battles between those who pay and those who benefit. Among the central issues of dispute in the early history of the United States were import tariffs, which benefited some states and hurt others.)

The problem becomes even more complicated when government can borrow money to finance benefits today while shifting costs onto future generations. Politicians compete for today's voters, who may discount tomorrow's voters' interests. The evidence from not just the United States but other advanced democracies suggests that they do. Virtually every modern democratic government eschews the American Founders' limitations on the size and scope of government; and virtually every such government has accumulated a heavy debt load alongside substantially unfunded future promises.

Finally, the growth of the *regulatory* state—both its rulemaking and its enforcement arms—provides the opportunity for making winners and losers without being limited by the need for taxing or borrowing. The Administrative Procedure Act and the modern rulemaking apparatus are designed to establish some modicum of fairness and to impose some cost-benefit principles on the regulatory process. But as we have seen, government actors in the executive branch have found ways to evade these constraints.

• • •

Whatever the merits of these critiques, the fact remains that democratic polities around the world have indeed opted for a significantly bigger government than the American Founders chose. This suggests that a return to the limited government envisioned in 1787 is highly unlikely, whatever its substantive merits.

The American social-insurance system may be poorly designed—and unsustainable in its current form, without modifications—but there is little public appetite for eliminating government safety nets altogether. Nor is some form of social-insurance system necessarily inconsistent with individual freedom—as the great twentieth-century exponent of classical liberalism, Friedrich Hayek, acknowledged even as he criticized the expanding Western welfare states in his landmark 1944 book, *The Road to Serfdom*. Not all libertarian thinkers agree with Hayek; but whether he is right or wrong, there is no plausible chance of returning to a pre–New Deal world without some significant government provision of a social safety net. The reality-based public debate is over the scope and structure of social-insurance provision—not its existence.

In some regards, the explosive growth in commerce and technology since the founding era—fueled in no small part by the American experiment itself—justifies a somewhat larger, more active government. Technological innovations in weaponry create public vulnerabilities that simply did not exist when external invaders had to send men with muskets on transoceanic voyages to threaten American shores. The Founders may well have been right that standing armies were a threat to liberty, but a citizen militia offers little protection against the threat of nuclear, chemical, or biological weapons.

Our modern commerce likewise informs the scope of the regulatory state, as this book explains. The general public has little longing to return to a world where commerce was governed by the classic contract-law doctrine *caveat emptor*, "let the buyer beware." After all, what we buy today is much harder for the average consumer to assess than the products available in the early years of the constitutional republic. People today carry around in their pockets technological wizardry dwarfing the capabilities of military supercomputers that existed within living memory. We generally eat foods harvested and processed in far-flung locales. We consume an array of chemicals that most of us wouldn't even recognize.

Even so, the notion that such complexity requires heavy-handed government oversight—be it *ex ante* regulation or *ex post* litigation—is often oversold. Repeat players in commerce have an incentive to behave, if they want to continue to sell to their customers. When a product's potential risks are easy to discern—say, hot coffee—there's little need for a government role. McDonald's has served billions of cups of the stuff for a reason. And even with more complicated products, modern technology also *enables* consumer knowledge. Anyone buying a car or a cell phone or a flat-screen TV need not understand all its inner workings to be an informed customer; he can get a vast array of safety data—synthesized by experts, based on testing—with a simple search on the Internet.

But precisely because consumer knowledge is inevitably incomplete, market checks alone can leave real information gaps related to safety and other concerns. Modern mass tort litigation emerged after a ubiquitous product, asbestos, turned out to have very real safety issues—which typically lay dormant for decades. Modern drug regulation in the United States began with amendments to the Food, Drug, and Cosmetic Act that were enacted in 1962 after the morning-sickness drug thalidomide (sold in Europe but not the United States) was shown to cause severe limb abnormalities in the children of some pregnant women who used it. Similarly, modern medical-device regulation traces to 1976 amendments to the food and drug statute enacted after studies attributed injuries to use of the Dalkon Shield intrauterine contraceptive device. These seminal cases are instructive. While I strongly believe that our modern regulatory and liability system is deeply flawed, this does not mean that I think a full return to the size and scope of government we saw in 1787 or 1900 is wise or beneficial.

Rulemaking Reform

Just as we will not be able to go back to the minimalist government of 1787, even were such retrenchment desirable, we will also not be able to reject wholesale the delegation of rulemaking authority by Congress to administrative agencies. There is no way to empower the scope of government action the public desires—and libertarian objections notwithstanding, the public does broadly desire it—without some significant layer of rulemaking delegation. I agree with Professor Richard Epstein, my colleague, that some level of delegated administration is inevitable in modern government.

That said, Justice Gorsuch's dissent last year in *Gundy v. United States*, calling on the Court to revisit its delegation doctrine, is a welcome invitation to think more carefully about *what* Congress may delegate. It's permissible for Congress to allow the executive branch to "fill in the details" of a statutory scheme—a standard that dates back to Chief Justice Marshall's 1825 decision in *Wayman v. Southard*. But it's something else entirely to punt the big legislative issues to the executive branch. As Justice Gorsuch's *Gundy* dissent emphasizes, the Supreme Court's "major questions doctrine" implicitly involves nondelegation principles. If Congress wants the FDA to regulate cigarettes, or the EPA to regulate greenhouse gases, or the Department of Homeland Security to exempt from immigration enforcement the longstanding residents who were brought to the country illegally as children, it should say so. Doubtless it's difficult as a practical matter to spur Congress to action on such major and controversial topics. But that's precisely the point. Sweeping changes to the social, political, or economic fabric—except for necessary short-term responses to a truly exigent crisis, like a war or a pandemic—ought to require broad social consensus.

Judicial efforts to rein in undue delegation of rulemaking will likely be limited to outer-bound cases. But nothing prevents Congress from tying administrative agencies' hands in the rulemaking arena. Two significant ideas bear mention: requiring Congress to sign off on all major rules before they take effect, and allowing all new agency-created rules to "sunset" unless Congress takes action to perpetuate them.

The first idea broadly describes the Regulations from the Executive In Need of Scrutiny (REINS) Act, which passed the U.S. House of Representatives multiple times in recent years. It borrows procedurally from other areas in which Congress has delegated its specific constitutional functions to the executive but retained its power of approval before the delegation becomes operative. I have suggested a more limited version of the REINS Act, which would require a congressional action at least for rulemaking with *criminal* penalties. This would end the practice of criminalization without representation and would force agencies better to contemplate the need for civil versus criminal enforcement remedies.

The most prominent example of a REINS Act approach is the way Congress has treated its constitutional power to levy tariffs since the 1930s. Congress has regularly delegated "trade negotiating authority" to the executive, allowing the executive branch to engage in negotiations over trade policies with foreign governments. (The idea is to break down trade barriers and facilitate commerce in a give-and-take, something that legislators are not well suited to do.) Successfully negotiated agreements must then go back to Congress for an up-or-down vote, on a "fast track," which means the negotiated agreement is not open to congressional amendments.

The REINS Act somewhat parallels the Congressional Review Act (CRA), which permits Congress to act, in a short time window, to *undo* administrative rulemaking. Precisely because the CRA requires congressional action, in a short period of time, it has rarely been used—save in 2017, when the new Congress undid a spate of rulemaking from late in the Obama administration. Because the REINS Act reverses the imperative—requiring the legislature to approve regulatory rules before they go into effect, rather than the inverse—it would set up a significantly higher hurdle for rulemaking agencies to clear. On the other hand, it would also give congressional imprimatur to approved bodies of rules, insulating them from procedural judicial review under the Administrative Procedure Act.

The "sunset" idea is somewhat more limited: the executive branch would not *have to* bring rules to Congress, but it would have an *incentive* to do so. The idea also appeals to those wishing to clear out regulatory deadwood. On the other hand—much like congressional laws and taxes that set expiration dates—the sunsetting could itself destabilize business and individual planning, at least for economically significant rules. As a "sunset" date approached, those making investment and other decisions would have to estimate the probability of a rule being extended or expiring. Even under the *existing* delegation standards, a change in administration can always jeopardize a rule; although under the *State Farm* "hard look" analysis, as we've seen, it is often a heavy lift to undo an old rule—indeed, harder in many respects than promulgating a new one.

What of *State Farm* and *Chevron* themselves? Given that so many justices have expressed concerns about the *Chevron* doctrine, it may well be in the Supreme Court's crosshairs. But diagnosing the problem is easier than figuring out a replacement. In his 2019 book, *The Dubious Morality of the Modern Administrative State*, Professor Epstein calls for replacing *Chevron* deference with *de novo* review—i.e., for courts to interpret statutory language empowering administrative rulemaking without regard to agencies' own interpretations. On its face, however, *Chevron* already does this, in the sense that deference is granted only in cases of statutory ambiguity—i.e., when an analysis of Congress's words would be indeterminate. If there really is no clear answer to what statutory text means, what are judges to do?

One possibility is for judges to nullify a statutory grant of power to the executive altogether, in the face of unclear text. If one reasons that any government regulation is an imposition on someone's individual liberty, this makes some sense, and it aligns with the criminal-law legality principle and other rule-of-law principles of notice. If Congress wants the executive to have some power to proscribe private conduct, it needs to say clearly what conduct the executive is empowered to proscribe. If the executive needs more power to implement the administration's agenda than is clearly offered in a law's text, it should go back to Congress—not simply act on the basis of ambiguous statutory language.

But whatever the theoretical appeal of this approach—doubtless more compelling to the libertarian than to the progressive—it is quite unlikely to happen. For one thing, it's hard to argue that a "nullification" rule necessarily follows from the constitutional design; it would seem to be a significant expansion of the power of judicial review. Second, it's simply difficult to imagine judges taking this step. As it was, when facing challenges to the Affordable Care Act, the Supreme Court reached tortured readings of *clear* statutory text to protect President Barack Obama's signature initiative—interpreting a regulatory penalty as a tax and reading "state" as "federal."

If not nullification, what then should courts do about ambiguous statutory text? Surely, justices should not just flip a coin to resolve the meaning. Professor Epstein suggests that there is always a *better* reading. But I'm not sure that's right, at least as a matter of semantic interpretation. (It may well be the case that there's always a better *policy* reading of a statute. But why is deciding the right policy in a complex statutory scheme a role for unelected, life-appointed judges? And would judges be likely to get the policy right? Most lawyers lack the economic training and understanding of Richard Epstein.)

Consider *Chevron* itself. On the face of the statute, it really was not clear what Congress meant by a "stationary source" of air pollution. The Reagan administration's decision to apply the term to an entire manufacturing facility rather than a single smokestack was certainly defensible. It was arguably the better reading, I suppose. But smokestacks are also stationary. As long as the agency's decision involved pollution sources that were stationary—not including moving objects like cars, trains, or planes—it's hard to see why one administration's preferred policy should necessarily tie the hands of the next—at least if the challenge is based on the meaning of the statute. Perhaps the better approach by the courts would be to reject the direct statutory challenge in such a case, while still permitting a challenge to the *policy* change truly at issue, under the deferential "arbitrary and capricious" standard articulated in the Administrative Procedure Act. In other words: the world of *State Farm.*

The real problem is not that courts have given agencies flexibility to act in the face of ambiguous statutory text, but that they have been far too willing to fall back on the *Chevron* doctrine to permit *strained* statutory readings by agencies, of statutory grants of power that were not truly ambiguous. In *Brand X*, for instance, the position of the Bush administration FCC that a cable company is an "information service" rather than a "telecommunications service," and thus exempt from regulation under the Telecommunications Act of 1996, strained credulity. If the administration's preferred regulatory scheme was the right path to take as a matter of policy, it needed to go back to Congress, not reverse the obvious implication of the statutory language. Likewise, it's hard to give the term "waters of the United States," as specified in the Clean Water Act under a preexisting interpretive doctrine, the far broader meaning subsequently attached to it by environmental administrators. Maybe the Supreme Court just needs to clarify, as it did with "*Auer* deference" in *Kisor v. Wilkie*: when we say "ambiguous," we mean really, *really* ambiguous.

As for the *State Farm* "hard look" review of agency decision making, it's difficult to square with the "arbitrary and capricious" standard in the Administrative Procedure Act itself. And it's hard to defend a one-way regulatory ratchet that is more deferential for new rules that give the federal government more control over private parties, and less deferential for ending old rules that constrain private actors. The current Supreme Court review schema too often acts as such a one-way ratchet. The better *substantive* review standard—at least as it logically follows under the statute that Congress passed, if not as a policy matter—is one that makes sure the *procedural* requirements were followed (notice and comment) and the resolution was not pretextual and comported with the statutory mandate. To be sure, a deferential review of substantive decisions would enable the executive branch to shift course from administration to administration. But that's consistent with the premise that elections have consequences. And nothing stops Congress from being more specific—and less deferential—if it wishes.

Indeed, Congress could also add a cost-benefit review requirement to the Administrative Procedure Act. Judges would most likely fall back substantially on process there, too—they're lawyers, not economists—but cost-benefit standards are already baked into much administrative rulemaking. Federal agencies and the D.C. courts focused on administrative law have considerable experience applying cost-benefit rationales. (As it is, since the Reagan administration, the Office of Information and Regulatory Affairs in the White House has performed cost-benefit reviews of many draft rules and regulations, often to significant effect.) Congress could also, of course, offer courts a decision map for resolving statutory or regulatory ambiguities—in effect, legislating adjustments to *Chevron* and *Auer*.

Enforcement Reform

One thing Congress should heed in any such reform efforts is the executive-branch temptation to eschew formal rulemaking by using *enforcement* powers—or the threat thereof—to realize regulatory goals. The Title IX guidance letters issued by the Obama administration, and the broad scope of many a deferred prosecution agreement, show just how much the executive branch can influence private conduct without either adopting a formal rule or adjudicating an actual case. Such tactics can expand the scope of government power without clear congressional authorization—or judicial review. The Trump Justice Department said it would no longer prosecute based on administrative "guidance" that failed to go through the notice-and-comment rulemaking prescribed in the Administrative Procedure Act—which was common in the Obama administration—and would stop the practice of funneling settlement payments to third parties. But any subsequent administration could revive such practices. And there is clearly still scope for the executive branch to bully private parties through other enforcement alternatives.

Although Congress cannot eliminate enforcement and prosecutorial discretion, it can develop processes wherein "guidance" documents and statements can be subjected to judicial review absent formal rulemaking. Congress could also limit prosecutors' ability to negotiate non-prosecution deals that enforce remedies not called for as statutory sanction.

In general, although the temptation to negotiate deferred prosecution agreements is obvious for both corporate defendants and federal prosecutors, the practice places enormous discretion in prosecutors' hands—with potentially sweeping economic and public policy ramifications. In essence, "regulation by threat" is a dubious end run around the administrative rulemaking process. To be sure, there are significant collateral risks to prosecuting a large corporate enterprise. But the answer may be to encourage more civil rather than criminal enforcement (you cannot jail a company, after all); to reduce harsh statutory collateral consequences, enabling companies better to negotiate or even litigate disputes (no one really wants to preclude the military from getting the best equipment, or seniors the best treatments through Medicare); and to empower companies to defend actual cases, including through defenses that show efforts at good-faith compliance (thus encouraging such efforts to be made).

If corporate offenses are egregious to the point of criminality, then a *responsible individual* should be held to criminal account—with a true showing of criminal intent, of course, not a strict-liability prosecution without any evidence of conscious wrongdoing. If it's impossible to make a criminal case against a responsible individual, it's dubious to threaten to enforce a criminal sanction against a corporate entity. As a general matter, government enforcement efforts should better distinguish between criminal and civil wrongdoing—*especially* for corporate officers, who can be deterred through both financial penalties and prospective jail time. And the government should make it *harder* to prosecute criminal cases for *malum prohibitum* offenses. Unless Congress says otherwise, the government should be forced to prove that an individual has a "guilty mind" to criminally convict him. The individual, in turn, should be able to make the case to the jury that his mistake was innocent—and ought to be excused on that basis.

Litigation Reform

As with the administrative state, the parallel system of regulation by litigation is by now ingrained, and difficult to undo in its entirety—even were such a step desirable as a policy matter. The U.S. Constitution does have a civil-jury requirement in the Seventh Amendment, even if its original conception had little to do with the then-limited world of tort law, and even if the requirement predates the merger of procedurally limited suits for damages in courts of law with the broader inquisitorial processes and remedies granted to courts of equity. The Supreme Court is almost certainly right that at least some forms of attorney advertising are protected speech under the First Amendment. And on the merits, the complexity of modern commerce does make some of the older rules questionable—such as the rules insulating virtually all product manufacturers from liability for virtually any product defect.

Indeed, there are certainly cases in which litigation after the fact is better than a bright-line *ex ante* administrative rule that would preclude beneficial private actions. Some libertarian defenders of the modern tort regime defend it based on just this premise. Others, more sympathetic to a broader government role, like to claim that litigation "fills in the gaps" left by regulators. But far too often, we get the worst of both worlds: overreaching administrative action and overreaching litigation. At a minimum, the prospect of regulation by lawsuit complicates any administrative agency cost-benefit analysis (or should, if the agency is doing cost-benefit analysis properly). And after-the-fact lawsuits can interfere with what the agency views as the right regulatory balance—as when an agency approves a pharmaceutical notwithstanding known risks, and then lawsuits punish the sale of the product when those known and disclosed risks cause the known and disclosed harmful effect.

As noted earlier in the book, the Supreme Court has taken some positive steps to rein in abusive litigation, beginning in the 1990s when the Court reframed evidentiary rules to weed out the worst "junk science" from federal courtrooms. A series of major Court decisions have together worked to block lower courts from certifying some national class action lawsuits. Another group of cases have together worked to empower private parties to enter into contracts that preclude some forms of class action litigation through alternative dispute resolution. And yet another line of cases has limited at least somewhat the "notice pleading" rules of civil procedure, in which a party need only state its claims in general terms without alleging particular facts to support them, before triggering sweeping discovery powers that impose costs on a civil defendant. More recently, the Court has even begun to limit the worst abuses of forum shopping, putting some jurisdictional limits around *International Shoe*.

These cases have all flowed from courts' interpretations of statutes enacted by Congress. And Congress has shown it can act, too. In 1986, Congress acted to protect vaccine manufacturers from industry-threatening lawsuits, substituting administrative compensation procedures. In 2001, in the wake of the September 11 terror attacks, Congress stepped in again with an administrative compensation process to sidestep potentially ruinous lawsuits against airlines. And in 1995 and 2005, Congress passed legislation cabining the scope of securities lawsuits and nationwide class actions. Also in 2005, Congress passed the Public Readiness and Emergency Preparedness Act, which shields from liability certain manufacturers responding to a crisis like a terror attack or declared public-health emergency—including an epidemic, an issue of current concern.

Still, litigation reform is difficult—in part because so much tort and liability law is a function of state versus federal law. There is basically no way to bring back the federal common law that Justice Brandeis declared nonexistent in his *Erie v. Tompkins* opinion in 1938, even were doing so legally right: federal courts would have to develop entire new doctrines. Some congressional leaders who would be predisposed to rein in lawsuit abuse are wary of stepping on states' toes—viewing the matter as one of states' rights rather than one of an inverted federalism that enables an outlier state in many cases to regulate implicitly interstate commerce.

But in at least some areas, Congress should act—especially when state tort and product liability litigation interferes with a federal regulatory scheme. In the 1976 Medical Device Amendments to the Food, Drug, and Cosmetic Act, Congress affirmatively preempted state product liability claims for FDA-approved devices. Congress could and should do the same for pharmaceuticals, reversing the Supreme Court's rule in *Wyeth v. Levine*. That's not because federal regulators will always get things right. But as powerfully demonstrated in the ongoing Covid-19 pandemic, regulators overwhelmingly err on the side of caution; far more lives are lost through regulatory delay than through premature approval of drugs that have unknown side effects or fail to work as advertised. Not all drugs are truly life-saving, of course; and Congress could consider alternative standards for alternative classes of drugs. But there's no reason why any state tort lawsuit should be allowed to override a regulatory decision to approve a drug; the normal case should be the opposite.

Some scholars, such as Alex Tabarrok of George Mason University, have convincingly argued that the FDA ought to scuttle "efficacy" review altogether. What matters is a drug's safety profile. Prescribing doctors can view the published, peer-reviewed evidence on efficacy, in addition to applying their own clinical judgments. That may not be a *universally* feasible approach: some drugs may indeed be unsafe, to a significant degree, yet preferable to the medical alternative of a life-threatening or debilitating disease or ailment. Doing a cost-benefit analysis requires assessing the benefit.

Fortunately, this is an area in which overlapping state tort law *could* in fact allow for complementary rather than competing regulatory approaches. There's no reason why Congress could not direct the FDA to adopt a two-tiered review process for pharmaceuticals. A full FDA safety and efficacy review process would preempt state tort lawsuits—protecting a drug manufacturer from after-the-fact liability. A safety-only review process—implicitly, the process currently in play for drugs prescribed off-label—would not foreclose state tort claims. Manufacturers could then weigh the costs and benefits of efficacy review; and prescribing doctors could weigh efficacy evidence themselves for drugs approved for safety only—as they currently do when prescribing off-label.

Beyond areas of commerce that Congress has expressly chosen to regulate, it could act to rein in the worst of lawsuit abuses through procedural reforms applicable in the federal courts. Class action litigation may have been created improvidently; it's hard to justify making sweeping changes to longstanding, nationally important litigation rules by delegation to law professors. And opt-out class actions have had many pernicious effects. We may be better off jettisoning them entirely. But the rules that young Arthur Miller wrote in the back of a car on the ferry to Martha's Vineyard are probably here to stay, at least in some form. Moreover, we do need some mechanism for pulling together a large number of common claims. The mass tort claims that flood courts with plaintiffs recruited through sophisticated advertising campaigns are hardly a universally better alternative.

Still, Congress has enacted major reforms involving class action lawsuits twice in the last twenty-five years for a reason: abuses in this arena are legion. In considering class action reform, it's important to understand that such cases almost never go to trial. Giant causes of action make defendants want to settle; and because the plaintiffs' lawyers are by definition unsupervised by actual plaintiffs, they have every incentive to cut a deal and move on to the next case. The critical decision points are thus at the front end—the decision to certify the class—and at the back end—the structuring of the settlement. Even as the Supreme Court has tightened certification standards, it is not the general rule that a defendant unhappy with a class-certification decision can appeal the decision right away—what lawyers call a right of "interlocutory" appeal. That should be the standard, to ensure that nationally important class lawsuits aren't regularly rubber-stamped by judges that lawyers filing on behalf of a national class seek out for their permissiveness. And on the back end, the Supreme Court should establish rules that clearly reject settlements that benefit the lawyers at the expense of the plaintiffs—a far too common practice.

For mass tort litigation, the most helpful action Congress could take might be to undo the unique American Rule that prevents successful defendants from recovering lawyers' fees in the event of a win in court. Knowing that defendants cannot possibly defend against every common case, plaintiffs' lawyers have every incentive to recruit bogus claims—as with the asbestos and silicosis case-processing efforts discussed in Chapter 10: lumping in bad cases with the good enables the lawyers to extract higher settlements in the aggregate (inevitably shortchanging their genuinely deserving clients). But if defendants could litigate the bogus cases and recover their legal fees with a win, plaintiffs' lawyers' incentives would suddenly change: they'd have every incentive to screen their mass tort cases for quality. Congress could make a simple modification to the existing Federal Rules of Civil Procedure to achieve this end. Rule 68 is an "offer of judgment" rule, designed to facilitate settlements. If one party makes an offer and the other rejects it, the party rejecting the offer must pay the other side's "costs" if an ultimate judgment "is not more favorable than the unaccepted offer." But the current rule excludes the most significant "cost" of litigation—attorney fees. There's no reason they couldn't be included; and existing methods of assessing fee awards in complicated cases, like class actions, could prevent abuses. (And state legislators would be well advised to adopt a loser-pays mechanism too—which would do much to enable small-business owners like Kathie Reece-McNeill to fight back against shakedown suits, without losing their businesses altogether, as she lost the Aztec Hotel.)

Reviving Federalism

Beyond preempting state lawsuits in areas fully regulated by federal agencies, what might Congress do to push back against antifederalist approaches that impose one outlier state's values on national commerce? One idea is to leverage the post-*Erie*, post–*International Shoe* forum-shopping norms to reorient states' tort-law incentives. The current regime creates incentives like those articulated by Richard Neely (former justice of West Virginia's supreme court): sock it to out-of-state companies, whose money can be redirected to in-state citizens. But there is no reason Congress can't make it easier to remove cross-state lawsuits to federal courts, as it did for class action litigation in 2005. All it has to do is remove "complete diversity" limits on federal court jurisdiction, for lawsuits above a certain dollar threshold—an approach that would do a great deal of good for improperly joined defendants like Hilda Bankston.

And what of states that nevertheless had substantive legal rules that were overly permissive, yet operative under *Erie*? Congress could base the operative state-law standard that applies in federal court on the rule in the state where the corporate defendant was incorporated or made its principal place of business. Such a "choice of law" reform has been developed by scholars including Professor Michael Krauss of George Mason University. Public-safety advocates would doubtless howl. Why wouldn't companies just flock to a new version of lowest-common-denominator state, that instead of being overly permissive of lawsuits let companies' products maim and kill? That needn't be the case—and there are workarounds, too complicated for treatment here but quite capable of leveraging federalism toward the appropriate balance. A proper federal choice-of-law rule would make tort litigation mirror the "genius" that Roberta Romano observed in the world of corporate law—converting the current "race to the bottom" in tort law to a "race to the top."

Reining in the Mike Moores, Eliot Spitzers, and Bill de Blasios of the world is trickier for Congress to achieve—beyond preempting their enforcement powers, which in some cases is appropriate. But absent such preemption, states' general "police powers" are broad. Still, there's no reason that Congress should *enable* state-led shakedown lawsuits that follow from *federal* law. Unfortunately, many modern federal statutes create "rights of action" that empower states to enforce a federal regulatory scheme—an open invitation for plaintiffs' lawyers to persuade ambitious state attorneys general and comptrollers to hire them to file damages suits on states' behalf. Congress should at least require states that contract out the work of federal law enforcement to use transparent hiring principles that deter abuse. The choice would still be left up to state leaders. But by encouraging states to adopt transparent practices and not to enter into bargains that give away state dollars as a windfall to campaign-donor attorneys, Congress could leverage the state-federal interplay to good effect.

Similarly, while Congress should not tell states how to manage their pension dollars—at least absent a federal bailout that props up underfunded pensions—there is still a case for legislative action in the area of stock market politics. The SEC should not adopt rules that facilitate state politicians' use of public-employee pension dollars to effect national policy through the corporate governance process. To be sure, state pension managers can choose to invest and divest their funds as they see fit—and communicate their wishes to corporate managers to the extent that such managers wish to take their calls. But the congressionally enacted statutes that give the SEC its securities-regulation mandate are designed to promote disclosure—to give investors the material investment-related information they need to buy and sell securities confidently in the national markets—not to permit social agitation that makes local elected officials de facto regulators of large companies trading on the stock exchanges. Reforming the SEC's power grab over corporate annual meetings would have many salutary effects—among them nudging state pension overseers to pay more attention to their investment choices than stock market politics.

• • •

As the size of government has grown, unaccountable elites have been given more and more power to govern the lives of individuals, associations, and businesses. In some cases, legislators have every incentive to punt difficult questions to unelected actors. It's hard to hold elected officials to account when they can point the finger elsewhere. Congress has delegated much of its constitutional power away for a reason.

In other cases, vested interests make it extremely difficult to change a status quo that empowers and enriches them. Growing the size of government creates winners and losers—and the winners in the game will fight hard to keep their spoils. The modern plaintiffs' bar is a highly sophisticated, organized entity that works aggressively to protect its interests—but it's not unique in that regard. Businesses that benefit from the current regime have little incentive to fix it, including big businesses for whom the regulatory state acts as a barrier to competition. Unelected actors in the system—bureaucratic rulemakers and enforcers—tend to enjoy their power. And elected politicians in city and state offices often have national ambitions.

Still, there is a path forward. It requires a multifaceted approach—including an eye toward not only rulemaking administrators but also prosecutors and other enforcers; toward not only private litigators but also state and local officials. The first step in this process is understanding the forces that underlie the regulatory behemoth, which this book has endeavored to elucidate.

The Unelected in a Pandemic

This book was largely drafted before a global pandemic left more than 100,000 Americans dead and much of America shuttered—with unemployment rates reaching heights unseen since the Great Depression. Unsurprisingly, advocates for even more government have seized on the crisis to make their case. Senator Bernie Sanders, the self-described "democratic socialist" who was runner-up in the Democratic Party's last two nominating contests, argues that America "is at a severe disadvantage compared to every other major country on earth because we do not guarantee health care to all people as a right." More broadly, the argument runs: if we only had more government, we'd be better equipped to prevent or handle a crisis like a viral pandemic. And to the central theme of this book: surely we shouldn't eschew expert opinion and place all our trust in elected politicians who lack the knowledge of virology and epidemiology required to understand the public-health issues at play!

At a fundamental level, the Covid-19 pandemic does exemplify the *need* for government. Public health is one of the classic government functions, along with public safety. We are all worse off if one individual physically harms another or takes another's property by force or fraud—which is why we have torts, property, and criminal law, and why every modern society has some form of policing to try to prevent such harms. And we are much better equipped to head off foreign invaders if we coordinate efforts and build capacity at scale—which is why every modern nation-state either has its own program of national defense or relies on foreign or international military protection. Public health combines the policing and defense functions of the state, at least when it concerns viruses transmitted from human to human. The unfettered liberty of an infected person can place other people at risk. And coordinated efforts can often be more effective than letting everyone individually choose a course of action.

But accepting those broad principles, there's something missing in Senator Sanders's morality tale. To be sure, East Asian governments in general worked much more effectively than the United States in containing this viral pandemic—doubtless helped by relatively recent experiences handling outbreaks of other SARS coronaviruses. But it's also the case that Western European governments—which mostly failed to contain the virus—have not only a high degree of rule by bureaucratic experts but also the national health and social-welfare systems that politicians like Bernie Sanders extol. (Contrary to Sanders's lamentations, government health-care spending in the United States actually tops that of most European countries, both per capita and as a percentage of the economy. Americans spend more on health care than Europeans not only privately but through government transfer programs as well. Our government spending on individuals' health care may be very misallocated, but we don't spend too little, relative to other developed nations.)

Moreover, at least in the earlier stages of the pandemic, the association between government spending and Covid-19 mortality has run in the opposite direction from what Senator Sanders suggests: more government spending and more centralization have been correlated with more, not fewer, coronavirus deaths. This pattern could change over time. But it's a plausible hypothesis that *leaner* governments may be more effective at performing their limited tasks than governments supporting massive welfare states, which have less bandwidth available to act decisively in a crisis.

•   •   •

Although the scope of the Covid-19 epidemic is at least as large as any we've seen in a hundred years—and the economic fallout deeper than anything we've seen since the Great Depression—our nation has dealt with viral pandemics since its earliest days. Only six years after the 1787 Constitutional Convention, a yellow fever epidemic hit Philadelphia, which then housed the fledgling federal government and was the nation's largest metropolitan area. (Philadelphia proper was smaller than New York City in the census only because the adjacent Northern Liberties District and Southwark—themselves among the nation's ten largest cities in 1790—were then separately incorporated, but would be annexed in 1854.) Philadelphia took a brutal hit from the epidemic. Some 10 percent of the city's population died in the summer of 1793. Alexander Hamilton, the treasury secretary, contracted yellow fever but survived. President George Washington moved the rest of the cabinet out of the city to Germantown.

The cabinet's nine-mile relocation measure was likely only marginally effective, in that yellow fever is contracted through mosquito bites, not human contact. But no one knew the mode by which the sickness was transmitted at the time. And lacking such knowledge, governments still tried to shut out external contacts as a means to prevent the spread of the disease. Baltimore and New York each forbade entry to those coming from Philadelphia in 1793—much as Rhode Island, Florida, and Texas sought to prevent entry by those fleeing Covid-19 hotspots in 2020.

In 1902, the U.S. Supreme Court formally sanctioned such limits on travel. In *Compagnie Francaise de Navigation a Vapeur v. Louisiana State Board of Health*, the Court upheld a state's refusal, in the wake of a yellow fever outbreak, to permit the passengers of a foreign vessel to disembark. Such powers are not absolute; courts have rejected travel limits deemed overbroad, or based on racial or socioeconomic classifications. But efforts to contain disease are longstanding uses of government power. And so too is public pushback against such efforts. The Spanish influenza outbreak of 1918–19 claimed more than 500,000 American lives, and tens of millions worldwide. But some citizens objected to public efforts to curb the epidemic—including those in San Francisco who formed the "Anti-Mask League."

Much of that history is lost to most Americans today, in no small part because public-health efforts by government and by private entities have proved so successful at eradicating the deadliest infectious diseases. In the late eighteenth century, a British doctor, Edward Jenner, discovered a smallpox vaccine. In the mid-nineteenth century, doctors in Britain discovered that cholera spread through London's water supply, and this knowledge led to a flurry of public sanitation projects in much of the developed world. After Jonas Salk discovered a polio vaccine in 1955, the West had largely won the battle against the old pathogens. Just twelve years later, the U.S. surgeon general purportedly exclaimed, "The time has come to close the book on infectious disease. We have basically wiped out infection in the United States."

The Unelected

Meanwhile, Congress reformed the food and drug laws to establish our modern testing protocols. To get to market today, a pharmaceutical product must go through years of multibillion-dollar tests to establish "safety" and "efficacy."

* * *

There is a cost to reorienting our laws in this fashion—to shifting from wholesale efforts to fight infection, to a regulatory regime that focuses more on preventing harms from treatments and vaccines than on harms from viruses and bacteria. "Germs no longer need to be smarter than our scientists, just faster than our lawyers," as my former colleague Peter Huber argued in 2007. "Public authorities are ponderous, rigid and slow; the new germs are nimble, flexible and fast. Drug regulators are paralyzed by the knowledge that error is politically lethal."

As I discussed in the introduction, exactly this paralysis stymied our initial pandemic response, as our regulators eschewed speed for perfection. Yes, the CDC's in-house testing design was flawed, thus compromising early testing results. But even had the CDC test worked perfectly, not nearly enough tests would have been available for large-scale testing on the South Korean model. When speed was of the essence, the agency was very, very slow.

Nor was the critical failure in testing strategy an isolated problem. It was March 25 before the FDA relaxed onerous rules on the manufacture of respirators and other personal protective equipment for medical professionals—weeks after there were reports of health-care workers reusing equipment or trying makeshift protection, or even going without it. On March 28, the FDA approved a new technology developed by the Ohio company Battelle for sterilizing protective medical equipment. The company's machines were capable of sterilizing up to 160,000 protective medical masks daily, but the FDA initially limited their usage to 10,000 masks per day. Even the availability of something as basic as ethyl-alcohol hand sanitizer was stalled by FDA oversight.

Democratic partisans hoping to score points have unsurprisingly pointed fingers at the Trump administration. Perhaps if the administration had not disbanded Obama-era teams and had left Obama-era holdovers in key positions and followed Obama-era playbooks, the agency response might have been better. To be sure, President Trump deserves criticism for early public statements that encouraged undue complacency about the epidemic risks—and for inconsistent statements that sowed public confusion during the crisis.

But the botched regulatory response in the United States generally owed little to the choices of political actors. The individuals running the FDA and the CDC are experts in their field, not hacks. The commissioner of the FDA, Stephen Hahn, is a distinguished oncologist who has authored hundreds of peer-reviewed articles and has executive experience running one of America's largest hospitals, Houston's MD Anderson. He's not a virologist or an epidemiologist, but the FDA is staffed with them. Robert Redfield, director of the CDC, is one of the nation's foremost researchers and clinicians specializing in viruses; he cofounded the Institute of Human Virology at the University of Maryland School of Medicine and led pathbreaking HIV research.

Thus, if the current pandemic crisis highlights the need for experts, the American response also shows the limits of relying on centralized expert command. Doctors and scientists who are the best in their field don't understand all fields. They are more than capable of designing a test that works (even if they sometimes err), but less capable of figuring out mass-production constraints and the necessary processes for large-scale manufacturing and distribution. We should always be careful not to succumb to hindsight bias, but the CDC's botched response contrasts with the speed of private companies in developing testing capability—making up lost ground in American testing, albeit too late to facilitate a Korean-style test-and-trace viral containment strategy.

• • •

The Covid pandemic also highlights problems with other facets of the unelected state. Consider the litigators, who can stymie the federal regulatory apparatus when it gets things *right*. It's telling that the *vaccine industry* itself was almost shuttered by tort litigation before Congress stepped in to create the Vaccine Injury Compensation Program in 1986. As Peter Huber noted thirteen years ago, the legal rule that a vaccine has "an implied guarantee of safety and sound design" is hard for a jury to interpret in a vacuum, apart from the maladies that the vaccine prevents—such as "cankers, pustules, sputum, fevers, diarrhea, dementia and emaciation," and, in the case of SARS-CoV-2, respiratory failure and death.

Covid-related lawsuits are already proliferating. According to a complaint-tracking website set up by the law firm Hunton Andrews Kurth, at least 2,278 Covid-related lawsuits had been filed in the United States by May 26. Eight states already had at least eighty Covid lawsuits: California,

Florida, Illinois, New Jersey, New York, Ohio, Pennsylvania, and Texas. New York led the way with 577 lawsuits already filed. And large personal injury firms had already set up dedicated websites, building on their marketing plans honed in asbestos and pharmaceutical mass tort litigation to trawl for clients.

Some of the early lawsuits alleged a failure to prevent exposure to the disease. On April 6, the family of a Walmart employee who died after contracting the virus sued the company for wrongful death. The wife of a man who died after contracting the virus on a Princess Cruise Lines voyage filed a similar wrongful-death lawsuit on April 14. Lawyers have filed class action suits against nursing homes that have suffered viral outbreaks, on behalf of residents; and against hospitals, on behalf of workers. On April 23, workers sued Smithfield Foods, a meat producer, which had experienced viral outbreaks in its plants, like many businesses in that industry. Five days later, President Trump invoked the Defense Production Act to protect meat and poultry processing and to help insulate such companies from liability that might imperil food supply chains.

While these lawsuits seek damages from businesses whose ongoing operations during the viral outbreak may have risked infecting workers or customers, *other* early lawsuits attacked businesses and other entities that shuttered operations to protect against the viral threat. Plaintiffs' lawyers filed suits seeking to recoup already-paid subscription fees from gyms. Universities going online-only faced lawsuits over room-and-board fees, as well as lawsuits alleging inadequate instruction.

Still other lawsuits have already targeted businesses working to sell products sanctioned by federal agencies and likely to enhance public safety. Shortly after the FDA finally worked to clear administrative hurdles to manufacturing alcohol-based hand sanitizers, lawyers hit manufacturers of sanitizer with class action lawsuits, based on state consumer-fraud laws—the same ones underlying the eleven-inch Subway litigation. The alleged fraud? Preexisting labels on the hand-sanitizer packaging said the product inside "Kills 99.9% of all germs"—a claim obviously not yet tested against the novel SARS-CoV-2 pathogen. Given the Supreme Court's determination that juries can apply state laws to punish companies even after federal agency approval of their product, such lawsuits can probably be expected to proceed—and essentially discourage businesses from providing vital sanitation supplies in a pandemic, unless or until they rework their packaging.

• • •

Doubtless, the Covid epidemic will reshape the way we think about policy. Bernie Sanders's case for a bigger American welfare state doesn't follow from the crisis, at least not immediately: nation-states with leaner governments have tended to outperform those with larger welfare states and more centralized structures. But the Covid outbreak certainly may strengthen the case for expanding government's size in some other respects.

For one: preparedness. Five years ago, Bill Gates argued for a large-scale government effort to get ready to face a likely pandemic. Gates suggested it made sense to think of the issue as we do national defense. We invest heavily in military personnel, and in new military equipment, even in peacetime—and even though we hope we won't need to use the personnel and equipment at all. America wasn't very well prepared when attacked on December 7, 1941, or on September 11, 2001. We're much better prepared for military and terror attacks now. And we should get ourselves better prepared for viral attacks after this epidemic, too.

A "viral defense force" would likely be significantly cheaper than the traditional military, and likely be money well spent. At a minimum, there's little excuse not to build and maintain real stockpiles of medical supplies and personal protective equipment that become necessary in epidemic outbreaks. We should also practice our response mechanisms to ready our ability to distribute supplies and personnel in an epidemic, and even to build new facilities and create new health-care capacity. The military obviously engages in training exercises; so should our pandemic preparedness teams. We needn't build a vast new government bureaucracy staffed with large numbers of health-care professionals; the response team could be largely manned by "reservist" doctors, physician assistants, and nurses who undergo viral-response training at regular intervals. But some sorts of efforts along these lines seem prudent.

As for the *process* of government decision making—the subject matter of this book—I think the broad case for reform I've outlined remains compelling. To be sure, our elected politicians have often dropped the ball during the pandemic, but the experts and other unaccountable governing elites have often failed us, too. Agencies have enforced counterproductive rules even when granted extraordinary powers to waive ordinary statutory mandates under a declared national emergency. The epidemic has highlighted how agencies can paralyze the development and distribution of drugs and medical devices, costing lots of lives. And the crisis has also shone light on our adjunct, shadow regulatory regime—the litigation system—which can be at cross-purposes with agency goals and can worsen health and economic outcomes alike.

We will not and should not get rid of the administrative state in its entirety—neither rulemakers nor enforcers. We will not and should not get rid of the adjunct litigation system either. And we certainly will not and should not get rid of federalism, a constitutional bedrock; state and local responses in the pandemic have certainly displayed their own sets of weaknesses and failures, but they've also shown the advantage of close-to-the-people decision making rather than relying on a one-size-fits-all approach from Washington.

A change is still in order. The Covid crisis has also reinforced how frustrated people of all political stripes have been with their government. That's nothing new, notwithstanding that control by one political party or the other comes and goes.

Our constitution is *supposed* to limit political outcomes (in ways that are also doubtless frustrating to those who'd prefer that the government do more). But it's also supposed to provide for accountable government, to channel public sentiment, to respond to the people's will.

This book has shown how each constitutional objective—limited government and accountable government—has been eroded, and in some cases inverted. Our government today is largely unbounded, and also largely unaccountable. Most Americans prefer some version of bigger government, certainly in relation to our Founders' original model. Some would prefer a government that's much bigger yet. Regardless, the votes cast in elections will not change large swathes of what government does to affect our lives. Rulemaking and enforcement will vary from administration to administration, but not in all cases—and our votes for Congress generally will make little difference to how the regulatory schemes shift over time. Our votes for national office will do almost nothing to affect the parallel litigation system, nor anything to influence the state and local officials from elsewhere endeavoring to change national policy.

Our lives are being substantially controlled by elites we don't vote for and can't remove from office. Moving back in the direction of a political regime that's more responsive to the voting public won't fix all our government's problems. It won't cure all public disaffection with government, or heal all political divisions. It's not a panacea. But it's a start.

ACKNOWLEDGMENTS

A book is the product of not only its author's own late nights but also many others' contributions, seen and unseen. There are far too many suppliers, cooks, and recipe writers in this author's kitchen to begin to acknowledge them all. What follows is but an abridged list of those who have made a meaningful impact, direct or indirect.

First, I'd like to thank Roger Kimball and the wonderful team at Encounter Books, which gave me this platform as a first-time book writer. Encounter is a national treasure, offering up books that matter to people whose decisions matter. Roger is among the most significant figures influencing the world of ideas in modern America—through his leadership of Encounter and *The New Criterion*, as well as at our mutual alma mater, Yale, and my employer, the Manhattan Institute for Policy Research; and through his own searing, erudite critiques of Western cultural and intellectual trends.

I believe those trends matter greatly. After World War II, Friedrich Hayek advised Antony Fisher, a former fighter pilot: "Keep out of politics, and make your case to the intellectuals—that is, the teachers, and the media—because they in turn influence the people." After a highly successful business career, Fisher went on to seed institutions oriented toward such intellectual influence, among them the Manhattan Institute.

I can't thank the Institute enough. Larry Mone, former MI president, took a chance on me as a young man, barely out of school, and nurtured my development—accepting my idiosyncrasies, covering my weaknesses, and amplifying my strengths. Larry believed in this book before it was written. Larry's successor, Reihan Salam, a public intellectual with uncommon human grace, is charting a bold new course continuing and amplifying Larry's legacy.

Think-tank presidents and scholars assume somewhat prominent public roles; but many others within their organizations work as hard, or harder, to enable their efforts' success. I'd like to offer a special thanks to the many long-serving Manhattan Institute personnel whose years of service alongside me enabled my best professional efforts—in particular Vanessa Mendoza, Howard Husock, Troy Senik, Leigh Harrington, Brian Anderson, Michael Barreiro, Matt Toyer, Peg O'Keefe, Howard Dickman, Michele Jacob, Taisha Camacho, Debbie Cherian, Jamie Meggas, Tatyana Kustas, Steve Malanga, Paul Beston, Jay Ruffino, Tony Rivera, Pat Rondinelli, Marilou David, Sarai Mason, Paul Howard, Lindsay Craig, Matthew Hennessey, David Des Rosiers, Eddie Craig, and Henry Olsen. Thanks to John Ketcham for able research assistance on this project. A very special thanks to Bernadette Serton, MI's book director, who guided and encouraged me throughout this process with wisdom and patience and empathy. And of course my deputy director, Rafael Mangual, as well as his predecessor, Isaac Gorodetski; their friendship and support and sometimes-unseen intellectual contributions, over many years, have been truly indispensable.

Although this may be the first book to tackle quite this set of legal and policy developments in quite this way, it is hardly the first writing to consider most of the ideas contained within. Intellectual inquiry is discursive. Manhattan Institute colleagues, past and present, have written on most of these issues, before me: Peter Huber, Wally Olson, Ted Frank, Marie Gryphon Newhouse, Lester Brickman, and the ubiquitous Richard Epstein. Each is mentioned somewhere in the book's text for a reason; their influence on my ideas is profound.

Nor are my colleagues alone. There are the giants on whose shoulders we all stand: Locke and Smith and Burke and Hayek and the rest. And then there are the many more modern thinkers whose intellectual fingerprints appear throughout this book, among them John Marini, Philip Hamburger, Joseph Postell, Frank Buckley, Christopher DeMuth, Peter Wallison, Adam White, Michael Greve, Randy Barnett, Harvey Silverglate, John Hasnas, Paul Larkin, Grant Gilmore, Jeff O'Connell, Philip Howard, Deborah Hensler, Michael Krauss, Kip Viscusi, Paul Rubin, Peter Schuck, John Langbein, John Witt, Alex Tabarrok, Paul Nolette, Niall Ferguson, William Goetzmann, Roberta Romano, and Stephen Bainbridge. The smudges are of course my own.

In the decades before I got to the Manhattan Institute, many mentors lighted my path. Again, there are too many such individuals to mention them all, and a large number with lasting influence I'll necessarily omit. But as the son of a teacher and the spouse of another, I fervently believe teachers matter; I want to name a few.

My postsecondary education was particularly guided by Chuck Lovelace, John Sanders, Michael Salemi, Razeen Sally, Jed Rubenfeld, George Priest, Henry Hansmann, and Ralph Winter. Each spent many hours over months or years contributing to my intellectual growth.

In my earlier years of education, two teachers bear special mention. Jim Dupree, in whose memory this book is dedicated, set me on this path. He, more than any other, kindled my interest in government, economics, law, and policy—and spurred my commitment to lifelong learning and pursuit of a career of the mind. Many seeds of this book germinated in the sitting room of his house, in wide-ranging hours-long discussions, often joined by his beloved, committed, and equally brilliant wife, B.

Almost as significant in shaping my early development, Karen Garrison, more than any other, taught me to read and interpret texts. And if Mr. Dupree refined my ability to express myself orally, Mrs. Garrison singularly molded my ability to express myself on paper—a particularly significant contribution to something like writing a book.

Beyond sponsors and colleagues and forebears and mentors, hundreds and hundreds of peers have contributed to my personal as well as intellectual growth over the years. I'd like to acknowledge a small subset whose friendship has been significant, longstanding, and ongoing: Kyle Hooper, Jonathan Whitlatch, Jason Thomas, Carmen Scoggins, Jennifer Lloyd Evans, Anna Barrett Smith, Mark Shelburne, Laura Passiment Pierro, Autumn Rierson Michael, Wendy Sarratt, Mark Gerson, Matt Fader, Bing Yuan, Ben Kerschberg, Mike Kaufman, Eliot Morgan, and Mark Crosby. I love and treasure each of you.

No one was more fundamental to this effort than my family. My dad, Jim III, is a larger-than-life figure who's left a mark larger yet, on his loved ones and the community around him. In addition to teaching me to hunt and fish, he filled my young mind with ideas and sparked my interest in the broader world; our dinner-table discussion regularly revolved around topics ranging from state and federal policy to international disputes. My mom, Harriett Eiler, is an educator, who taught me to read and write and so much else—and to ask questions and think on my own. She was always my most committed caregiver, and she was and remains my fiercest advocate. More than anything, my parents have always offered unconditional love and support.

My wife, Tahira, chose me many years ago and has stuck by me ever since, through every hardship and in each new adventure. Throughout it all she has remained my biggest fan, my most trustworthy ally, my closest confidante, my most engaging interlocutor, and my dearest friend. Words cannot do justice to the value of her contributions, which obviously go far beyond the penning of this book.

Finally, the two in whose honor this book is dedicated, along with the memory of Jim Dupree: my children, James Reuben V and Elizabeth Coble, Ben and Liz. Along with Tahira, they have endured the negative side effects of this effort—the absent evenings, the cranky mornings, and the days and weeks of neglected parenting duties. I pray that the neglect was not at too great a cost; I hope that the effort might, in some small way, have a positive impact on the world they will grow up to inhabit.

NOTES

INTRODUCTION

1 Defense Production Act of 1950, Pub. L. 81–774, 64 Stat. 798.

1 *emergency legislation:* Coronavirus Aid, Relief, and Economic Security Act, Pub. L. 116–136 (2020).

2 *CDC developed a new testing protocol:* Centers for Disease Control, Transcript of Update on 2019 Novel Coronavirus (2019-nCoV), Jan. 21, 2020.

3 *FDA approved an emergency authorization:* Determination of a Public Health Emergency and Declaration that Circumstances Exist Justifying Authorizations Pursuant to Section 564(b) of the FD&C Act (Feb. 4, 2020); Food and Drug Administration, Emergency Use Authorization, CDC 2019-Novel Coronavirus (2019-nCoV) Real-Time RT-PCR Diagnostic Panel (Feb. 4, 2020).

3 *granted its first non-CDC testing authorization:* Food and Drug Administration, Emergency Use Authorization, Roche Molecular Systems, Inc., cobas SARS-CoV-2 (Mar. 12, 2020).

3 *required to mail in CD-ROMs:* Robert P. Baird, "What Went Wrong with Coronavirus Testing in the U.S.," *New Yorker*, Mar. 16, 2020.

3 *United States had administered only 125 tests:* Larry Buchanan et al., "U.S. Lags in Coronavirus Testing After Slow Response to Outbreak." *N.Y. Times*, Mar. 17, 2020.

4 *Franklin quipped:* Gillian Brockell, "'A Republic, If You Can Keep It': Did Ben Franklin Really Say Impeachment Day's Favorite Quote?" *Washington Post*, Dec. 18, 2019.

5 *ruled slavery unconstitutional in 1783: Commonwealth v. Jennison* (Massachusetts, 1783, Unreported).

6 *Friedrich Hayek who believed:* F. A. Hayek, *The Constitution of Liberty* (1960).

7 *300,000 federal crimes on the books…:* Julie Rose O'Sullivan, "The Federal Criminal 'Code': Return of Overfederalization, 37 *Harvard Journal of Law & Public Policy* 57, 58 (2014).

9 *law professors from Yale and the University of Michigan:* Charles E. Clark, "The Federal Rules of Civil Procedure: A New Federal Civil Procedure," 44 *Yale Law Journal* 387, 1291 (1935); Charles E. Clark, "Edson Sunderland and the Federal Rules of Civil Procedure," 58 *Michigan Law Review* 6 (1959); Michael E. Smith, "Judge Charles E. Clark and The Federal Rules of Civil Procedure," 85 *Yale Law Journal* 914 (1976).

9 *a Harvard law professor and his young protégé:* Benjamin Kaplan, "Continuing Work of the Civil Committee: 1966 Amendments of the Federal Rules of Civil Procedure (I)," 81 *Harvard Law Review* 356 (1967).

9 *during a ferry crossing over to Martha's Vineyard:* Arthur R. Miller, "Some Very Personal Reflections on the Rules, Rulemaking, and Reporters," 46 *University of Michigan Journal of Law Reform* 651, 652 (2013).

9 *"vote with their feet":* Ilya Somin, *Free to Move: Foot Voting, Migration, and Political Freedom* (2020).

10 *"race to the top"… "race to the bottom":* William L. Cary, "Federalism and Corporate Law: Reflections upon Delaware," 83 *Yale Law Journal* 663, 705 (1974); Ralph K. Winter, "State Law, Shareholder Protection, and the Theory of the Corporation," 6 *Journal of Legal Studies* 251 (1977).

11 *a Maryland doctor:* Ronald E. Kramer, "The Administrative State and The Death of Peter Gleason, MD: An Off-Label Case Report," 15 *Journal of Clinical Sleep Medicine* 529 (2019).

11 *a Michigan real estate developer: Rapanos v. United States,* 547 U.S. 715 (2006).

11 *a New Mexico auto-racing champion:* Excerpts of Testimony and Questioning of Bobby Unser Before the Judiciary Committee of the House of Representatives Subcommittee on Commercial and Administrative Law, May 7, 1998.

12 *a California entrepreneur:* James Figueroa, "Monrovia's Aztec Hotel in Management Dispute of Historic Proportions," *Pasadena Star-News,* May 28, 2011.

12 "I'm Just a Bill," *Schoolhouse Rock!,* Season 3, Episode 5, Mar. 27, 1976.

12 *The modern reality was spoofed:* "How a Bill Does Not Become a Law," *Saturday Night Live,* Season 40, Episode 7, Nov. 22, 2014.

13 *action taken by President Barack Obama:* President Barack Obama, Remarks by the President in Address to the Nation on Immigration (Nov. 20, 2014); Fixing Our Broken Immigration System Through Executive Action – Key Facts, U.S. Dep't of Homeland Security (Aug. 19, 2015).

13 *Federal courts reviewed various pieces of the president's executive actions: Texas v. United States,* 809 F.3d 134, (5th Cir. 2015), *aff'd by an equally divided court,* 136 S. Ct. 2271 (2016) (per curiam); *Texas v. United States,* 328 F. Supp. 3d 662 (S.D. Tex. 2018); *Regents of the University of California v. Department of Homeland Security,* 908 F.3d 476 (9th Cir. 2018), *cert. granted,* 139 S. Ct. 2779 (2019).

CHAPTER 1. LEGISLATING WITHOUT CONGRESS

17 For more on Gleason's story, see Ronald E. Kramer, "The Administrative State and The Death of Peter Gleason, MD: An Off-Label Case Report," 15 *Journal of Clinical Sleep Medicine* 529 (2019).

17 *"engaging in interstate commerce of a misbranded drug": United States v. Gleason,* Superseding Indictment, Case 1:06-cr-00229-ENV (E.D.N.Y. July 25, 2007).

17 *Xyrem was a legal drug:* U.S. Food & Drug Administration, Drug Approval Package, Xyrem (Sodium Oxybate) Oral Solution, App. No.: 21-196, July 17, 2002.

18 *it is not illegal for doctors to prescribe drugs: Buckman Co. v. Plaintiffs' Legal Committee,* 531 U.S. 341, 350 (2001).

18 *studies published in peer-reviewed medical journals:* Todd J. Swick, "Sodium Oxybate: A Potential New Pharmacological Option for the Treatment of Fibromyalgia Syndrome," 3 *Therapeutic Advances in Musculoskeletal Disease* 167 (2011).

18 *studies estimate that 21 percent:* David C. Radley et al., "Off-Label Prescribing among Office-Based Physicians," 166 *Archives of Internal Medicine* 1021–26 (2006).

18 *79 percent of all pediatric prescriptions:* S. S. Shah et al., "Off-Label Drug Use in Hospitalized Children," 161 *Archives of Pediatrics & Adolescent Medicine* 282–90 (2007) (published correction appears in 161 *Archives of Pediatrics & Adolescent Medicine* 655 (2007)).

18 *Mr. Caronia also challenged his conviction: United States v. Caronia*, 703 F.3d 149 (2nd Cir. 2012).

19 *written by the FDA, not by Congress:* 21 U.S.C. § 331(a) (prohibiting "introduction or delivery for introduction into interstate commerce of any...drug...that is...misbranded"); 21 C.F.R. § 201.128 (regulation interpreting the statute to mean "oral or written statements" indicating a drug use "for a purpose for which it is neither labeled nor advertised").

19 *300,000 federal crimes are on the books:* Julie Rose O'Sullivan, "The Federal Criminal 'Code': Return of Overfederalization, 37 *Harvard Journal of Law & Public Policy* 57, 58 (2014).

19 *added 201,838 new rules:* Clyde Wayne Crews Jr., *10,000 Commandments: An Annual Snapshot of the Federal Regulatory State* (2019).

19 Executive Order 13771, Reducing Regulation and Controlling Regulatory Costs, 82 Fed. Reg. 9339 (Feb. 3, 2017).

19 *"the most far-reaching regulatory reform in American history":* Remarks by President Trump on Deregulation, Dec. 14, 2017.

19 *added 61,308 pages:* Clyde Wayne Crews Jr., *10,000 Commandments: An Annual Snapshot of the Federal Regulatory State* (2018), at 25–27 ("The last time the annual page count was this low was in 1993."; "by the time Trump was inaugurated on January 20, 2017, the Obama administration had already added 7,630 pages to the *Federal Register*"; "at the end of Obama's final calendar year of 2016, the number of *Federal Register* pages stood at 95,854").

20 *3,281 and 3,368, respectively:* Clyde Wayne Crews Jr., *10,000 Commandments: An Annual Snapshot of the Federal Regulatory State* (2019), at 32.

20 *Keystone XL:* Memorandum of January 24, 2017, Construction of the Keystone XL Pipeline, 2017-02035.

20 *Dakota Access:* Memorandum from Todd Semonite, Lieutenant General, Army Corp of Engineers, Feb. 3, 2017.

20 *"only to make laws, and not to make legislators":* John Locke, *Second Treatise of Civil Government* (1690).

20 *"no liberty":* Charles de Secondat, Baron de Montesquieu, *The Spirit of the Laws* (1748).

22 *"by such route as the President...":* Annals of Congress, 2d Cong., 1st sess. (Dec. 17, 1791).

22 *Cargo of the Brig Aurora v. United States*, 11 U.S. (7 Cranch) 382 (1813).

23 *Wayman v. Southard*, 23 U.S. (10 Wheat.) 1 (1825).

25 Coinage Act of 1873, Pub. L. 42–131, 17 Stat. 424.

25 Coinage Act of 1792, Pub. L. 2–16, 1 Stat. 246.

26 *National Bureau of Economic Research estimates:* National Bureau of Economic Research, US Business Cycle Expansions and Contractions.

26 *industrial production soared:* Eric Hobsbawm, *The Age of Empire (1875-1914)* (1989).

26 Bland-Allison Act, Pub. L. 45–20, 20 Stat. 25 (1878).

26 Sherman Silver Purchase Act, Pub. L. 51–708, 26 Stat. 289 (1890).

26 *"Cross of Gold":* Michael Kazin, *A Godly Hero: The Life of William Jennings Bryan* (2006).

26 Interstate Commerce Act of 1887, Pub. L. 49–104, 24 Stat. 379.

26 Sherman Antitrust Act of 1890, Pub. L. 51–647, 26 Stat. 209.

26 *commission's powers were "meager":* James Landis, *The Administrative Process* (1938).

27 Tariff Act of 1890, Pub. L. 51–1244. 26 Stat. 567–625.

27 *Field v. Clark*, 143 U.S. 649 (1892).

28 *J. W. Hampton, Jr. & Co. v. United States*, 276 U.S. 394 (1928).

29 *"a new deal for the American people":* Franklin Delano Roosevelt, Acceptance Speech to the 1932 Democratic Convention.

29 National Industrial Recovery Act of 1933, Pub. L. 73–67, 48 Stat. 195.

29 Hepburn Act, Pub. L. 59–337, 34 Stat. 584 (1906).

29 Pure Food and Drug Act of 1906, Pub. L. 59–384, 34 Stat. 768.

29 Federal Reserve Act of 1913, Pub. L. 63–43, 38 Stat. 251.

29 Federal Trade Commission Act of 1914, Pub. L. 63–311, 38 Stat. 717.

30 *Panama Refining Co. v. Ryan*, 293 U.S. 388 (1935).

31 *A. L. A. Schechter Poultry Corp. v. United States*, 295 U.S. 495 (1935).

32 *The Supreme Court rejected an opportunity to revive: Mistretta v. United States*, 488 U.S. 361 (1989).

33 *Gundy v. United States*, 588 U.S. ____, 139 S. Ct. 2116 (2019).

33 Adam Walsh Child Protection and Safety Act, Pub. L. 109–248, 120 Stat. 587 (2006).

CHAPTER 2. ADMINISTERING WITHOUT THE EXECUTIVE

35 *"hard at work"/ "acting director":* Nik DeCosta-Klipa, "The Story Behind the Strange Controversy Engulfing Elizabeth Warren's Brainchild Agency," *Boston Globe*, Nov. 29, 2017.

35 Dodd-Frank Wall Street Reform and Consumer Protection Act, Pub. L. 111–203, 124 Stat. 1376 (2011).

36 Federal Vacancies Reform Act of 1998, Pub. L. 105–277, 112 Stat. 2681.

36 *the Office of Legal Counsel…opined:* Memorandum for Donald F. McGahn II, Nov. 25, 2017; Memorandum, Mary E. McLeod, General Counsel, CFPB, Nov. 25, 2017.

36 *federal judge refused to grant:* Katie Rogers & Tara Siegel Bernard, "President Wins Round in the Battle for the Consumer Bureau," *N.Y. Times*, Nov. 28, 2017.

36 *"Congress determined that [the CFPB] needed...":* English v. Trump, Memorandum in Support of Plaintiff's Motion for Preliminary Injunction, Case No. 1:17-cv-02534 (D.D.C. Dec. 6, 2017).

37 *"species of power which...":* Cong. Register, I, 499–507, *Gazette of the U.S.*, 24 June 1789.

37 *"I destine a part of the money only...":* Dunlap's American Daily Advertiser, 12 Mar. 1793.

37 *"perplexity and confusion will inevitably ensue":* Leonard D. White, *The Federalists: A Study in Administrative History* (1967).

37 *"worst evil that can happen...":* Letter from John Adams to Thomas Pickering, Oct. 31, 1797.

37 *"unity of object and action":* Leonard D. White, *The Federalists: A Study in Administrative History* (1967).

38 *"tended to sap the foundation...":* Remarks of Senator Calhoun, Feb. 9, 1835.

38 *Calhoun's transparency legislation:* The Works of John C. Calhoun, Vol. 2 (2017), at 241; Annual Report of the United States Civil Service Commission, Vol. 15 (1899).

38 *"early decision"... "at will"... "uniformly sanctioned it":* Remarks of Daniel Webster, Feb. 16, 1835.

39 *"ominous to the stability of our institutions":* Charles Francis Adams, "An Appeal from the New to the Old Whigs" (1835).

39 *"the Whigs and their ideological successors...":* Joseph Postell, *Bureaucracy in America: The Administrative State's Challenge to Constitutional Government* (2017).

40 *"monied interest":* President Jackson's Veto Message Regarding the Bank of the United States, July 10, 1832.

40 *"the entire executive power is vested...":* Leonard D. White, *The Jacksonians: A Study of Administrative History, 1829-1861* (1954).

40 *"agent or representative of Congress":* Richard J. Ellis, *The Development of the American Presidency* (2012).

40 *Jackson responded with a "protest":* Leonard D. White, *The Jacksonians: A Study of Administrative History, 1829-1861* (1954).

41 Tenure of Office Act, Pub. L. 39–154, 14 Stat. 430 (1867).

41 *Myers v. United States*, 272 U.S. 52 (1926).

42 *"Postmasters of the first, second,...":* Act of July 12, 1876, Pub. L. 44–179, 19 Stat. 80.

43 New York Customs House operation: Commissions to Examine Certain Customs Houses of the United States (Jay Commission) (1877); George F. Howe, "The New York Custom-House Controversy, 1877-1879," 18 *Mississippi Valley Historical Review* (1931); George F. Howe, *Chester A. Arthur, A Quarter-Century of Machine Politics* (1934); Thomas C. Reeves, *Gentleman Boss: The Life of Chester A. Arthur* (1975); Jay Cost, *A Republic No More: Big Government and the Rise of American Political Corruption* (2015).

44　Pendleton Civil Service Reform Act of 1833, Pub. L. 47–27, 22 Stat. 403.

44　Woodrow Wilson, *Congressional Government: A Study in American Politics* (1885).

45　Interstate Commerce Act of 1887, Pub. L. 49–104, 24 Stat. 379.

45　Woodrow Wilson, "The Study of Administration," 2 *Political Science Quarterly* 197 (1887).

45　*"unphilosophical bulk of mankind": Ibid.*

45　*"democracies have ever been spectacles…":* James Madison, *The Federalist* no. 10.

46　*"combination in business should be…":* Harold Howland, *Chronicles of America: Theodore Roosevelt and His Times* (1921).

46　*"dissolution"… "purely negative"… "of little permanent avail":* Theodore Roosevelt, *Theodore Roosevelt: An Autobiography* (1913).

46　Federal Reserve Act of 1913, Pub. L. 63–43, 38 Stat. 251.

47　*Federal Open Market Committee:* Banking Act of 1933, Pub. L. 73–66, 48 Stat. 162.

47　Federal Trade Commission Act of 1914, Pub. L. 63–311, 38 Stat. 717.

47　Clayton Antitrust Act of 1914, Pub. L. 63–212, 38 Stat. 730.

47　*"Effective as of this date, you are hereby removed…":* Humphrey's Executor v. United States, 295 U.S. 602 (1935).

48　*"submerged in a bowl of alphabet soup":* William Safire, *Safire's Political Dictionary* (2008).

49　*Free Enterprise Fund v. Public Company Accounting Oversight Board,* 561 U.S. 477 (2010).

49　*Ninth Circuit and the D.C. Circuit federal courts of appeals upheld: Consumer Financial Protection Bureau v. Seila Law LLC,* 923 F.3d 680 (9th Cir. 2019), *cert. granted,* No. 19-7, 2019 WL 5281290 (Oct. 18, 2019); *PHH Corp. v. Consumer Financial Protection Bureau,* 839 F.3d 1 (D.C. Cir. 2016).

49　*Collins v. Mnuchin,* 938 F.3d 553 (5th Cir. 2019).

CHAPTER 3.　JUDGING WITHOUT THE JUDICIARY

51　*Rapanos v. United States,* 547 U.S. 715 (2006).

51　*settled a legal dispute:* Rapanos Clean Water Act Settlement, Dec. 29, 2008.

51　Clean Water Act, Pub. L. 92–500, 86 Stat. 816 (1972).

51　*"interstate wetlands"… "are or would be used as habitat":* 33 C.F.R. § 328.3(a)(2) (2004); 51 Fed. Reg. 41217 (1986).

51　*"ephemeral streams"… "drainage ditches":* 33 C.F.R. § 328.3(a)(5), 65 Fed. Reg. 12823 (2000).

51　*"the presence of litter and debris": Ibid.;* 33 CFR § 328.3(e).

52　*"navigable in fact": The Daniel Ball,* 77 U.S. (10 Wall.) 557 (1871).

52　*But that interpretation was challenged in a lawsuit: Natural Resources Defense Council v. Callaway,* 392 F. Supp. 685 (D.D.C. 1975).

52　*the government settled that lawsuit:* Jeffrey K. Stine, "Regulating Wetlands in the 1970s: U.S. Army Corps of Engineers and the Environmental Organizations," 27 *Journal of Forest History* 60 (1983).

52 *"asserted federal jurisdiction over...":* Callaway, 392 F. Supp. at 686.

52 *United States v. Riverside Bayview,* 474 U.S. 121 (1985).

53 *settled with the government for almost $1 million:* Press Release, U.S. Department of Justice, John Rapanos Agrees to Pay for Clean Water Act Violations, Dec. 29, 2008 ("Rapanos has agreed to pay a $150,000 civil penalty and will spend an estimated $750,000 to mitigate for 54 acres of wetlands....").

53 *Little v. Barreme,* 6 U.S. 170 (1804).

54 *Interstate Commerce Commission v. Illinois Central Railroad Co.,* 215 U.S. 452 (1910).

54 *"could not be achieved":* James Landis, *The Administrative Process* (1938).

55 *Gray v. Powell,* 314 U.S. 402 (1941).

55 Bituminous Coal Act of 1937, Pub. L. 75–127, 50 Stat. 72.

55 *NLRB v. Hearst Publications,* 322 U.S. 111 (1944).

55 National Labor Relations Act of 1935, Pub. L. 74–198, 49 Stat. 449.

55 *Skidmore v. Swift & Co.,* 323 U.S. 134 (1944).

56 Fair Labor Standards Act of 1938, Pub. L. 75–718, 52 Stat. 1060.

57 Roscoe Pound, "Executive Justice," 55 *American Law Register* 137 (1907).

57 Report of the Special Committee on Administrative Law, 1938 A.B.A. Ann. Rep.

58 *"one-man committee":* Daniel R. Ernst, *Tocqueville's Nightmare: The Administrative State Emerges in America, 1900-1940* (2014).

58 *"a flood of wildly bombastic articles...":* Dan Ernst, "The Special Committee on Administrative Law," *Legal History Blog,* Sept. 27, 2008.

58 Walter-Logan Act: James M. Landis, "Crucial Issues in Administrative Law. The Walter-Logan Bill," 53 *Harvard Law Review* 1077 (1940).

58 *Pound testified before a Senate subcommittee:* Statement of Dean Roscoe Pound, Harvard Law School, Cambridge, Mass., Before a Subcommittee of the U.S. Senate Committee on the Judiciary, May 14, 1938.

59 Administrative Procedure Act, Pub. L. 79–404, 60 Stat. 237 (1946).

60 *Motor Vehicle Manufacturers Association v. State Farm Mutual Automobile Insurance Co.,* 463 U.S. 29 (1983).

60 *Chevron v. Natural Resources Defense Council,* 467 U.S. 837 (1984).

60 National Traffic and Motor Vehicle Safety Act, Pub. L. 89–563, 80 Stat. 718 (1966).

60 *mandated that all new cars include seat belts:* 37 Fed. Reg. 3911 (1972).

60 *"ignition interlock":* 37 Fed. Reg. 3911 (1972); *Chrysler Corp. v. Department of Transportation,* 472 F.2d 659 (6th Cir. 1972).

60 Motor Vehicle and School Bus Safety Amendments of 1974, Pub. L. 93-492, 88 Stat. 1482.

60 *"passive restraints":* 34 Fed. Reg. 11148 (1969).

60 *"full passive protection...":* 37 Fed. Reg. 3911 (1972).

60 *Department of Transportation put off the date:* 40 Fed. Reg. 16217 (1975).

60 *William T. Coleman, announced a new rulemaking process:* 41 Fed. Reg. 24070 (1976).

60 *issued a new rule, once again requiring passive-restraint safety:* 42 Fed. Reg. 34289 (1977); 49 CFR § 571.208 (1978).

60 *appellate court approved the regulation: Pacific Legal Foundation v. Department of Transportation,* 593 F.2d 1338 (D.C. Cir. 1979), *cert. denied,* 444 U.S. 830 (1979).

61 *reopened the department's passive-restraint rulemaking:* 46 Fed. Reg. 12033 (1981).

61 *Secretary Lewis extended the deadline:* 46 Fed. Reg. 21172 (1981).

61 *the secretary rescinded the mandate altogether:* Notice 25, 46 Fed. Reg. 53419 (1981).

61 *"lifesaving potential of airbags…": State Farm,* 463 U.S. at 38–39 (citing Notice 25).

62 *But in fact there was substantial additional evidence:* Richard A. Epstein, *The Dubious Morality of Administrative Law* (2019).

62 Merrick B. Garland, "Deregulation and Judicial Review," 98 *Harvard Law Review* 505 (1985).

63 *Anne Gorsuch:* Brady Dennis & Chris Mooney, "Neil Gorsuch's Mother Once Ran the EPA. It Didn't Go Well," *Washington Post,* Feb. 1, 2017.

63 Clean Air Act of 1963, Pub. L. 88–206, 77 Stat. 392.

63 Clean Air Act Amendments of 1977, Pub. L. 95–95, 91 Stat. 685.

63 *in August 1980, the EPA had reversed its earlier judgment:* 45 Fed. Reg. 52697 (1980).

64 *new regulation returning the reading of "source" to its earlier definition:* 46 Fed. Reg. 16281 (1981).

65 *meaning of the word "is":* President Clinton's Grand Jury Testimony, Part 4, Aug. 17, 1998.

65 Communications Act of 1934, Pub. L. 73–416, 48 Stat. 1064.

65 Telecommunications Act of 1996, Pub. L. 104–104, 110 Stat. 56.

66 *And the FCC initially decided:* In re Federal-State Joint Board on Universal Service, 13 FCC Rcd. 11501 (1998).

66 *the FCC now decided that cable companies:* In re Inquiry Concerning High-Speed Access to the Internet Over Cable and Other Facilities, 17 FCC Rcd. 4798 (2002).

66 *the U.S. Court of Appeals for the Ninth Circuit ruled: AT&T Corp. v. Portland,* 216 F.3d 871 (9th Cir. 2000).

66 *National Cable & Telecommunications Association v. Brand X Internet Services,* 545 U.S. 967 (2005).

66 *"common carriers":* In re Protecting and Promoting the Open Internet, 30 FCC Rcd. 5601 (2015).

66 *reversed course and repealed its "net neutrality" rule:* In re Restoring Internet Freedom, 33 FCC Rcd. 311 (2018).

66 *surrounded the FCC leader's residence:* Hamza Shaban, "FCC Chairman Ajit Pai Says His Children Are Being Harassed Over Net Neutrality," *Washington Post,* Nov. 27, 2017; Cecilia Kang, "Man Charged with Threatening to Kill Ajit Pai's Family," *N.Y. Times,* June 29, 2018.

67 *"clean water" rule that further expanded:* 80 Fed. Reg. 37053 (2015).

67 *district and appellate courts blocked its implementation: State of North Dakota et al. v. U.S. Environmental Protection Agency*, 127 F. Supp. 3d 1047 (D.N.D. 2015); *State of Georgia v. Pruitt*, 326 F. Supp. 3d 1356 (S.D. Ga. 2018); *In re Dept. of Defense*, 817 F. 3d 261 (6th Cir. 2016), *rev'd, National Association of Manufacturers. v. Department of Defense*, 583 U.S. ____, 138 S. Ct. 617 (2018).

67 *President Trump ordered the EPA:* Presidential Executive Order on Restoring the Rule of Law, Federalism, and Economic Growth by Reviewing the "Waters of the United States" Rule, Feb. 28, 2017.

67 *agency subsequently announced:* 82 Fed. Reg.12532 (2017).

67 *Trump administration announced:* Coral Davenport & Lisa Friedman, "Trump Administration Rolls Back Clean Water Protections," *N.Y. Times*, Sept. 12, 2019.

68 *"executive bureaucracies to swallow…": Gutierrez-Brizuela v. Lynch*, 834 F.3d 1142 (10th Cir. 2016).

68 *Justice Thomas signaled: Baldwin v. United States*, No. 19–402, 589 U. S. _____ (2020) (Thomas, J., dissenting).

CHAPTER 4. REGULATING WITHOUT RULEMAKING

71 *Matt Boermeester:* Zach Helfand, "Kicker Matt Boermeester Was Removed from USC after an Unfair Investigation, Girlfriend Says," *L.A. Times*, July 30, 2017. In May 2020, Boermeester was successful in the latest stage of ongoing litigation against USC. *See Boermeester v. Carry*, B290675 (Cal. App. 2d May 28, 2020).

71 Higher Education Amendments of 1972, Pub. L. 92–318, 86 Stat. 235.

71 *created by a "policy interpretation":* A Policy Interpretation: Title IX and Intercollegiate Athletics, 44 Fed. Reg. 239 (1979).

71 *nineteen-page "dear colleague" letter:* Letter from Assistant Secretary for Civil Rights Russlynn Ali, Apr. 4, 2011.

72 *"I am the one involved…":* Alice B. Lloyd, "Behind the Curious Case of USC's Star-Crossed Student Athletes," *Washington Examiner*, Aug. 21, 2017.

72 *"I want to be very clear…":* Eric He & Emma Peplow, "Girlfriend of Former Kicker Matt Boermeester Says His Removal Was the Result of Unfair Investigation," *Daily Trojan*, July 31, 2017.

72 *USC had been placed under investigation:* Russell Goldman, "USC Statement on Title IX Investigation," *ABC News*, July 24, 2013.

73 *Bowles v. Seminole Rock & Sand*, 325 U.S. 410 (1945).

73 Emergency Price Control Act of 1942, Pub. L. 77–421, 56 Stat. 23.

73 Maximum Price Regulation No. 188, 7 Fed. Reg. 5872, 7967, 8943 (1942).

74 *"[Seminole Rock] developed a doctrine of deference…": Perez v. Mortgage Bankers Association*, 575 U.S. _____, 135 S.Ct. 1199 (2015) (Thomas, J., concurring).

75 *Marbury v. Madison*, 5 U.S. 137 (1803).

75 *Auer v. Robbins*, 519 U.S. 452 (1997).

75 Fair Labor Standards Act of 1938, Pub. L. 75–676, 52 Stat. 1060.

75 *"salary-basis test":* 5 Fed. Reg. 4077 (1940).

75 *As codified in a regulation from 1954:* 19 Fed. Reg. 4405 (1954).

77 "Development, Issuance, and Use of Guidance Documents": 62 Fed. Reg. 8961 (1997).

77 Richard A. Epstein, "The Role of Guidances in Modern Administrative Procedure: The Case for *De Novo* Review," 8 *Journal of Legal Analysis* 47 (2016).

77 *typically invoke administrative agencies' expertise: See, e.g.,* Tr. of Oral Arg. in *Kisor v. Wilkie*, O.T. 2018, No. 15, p. 10 ("JUSTICE BREYER: [T]here are hundreds of thousands, possibly millions of interpretive regulations. I mean … the Court deferred to the understanding of the FDA that a particular compound should be treated as a single new active moiety, which consists of a previously approved moiety, joined by a non-ester covalent bond to a lysine group.").

77 *interpreting* words—*the stuff of written regulations: Ibid.,* p. 13 ("JUSTICE ALITO: [D]o you think the FCC knows a lot more about the meaning of the word 'relevant' than federal district judges?").

78 *the Clinton Labor Department issued opinion letters:* Opinion Letter, Mortgage Loan Officers/Exempt Status 6A LRR, Wages and Hours Manual 99:8249 (May 17, 1999); Opinion Letter, Loan Officers/Exempt Status, 6A LRR, Wages and Hours Manual 99:8351 (Feb. 16, 2001).

78 *The Bush administration…issued a letter in 2006:* Opinion Letter, FLSA 2006-31 (Sept. 8, 2006).

78 *the Obama Labor Department…again reversed course:* Administrator's Interpretation No. 2010-1 (Mar. 24, 2010).

78 *rubber-stamped the change: Perez v. Mortgage Bankers Association,* 575 U.S. _____, 135 S.Ct. 1199 (2015).

79 *The 2016 letter advised colleges:* Dear Colleague Letter on Transgender Students, May 13, 2016.

80 *guidance document covering these issues for secondary schools:* Examples of Policies and Emerging Practices for Supporting Transgender Students, U.S. Department of Education, May 2016.

80 *"may provide separate toilet, locker room…":* 34 C.F.R. § 106.33.

80 *"bureaucratic processes to push for greater justice":* Emily Esque: Fighting for Justice through Bureaucratic Black Magic: About Emily, http://www.emily-esque.com/ ("Noting the lack of organizations focusing on administrative law with respect to trans rights, Emily has carved out a niche and uses bureaucratic processes to push for greater justice.") (accessed June 14, 2020).

80 *"Title IX regulations permit schools…":* Letter from James A. Ferg-Cadima, Acting Deputy Assistant Secretary for Policy, Office for Civil Rights, U.S. Department of Education, to Emily T. Prince, Esq., Jan. 7, 2015.

80 *document from December 2014:* Questions and Answers on Title IX and Single-Sex Elementary and Secondary Classes and Extracurricular Activities, Dec 1, 2014.

81 *"diagnosed with gender dysphoria…": G.G. v. Gloucester County School Board,* 822 F.3d 709 (4th Cir. 2016), *vacated, Gloucester County School Board v. G.G.,* 137 S. Ct. 1239 (2017) (mem.).

81 *On February 22, 2017:* Dear Colleague Letter, Feb. 22, 2017.

81 Executive Order 13777, 82 Fed. Reg. 12285 (2017).

82 *a memorandum in November 2017:* Memorandum for All Components, Nov. 16, 2017.

82 *Kisor v. Wilkie,* 588 U.S. _____, 139 S. Ct. 2400 (2019).

82 *Veterans Affairs regulation:* 38 C.F.R. § 3.156(c)(1) (2013).

83 *the Federal Circuit decided: Kisor v. Shulkin,* 869 F. 3d 1360, 1368 (Fed. Cir. 2017), *aff'd, Kisor v. Wilkie,* 588 U.S. _____, 139 S. Ct. 2400 (2019).

CHAPTER 5. CRIMINALIZING EVERYTHING

85 Testimony, Bobby Unser, Hearing Before the House Subcommittee on Commercial and Administrative Law of the Committee on the Judiciary, May 7, 1998.

85 *United States v. Unser,* 165 F.3d 755 (10th Cir. 1999).

86 *"make provisions for the protection against…":* 16 U.S.C. § 551 ("any violation of … such rules and regulations shall be punished by [criminal fines or imprisonment]").

86 *an estimated 300,000 criminal offenses:* Julie Rose O'Sullivan, "The Federal Criminal 'Code': Return of Overfederalization, 37 *Harvard Journal of Law & Public Policy* 57, 58 (2014).

86 *For Bobby Unser, the operative violation:* 36 C.F.R. § 261.16(a) (1995).

87 *Courts have limited* [ex post facto] *prohibition to the criminal-law context: Calder v. Bull,* 3 U.S. (3 Dall.) 386 (1798).

87 *Caligula had famously posted his edicts high:* Richard S. Kay, "Original Intention and Public Meaning in. Constitutional Interpretation," 103 *Northwestern University Law Review* 703 (2009). Although the posting of edicts out of sight is usually attributed to Caligula, Justice Scalia attributed it to Nero. Antonin Scalia, *A Matter of Interpretation: Federal Courts and the Law* (1997), at 17 (discussing "the trick the emperor Nero was said to engage in: posting edicts high up on the pillars, so that they could not be easily read").

88 *nine major felonies under the common law:* Francis Wharton, *Treatise on the Criminal Law of The United States* (1846).

88 *[sodomy] no longer deemed criminal under the Supreme Court's interpretation: Lawrence v. Texas,* 539 U.S. 558 (2003).

88 *common-law misdemeanor offenses:* Richard M. Jackson, "Common Law Misdemeanors," 6 *Cambridge Law Journal* 193 (1937).

88 Crimes Act of 1790, Pub. L. 1–9, 1 Stat. 112.

88 Harvey Silverglate, *Three Felonies a Day: How the Feds Target the Innocent* (2009).

89 *Legally Blonde* (Marc Platt & Ric Kidney, 2001).

89 *"an unwarrantable act without a vicious will…":* William Blackstone, *Commentaries on the Laws of England* (1765).

89 *"Even a dog distinguishes…":* Oliver Wendell Holmes Jr., *The Common Law* (1881).

90 *Regina v. Faulkner,* 13 Cox C.C. 550 (1877).

90 *Lawrence Lewis:* Gary Fields & John R. Emshwiller, "A Sewage Blunder Earns Engineer a Criminal Record," *Wall Street Journal,* Dec. 12, 2011; Lawrence Lewis, Testimony Before the Over-Criminalization Task Force of the U.S. House Committee on the Judiciary, Regulatory Crime: Identifying the Scope of the Problem (Oct. 30, 2013).

90 Clean Water Act, Pub. L. 92–500, 86 Stat. 816 (1972).

90 *"the prosecution of minor offenses":* Tenement House Department of City of New York v. McDevitt, 109 N.E. 88 (N.Y. 1915).

90 *Morissette v. United States,* 342 U.S. 246 (1952).

91 National Association of Criminal Defense Lawyers & Heritage Foundation, *Without Intent: How Congress Is Eroding the Criminal Intent Requirement in Federal Law* (2010).

91 *Mackinac Center for Public Policy in Michigan:* Michael J. Reitz, Criminal Minds: Defining Culpability in Michigan Statutes (Mackinac Center for Public Policy, Dec. 10, 2013); James R. Copland et al., Overcriminalizing the Wolverine State: A Primer and Possible Reforms for Michigan, Issue Brief 31 (Manhattan Institute for Policy Research, Oct. 2014).

92 *requirement that a defendant's act be "knowing":* Fifth Circuit Pattern Jury Instructions, § 1.35 (1990); *West's Encyclopedia of American Law* (2d ed. 2008) ("When the term knowingly is used in an indictment, it signifies that the defendant knew what he or she was going to do and, subject to such knowledge, engaged in the act for which he or she was charged."); John Bouvier, *A Law Dictionary, Adapted to the Constitution and Laws of the United States* (1856) ("The word 'knowingly,' or 'well knowing,' will supply the place of a positive averment in an indictment or declaration, that the defendant knew the facts subsequently stated.").

92 *law of criminal conspiracy:* Ted Prim, "The *Mens Rea* Requirement for Conspiracy: The Model Penal Code and the Progressive Law of Judge Learned Hand," 40 *Missouri Law Review* 467 (1975).

92 *"felony murder":* James J. Tomkovicz, "The Endurance of the Felony-Murder Rule: A Study of the Forces that Shape Our Criminal Law," 51 *Washington & Lee Law Review* 1429 (1994).

92 *Seinfeld* (West-Shapiro Productions & Castle Rock Entertainment, episodes 179 & 180, 1998).

92 *"Good Samaritan" law: Seinfeld* dubbed the fictitious law in question a "Good Samaritan" law—based on the Biblical Parable of the Good Samaritan as recounted in *Luke* 10:29–37. The term is typically applied instead to laws *shielding* from legal action those who offer charitable assistance. A version applies in every state. *See, e.g.,* Maryland Courts and Judicial Proceedings Code § 5-603; Virginia § 8.01-225; N.C. § 20-166, § 90-21.14; S.C. § 15-1-310; Tennessee § 63-6-218; Georgia § 51-1-29. The fictitious law in *Seinfeld* might better have been dubbed a "duty to rescue" law. There is no such legal duty to come to another's aid in U.S. common-law tradition. *See, e.g., Buch v. Amory Manufacturing Co.,* 44 A. 809 (N.H. 1898); *People v. Beardsley,* 113 N.W. 1128 (Mich. 1907). Some states, however, have enacted duty-to-rescue laws that

criminalize failures to aid others under certain conditions. *See, e.g.,* Wis. Stat. §
940.34.

92 *Hanousek v. United States,* 176 F. 3d 1116 (9th Cir. 1999).

93 *Hanousek v. United States,* 528 U.S. 1102 (2000) (Thomas, J., dissenting in denial
of certiorari).

93 *"command or direction":* Rex v. Huggins & Barnes, 2 Strange 883 (K.B. 1730).

94 *United States v. Dotterweich,* 320 U.S. 277 (1943).

94 *"responsible corporate officer":* The doctrine was further established in *United
States v. Park,* 421 U.S. 658 (1975). *See* Kathleen F. Brickey, "Criminal Liability of
Corporate Officers for Strict Liability Offenses—Another View," 35 *Vanderbilt
Law Review* 1337 (1984).

95 *a fisherman who threw three fish back:* Yates v. United States, 574 U.S. 528 (2015).

95 *Florida seafood importer:* United States v. McNab, 331 F.3d 1228 (11th Cir. 2003).

95 *Honduran regulatory code in combination with a federal law:* Lacey Act, 16 U.S.C.
§ 3372(a)(2)(A) (criminalizing taking, possessing, transporting, or selling "fish
or wildlife . . . in violation of . . . any foreign law").

CHAPTER 6. OFFERS YOU CAN'T REFUSE

97 On the FedEx case: James R. Copland & Rafael A. Mangual, "Thank You
FedEx, for Standing Up to the Feds," *RealClearMarkets,* June 21, 2016; James R.
Copland & Rafael A. Mangual, Justice Out of the Shadows: Federal Deferred
Prosecution Agreements and the Political Order (Manhattan Institute for
Policy Research, June 2016).

97 *"novel prosecution":* Jay Rosenblatt, "Novel FedEx Drug-Shipping Case Left to
Skeptical Judge at Trial," *Bloomberg,* June 13, 2016.

97 *United Parcel Service:* Deferred Prosecution Agreement, U.S. Department of
Justice, Re: United Parcel Service (Mar. 29, 2013).

98 *the government sought $1.6 billion in fines:* Indictment, *United States v. FedEx
Corp.,* C.R. 14 380 (N.D. Cal., July 17, 2014).

98 *The Godfather* (Albert S. Ruddy, 1972).

99 *one in five of the Fortune 100 companies:* James R. Copland & Rafael A. Mangual,
The Shadow Regulatory State at the Crossroads: Federal Deferred Prosecution
Agreements Face an Uncertain Future (Manhattan Institute for Policy
Research, June 2017).

99 *total more than $50 billion:* Gibson-Dunn, 2019 Year-End Update on Corporate
Non-Prosecution Agreements and Deferred Prosecution Agreements (Jan. 8,
2020).

99 *"companies cannot be sent to jail":* Rahul Rose, "Caldwell: Settlement a 'More
Powerful Tool' Than Convictions," *Global Investigations Review* (Dec. 3, 2014).

100 *between the Justice Department and Salomon Brothers:* Press Release, U.S.
Department of Justice, Department of Justice and SEC Enter $290 Million
Settlement with Salomon Brothers in Treasury Securities Case (May 20, 1992).

100 *their numbers have grown dramatically:* James R. Copland & Rafael A. Mangual,
The Shadow Regulatory State at the Crossroads: Federal Deferred Prosecution
Agreements Face an Uncertain Future (Manhattan Institute for Policy

Research, June 2017); Gibson-Dunn, 2019 Year-End Update on Corporate Non-Prosecution Agreements and Deferred Prosecution Agreements (Jan. 8, 2020).

100 *still heavily governs European democracies:* Sara Sun Beale & Adam G. Safwat, "What Developments in Western Europe Tell Us about American Critiques of Corporate Criminal Liability," 8 *Buffalo Criminal Law Review* 89 (2004).

100 *A few cases in the seventeenth and eighteenth centuries:* Kathleen F. Brickey, "Corporate Criminal Accountability: A Brief History and an Observation," 60 *Washington University Law Quarterly* 393 (1982).

100 *more than 10,000 municipal corporations: Ibid.* (citing *Two Centuries' Growth Of American Law 1701-1901* (1901)).

101 *the State of New York indicted the city of Albany: People v. Corporation of Albany,* 11 Wend. 539 (N.Y. Sup. Ct. 1834).

101 *"for any crime of which a corrupt intent…": United States v. MacAndrews & Forbes Co.,* 149 F. 836 (1907).

101 *State v. Morris & Essex Railroad Co.,* 23 N.J.L. 360 (1852).

101 *Telegram Newspaper Co. v. Commonwealth,* 52 N.E. 445 (Mass. 1899).

101 Elkins Act of 1903, Pub. L. 57–708, 32 Stat. 847.

102 *New York Central & Hudson River Railroad Co. v. United States,* 212 U.S. 481 (1909).

102 *courts have assumed that crimes written into law: United States v. Blood,* 435 F.3d 612 (6th Cir. 2006); *United States v. Sun-Diamond Growers,* 138 F.3d 961 (D.C. Cir. 1998).

102 *for offenses of low-level employees: United States v. Dye Construction Co.,* 510 F.2d 78, 82 (10th Cir. 1975).

102 *for actions that are contrary to corporate policy: Dollar Steamship Co. v. United States,* 101 F.2d 638 (9th Cir. 1939); *United States v. Hilton Hotels Corp.,* 467 F.2d 1000 (9th Cir. 1972).

102 *even if the individual employees in question lacked the level of knowledge: United States v. Bank of New England,* 821 F.2d 844 (1st Cir. 1987).

102 *U.S. Sentencing Commission:* Comprehensive Crime Control Act of 1984, Pub. L. 98–473, 98 Stat. 1976.

102 *"guidelines" to ensure consistency:* United States Sentencing Commission, 2018 Guidelines Manual Annotated (Nov. 1, 2018).

102 *"credit" to corporations for "cooperating":* Supplementary Report on Sentencing Guidelines for Organizations (August 1991).

103 *Salomon Brothers reached the first non-prosecution agreement:* Press Release, U.S. Department of Justice, Department of Justice and SEC Enter $290 Million Settlement with Salomon Brothers in Treasury Securities Case (May 20, 1992).

103 *over the first decade after the sentencing guidelines were adopted:* James R. Copland & Isaac Gorodetski, Without Law or Limits: The Continued Growth of the Shadow Regulatory State (Manhattan Institute for Policy Research, Mar. 2015).

103 *Arthur Andersen LLP v. United States,* 544 U.S. 696 (2005); Daniel Diermeier et al., Arthur Andersen (C): The Collapse of Arthur Andersen (Kellogg Case Publishing, 2011).

104 *David Duncan:* "Charge Dropped Against Accountant David Duncan," *Houston Chronicle,* Dec. 15, 2005.

104 *KPMG:* Carrie Johnson, "Charge Against KPMG Dropped," *Washington Post,* Jan. 4, 2007.

104 *"debarred":* 48 C.F.R. § 9.406-2.

104 *"excluded":* 42 U.S.C. § 1320a-7.

104 *can lose government licenses:* 7 U.S.C. § 252.

104 *the year following Andersen's conviction:* Gibson-Dunn, 2019 Year-End Update on Corporate Non-Prosecution Agreements and Deferred Prosecution Agreements (Jan. 8, 2020).

105 *"off-label" uses:* James R. Copland & Paul Howard, Off-Label, Not Off-Limits: The FDA Needs to Create a Safe Harbor for Off-Label Drug Use (Manhattan Institute for Policy Research, Dec. 2012).

105 *GlaxoSmithKline:* Katie Thomas and Michael S. Schmidt, "Glaxo Agrees to Pay $3 Billion in Fraud Settlement," *N.Y. Times,* July 2, 2012.

105 *"unprecedented in both size and scope":* Press Release, U.S. Department of Justice, GlaxoSmithKline to Plead Guilty and Pay 3 Billion to Resolve Fraud Allegations and Failure to Report Safety Data (July 2, 2012).

105 *Pfizer:* Mark Ratner, "Pfizer Settles Largest Ever Fraud Suit for Off-Label Promotion," 27 *Nature Biotechnology* 961 (2009).

105 *Abbott:* Press Release, U.S. Department of Justice, Abbott Labs to Pay $1.5 Billion to Resolve Criminal & Civil Investigations of Off-label Promotion of Depakote (May 7, 2012).

106 *Eli Lilly:* Zosia Kmietowicz, "Eli Lilly Pays Record $1.4bn for Promoting Off-Label Use of Olanzapine," *BMJ,* Jan. 20, 2009.

106 *the Second Circuit overturned: United States v. Caronia,* 703 F.3d 149 (2nd Cir. 2012).

107 *Bank of America:* Press Release, U.S. Department of Justice, Bank of America to Pay $16.65 Billion in Historic Justice Department Settlement for Financial Fraud Leading up to and During the Financial Crisis (Aug. 21, 2014).

107 *JPMorgan Chase:* Deferred Prosecution Agreement, U.S. Department of Justice, RE: JPMorgan Chase Bank, N.A. (Jan. 6, 2014).

107 *Citigroup:* Press Release, U.S. Department of Justice, Justice Department, Federal and State Partners Secure Record $7 Billion Global Settlement with Citigroup for Misleading Investors About Securities Containing Toxic Mortgages (July 14, 2014).

108 *ACORN:* Charlie Savage, "Audit Finds Acorn Received Some Federal Grant Money Through Its Affiliates," *N.Y. Times,* Nov. 20, 2009.

108 *ACORN dissolved:* Brian Montopoli, "ACORN, Stung by Scandal, to be Dissolved," *CBS News,* Mar. 22, 2010.

108 *"power of the purse":* Kate Stith, "Congress' Power of the Purse," 97 *Yale Law Journal* 1343 (1988).

108 *billions to outside third-party groups:* Karen Freifeld & David Shepardson, "Justice Department halts settlements funding outside groups," *Reuters,* June 7, 2017.

108 *new attorney general, Jeff Sessions:* Press Release, U.S. Department of Justice, Attorney General Jeff Sessions Ends Third Party Settlement Practice, June 7, 2017.

109 Speedy Trial Act, Pub. L. 93–619, 88 Stat. 2080 (1974).

109 Foreign Corrupt Practices Act, Pub. L. 95–213, 91 Stat. 1494 (1977).

109 *companies that self-reported just such low-level corruption: See, e.g.,* Non-Prosecution Agreement, U.S. Department of Justice, Re: Ralph Lauren Corporation (Apr. 22, 2013); Non-Prosecution Agreement, U.S. Securities and Exchange Commission, Re: Ralph Lauren Corporation (Apr. 22, 2013). *See also* James R. Copland & Isaac Gorodetski, The Shadow Lengthens: The Continuing Threat of Regulation by Prosecution (Manhattan Institute for Policy Research, Feb. 2014).

109 *"safe harbor": United States v. Kay,* 359 F.3d 738 (5th Cir. 2004).

109 *doing business in U.S. dollars:* Paul Enzinna, The Foreign Corrupt Practices Act: Aggressive Enforcement and Lack of Judicial Review Create Uncertain Terrain for Businesses (Manhattan Institute for Policy Research, Jan. 2013).

109 *sending emails that were routed through: Ibid.*

110 *HSBC:* Press Release, U.S. Department of Justice, HSBC Holdings PLC and HSBC Bank USA N.A. Admit to Anti Money Laundering and Sanctions Violations, Forfeit $1.256 Billion in Deferred Prosecution Agreement (Dec. 11, 2012); Deferred Prosecution Agreement, U.S. Department of Justice, Re: HSBC Bank USA, N.A. and HSBC Holdings, PLC (Dec. 11, 2012).

110 Bank Secrecy Act, Pub. L. 91–508, 84 Stat. 1114 (1970).

110 *abandoned an array of business activities in Asia and Latin America:* Patrick Jenkins, "HSBC Mindful of Sharp Edges on Its 'Sword of Damocles,'" *Financial Times,* Sept. 16, 2013.

CHAPTER 7. LITIGATION NATION

111 *Kathie Reece-McNeill:* Marjie Lundstrom & Sam Stanton, "Room for Compromise," *Sacramento Bee,* Nov. 14, 2006.

111 *"frequent filers":* Manhattan Institute, *Trial Lawyers, Inc. Update: Wheels of Fortune* (Nov. 2014).

112 *"American Rule": See* U.S. Department of Justice, Civil Resource Manual, 220. Attorney's Fees (May 1998) ("The general rule in this country, the so-called 'American Rule' is that each party must pay its own attorney's fees."). *See also Alyeska Pipeline Service Co. v. Wilderness Society,* 421 U.S. 240 (1975) ("the general 'American rule' [is] that the prevailing party may not recover attorneys' fees as costs or otherwise").

112 *Reece-McNeill lost control of the property:* James Figueroa, "Monrovia's Aztec Hotel in Management Dispute of Historic Proportions," *Pasadena Star-News,* May 28, 2011.

112 *a "private" law system: See generally* John C. Coffee, Jr., "Understanding the Plaintiffs Attorney: The Implications of Economic Theory for Private Enforcement of Law Through Class and Derivative Actions," 86 *Columbia Law Review* 669 (1986). *Cf.* Susan Rose-Ackerman, "Regulation and the Law of Torts," 81 *American Economic Review* 54 (1991) ("Tort law is 'private' law. Regulation by statute is 'public' law.").

113 *only fifty-seven cents on every dollar:* Paul Hinton et al., Costs and Compensation of the U.S. Tort System (U.S. Chamber of Commerce Institute for Legal Reform, Oct. 2018).

113 *over $400 billion annually: Ibid.*

113 *almost a 10 percent bump up on regular taxation: See* Tax Policy Center Briefing Book (2018) (estimating total federal, state, and local taxation in the U.S. as 24 percent of gross domestic product).

113 *about three times the comparable litigation costs:* Paul Hinton et al., Costs and Compensation of the U.S. Tort System (U.S. Chamber of Commerce Institute for Legal Reform, Oct. 2018).

113 *Doctors and hospitals often order unnecessary... tests: See* Ronen Avraham & Max Schanzenbach, "The Impact of Tort Reform on Intensity of Treatment: Evidence from Heart Patients," 39 *Journal of Health Economics* 273 (2015) (finding "strong evidence that treatment intensity declines after a cap on non-economic damages"); Ronen Avraham et al., "The Impact of Tort Reform on Employer-Sponsored Health Insurance Premiums," 28 *Journal on Law, Economics & Organization* 657 (2012) (finding "direct evidence that tort reform reduces healthcare costs in aggregate").

113 *tugging on heartstrings:* Adam Liptak & Michael Moss, "The 2004 Campaign: The North Carolina Senator; In Trial Work, Edwards Left A Trademark," *N.Y. Times,* Jan. 31, 2004.

113 *tort litigation in the United States is unique: See generally The Liability Maze: The Impact of Liability Law on Safety and Innovation* (Peter W. Huber and Robert E. Litan, eds., 1991); Geoffrey C. Hazard, Jr., "Two Valuable Treatises on Civil Procedure," 37 *N.Y.U. Journal of International Law & Policy* 611, 620 (2005) ("The distinctive features of the U.S. system are jury trial, pretrial witness depositions, broad documents discovery, judges selected primarily on popular and political bases rather than professional standing, and the 'American rule' concerning litigation costs and expenses.")

114 *"trial by ordeal": See generally* Robert Bartlett, *Trial by Fire and Water* (1986).

114 *Antifederalist critics: The Anti-Federalist Papers and the Constitutional Convention Debates: The Clashes and Compromise that Gave Birth to Our Government* (Ralph Ketcham, ed., Signet, 15th ed., 2003).

114 *one of the rights lacking was protection for civil juries:* Essay of a Democratic Federalist, Oct. 17, 1787 (worrying about "the entire abolition of the trial by jury in civil cases"); Federal Farmer, Letters to the Republican, Nov. 8, 1787 ("The trial by jury is very important in another point of view. It is essential in every free country, that common people should have a part and share of influence, in the judicial as well as in the legislative department."); Remarks of Patrick Henry to the Virginia Ratifying Convention, June 20, 1788 (worrying that the Supreme Court "will, in its operation, destroy the trial by jury").

114 *"a valuable safeguard to liberty":* Alexander Hamilton, *The Federalist* no. 83 (1788).

114 *"for non-compliance with, or breach of the laws of the customs...":* Letter of Centinel (II), To the People of Pennsylvania, Oct. 24, 1787.

115 *revolved around debtor-creditor relations: See* Bruce H. Mann, *Republic of Debtors: Bankruptcy in the Age of American Independence* (2002); Charles W. Wolfram,

"The Constitutional History of the Seventh Amendment," 57 *Minnesota Law Review* 639, 704 (1973).

115 *overturn hosts of tort-reform laws enacted by the states' elected legislatures:* Victor E. Schwartz & Leah Lorber, "Judicial Nullification of Civil Justice Reform Violates the Fundamental Federal Constitutional Principle of Separation of Powers: How to Restore the Right Balance," 32 *Rutgers Law Journal* 907 (2001) (summarizing cases); Victor E. Schwartz, "Judicial Nullification of Tort Reform: Ignoring History, Logic, and Fundamentals of Constitutional Law," 31 *Seton Hall Law Review* 688 (2001).

115 *The ability to sue the manufacturer of a product: See MacPherson v. Buick Motor Co.,* 111 N.E. 1050 (N.Y. 1916).

115 *a plaintiff in that era had to be alive to pursue a claim: See Baker v. Bolton,* 170 Eng. Rep. 1033 (K.B. 1808); *Carey v. Berkshire Railroad,* 55 Mass. 475 (1848).

115 *neither defendants nor plaintiffs...could appear as witnesses in court: See* John Henry Wigmore, *A Treatise on the Anglo-American System of Evidence in Trials at Common Law: Including the Statutes and Judicial Decisions of All Jurisdictions of the United States and Canada* § 575 (Little, Brown, 3rd ed., 1940).

115 *as "rudimentary":* John H. Langbein et al., *History of the Common Law: The Development of Anglo-American Legal Institutions* (Aspen 2009), at 888.

116 *"not a proper subject for a law book":* Book Notice, 5 *American Law Review* 340 (1871).

116 *tort litigation increased...to 40.9 percent in 1910: See* John Fabian Witt, *The Accidental Republic: Crippled Workingmen, Destitute Widows, and the Remaking of American Law* (2004), at 59.

116 *Gibbons v. Pepper,* 1 Ld. Raym. 38 (K.B. 1695).

116 *cases in Boston...had jumped 6,500 percent: See* John Fabian Witt, *The Accidental Republic: Crippled Workingmen, Destitute Widows, and the Remaking of American Law* (2004) (citing increase from "a dozen or so" such suits in Boston to "over 800" in twenty years).

116 *"blocking...calendars with a mass of litigation...":* Elon R. Brown, Some Faults of Legal Administration, Report to the New York State Bar, Dec. 14, 1907 (*available at* New York State Bar Association, Proceedings of the Thirty-First Annual Meeting Held at New York, January 21, 24–25, 1908, and Charter Constitution By-laws, List of Members Officers and Committees and Reports for 1907, at 136).

116 *city of Boston grew just under 55 percent from 1880 to 1900:* U.S. Census records show the population of Boston increasing from 362,839 in 1880 to 560,892 in 1900.

116 *lighted explosive squibs: Scott v. Shepherd,* 96 Eng. Rep. 525 (K.B. 1773).

116 *runaway hot-air balloons: Guille v. Swan,* 19 Johns. 381 (N.Y. Sup. Ct. 1822).

116 *"trespass on the case": See Reynolds v. Clarke,* 92 Eng. Rep. 410 (K.B. 1726) (defining distinction between tort of "trespass" and that of "trespass on the case"); *Williams v. Holland,* 131 Eng. Rep. 848 (C.P. 1833) (allowing suit in case when defendant negligent).

117 *unless the defendant was "negligent": Brown v. Kendall,* 60 Mass. 292 (1850)

(holding that "if it appears that the defendant... unintentionally hit and hurt the plaintiff" then the plaintiff can only recover if establishing the defendant's "fault, negligence, carelessness, or want of prudence"). *Cf.* Gary Schwartz, "Tort Law and the Economy in Nineteenth-Century America: A Reinterpretation," 90 *Yale Law Journal* 1717 (1981) (arguing that negligence principle was already well-established in early American cases before industrial transformation).

117 *forbade plaintiffs from recovering... if... negligent: Butterfield v. Forrester*, 103 Eng. Rep. 926 (K.B. 1809); *Brown v. Kendall*, 60 Mass. 292 (1850).

117 *Farwell v. Boston & Worcester Railroad Corporation*, 4 Met. 49 (Mass. 1842).

117 *allowed recovery for "wrongful death"*: Richard A. Epstein, *Cases & Materials on Torts* (Aspen, 7th ed., 2000), at 904 ("Today no state has any general limitation for damages in wrongful death actions, although a number of states retain special limitations for certain types of cases."). *See also* John Fabian Witt, "From Loss of Services to Loss of Support: The Wrongful Death Statutes, the Origins of Modern Tort Law, and the Making of the Nineteenth-Century Family," 25 *Law & Social Inquiry* 717 (2000).

117 *By the late nineteenth century, courts had also relaxed the bar: See* Wex S. Malone, "The Genesis of Wrongful Death," 17 *Stanford Law Review* 1043 (1965).

117 *beginning with Massachusetts in 1887: See, e.g.*, Massachusetts Employer's Liability Act, 1887 Mass. Acts 566.

117 Federal Employers' Liability Act, Pub. L. 60–149, 35 Stat. 65 (1908).

117 *these workplaces were very dangerous: See* John Fabian Witt, *The Accidental Republic: Crippled Workingmen, Destitute Widows, and the Remaking of American Law* (2004) (finding that "railroad worker death rates were 314 per 100,000 workers per year" and that "coal miner fatality rates were comparable").

117 *workers' compensation laws: See* Richard A. Epstein, "The Historical Origins and Economic Structure of the Workers' Compensation Act," 16 *Georgia Law Review* 775 (1982).

118 Simon Greenleaf, *Treatise on the Law of Evidence* (1842).

118 *Connecticut was the first... most other states soon followed:* George Fisher, "The Jury's Rise as Lie Detector," 107 *Yale Law Journal* 575, 669 (1997).

118 *a new code of civil procedure: See* Stephen N. Subrin, "David Dudley Field and the Field Code: A Historical Analysis of an Earlier Procedural Vision," 6 *Law & Historical Review* 311 (1988).

118 *early sixteenth century... rule that the loser in litigation paid:* 23 Henry VIII, c. 15 (1531) (allowing successful defendants to recover fees in a variety of causes of action, including trespass and case).

118 *Limiting legal costs to the level of damages: See* Arthur L. Goodhart, "Costs," 38 *Yale Law Journal* 849 (1929).

118 *Requiring courts to approve fees:* 2 Geo. II, c. 23 (1729).

119 *published fee schedules: See, e.g.*, John Palmer, The Attorney and Agent's New Table of Costs (London 1812).

119 *in the new American republic:* John Leubsdorf, "Toward a History of the American Rule on Attorney Fee Recovery," 47 *Law & Contemporary Problems* 9 (1984).

119 *"The losing party, ought…"*: First Report of the Commissioners on Practice and Pleading, Code of Procedure (N.Y. 1848), at 206–07.

119 *"champerty"*: *Black's Law Dictionary* 262 (9th ed. 2009); Statute of Westminster I (1275).

119 *"a vice"*: Lester Brickman, *Lawyer Barons: What Their Contingency Fees Really Cost America* (2012), at 20.

120 Walter Olson, *The Litigation Explosion: What Happened When America Unleashed the Lawsuit* (1991).

120 *Major's Executor v. Gibson*, 1 Pat. & H. 48 (Va. Spec. Ct. App. 1855).

121 *a plaintiffs' lawyer may have to do very little work*: See, e.g., Lester Brickman, "Contingent Fees without Contingencies: Hamlet without the Prince of Denmark?," 37 *UCLA Law Review* 29 (1989).

121 *"nuisance suits"*: Marie Gryphon (Newhouse), Greater Justice, Lower Cost: How a "Loser Pays" Rule Would Improve the American Legal System (Manhattan Institute for Policy Research 2008).

122 *"a pattern of unethical behavior…"*: *Molski v. Mandarin Touch Restaurant*, 359 F.Supp.2d 924, at 934 (C.D. Cal. 2005), *aff'd sub nom. Molski v. Evergreen Dynasty Corp.*, 500 F.3d 1047 (9th Cir. 2007), *cert. denied*, 129 S. Ct. 594 (2008).

122 *Frankovich built a multimillion-dollar practice*: See Tom McNichol, "Targeting ADA Violators," *California Lawyer* (Jan. 2012); Carol Lloyd, "ADA Accessibility Lawsuits Causing Headaches for Small Business Owners," *SFGate*, June 13, 2008; Ron Russell, "Wheelchairs of Fortune: Attorney Tom Frankovich and His Disabled Clients Sue Small Businesses to Make Them Accessible—And Make Millions," *SF Weekly*, July 25, 2007.

122 *"rapacity" of these agents*: "The Solicitation of Accident Cases," 63 *American Law Review* 135, 140 (1929); Peter Karsten, "Enabling the Poor to Have Their Day in Court: The Sanctioning of Enabling the Poor to Have Their Day in Court: The Sanctioning of Contingency Fee Contracts, a History to 1940," 47 *DePaul Law Review* 231 (1998).

CHAPTER 8. LAWYERS WITHOUT CLIENTS

125 *advertising campaign*: Peter Rugg, "The 'Five-Dollar Footlong' Subway Song Was the Greatest Jingle of our Time," *Inverse*, Feb. 5, 2016.

125 *In re Subway Footlong Sandwich Marketing & Sales Practices Litig.*, 869 F.3d 551 (7th Cir. 2017).

125 *Class action lawsuits*: See Fed. R. Civ. Pro. 23.

125 *"I have the greatest practice of law…"*: Neil Weinberg, "Shakedown Street," *Forbes*, Feb. 11, 2008.

126 *Three in ten class action lawsuits*: Carlton Fields & Jorden Burt, The 2015 Carlton Fields Jorden Burt Class Action Survey: Best Practices in Reducing Cost and Managing Risk in Class Action Litigation.

126 *54 percent faced a class action lawsuit*: Ibid.

127 *Supreme Court defined the procedural rules in equity cases*: See Act of May 8, 1792, Pub. L. 1–36, 1 Stat. 275.

127 *American Bar Association*: See, e.g., Report of the Committee on Uniformity of Procedure and Comparative Law, ABA Report No. 19 (1896).

127 *David Dudley Field: See* Daun Van Ee, *David Dudley Field and the Reconstruction of the Law* (1986). *Cf.* David Dudley Field, "Codification in the United States," 1 *Juridical Review* 18 (1889).

127 *William Howard Taft: See* Stephen N. Subrin, "How Equity Conquered Common Law: The Federal Rules of Civil Procedure in Historical Perspective," 135 *University of Pennsylvania Law Review* 909 (1987). *See also* William Howard Taft, "Possible and Needed Reforms in Administration of Justice in Federal Courts: Better Results Would be Secured by Measures Permitting Judicial Team-Work in Handling Business of District Court, Increasing Discretionary Appellate Jurisdiction of Supreme Court, Abolishing Separate Courts of Law and Equity, and Providing for Reconciling Two Forms of Procedure by Rules of Court," 8 *A.B.A. Journal* 601 (1922).

128 Rules Enabling Act, Pub. L. 73–415, 48 Stat. 1064 (1934).

128 *"Clark was impressed…"*: Subrin, 135 *University of Pennsylvania Law Review* at 966.

128 *"furnish the substantial model…"*: Charles E. Clark & James W. Moore, "A New Federal Civil Procedure I: The Background," 44 *Yale Law Journal* 387, 434–35 (1935).

129 *"true nature of the controversy"*: Edson R. Sunderland, "Improving the Administration of Civil Justice," *in* 167 *Annals of the American Academy of Political and Social Science* 60 (1933).

129 *Up to that point, legal rights of discovery were extremely limited: See* Stephen N. Subrin, "Fishing Expeditions Allowed: The Historical Background of the 1938 Federal Discovery Rules," 39 *Boston College Law Review* 691 (1998).

129 *completely unprecedented, as he freely admitted:* Proceedings of Advisory Committee on Uniform Rules of Civil Procedure for the District Court of the United States (Nov. 17, 1935) (Sunderland: "There is no very well settled system which will embrace the various objects that I have sought to attain…. [One] Rule would be supported by experience in one State or jurisdiction, and another by experience in another State or jurisdiction. You cannot find justification for all of these anywhere. It is strictly an eclectic provision which I have brought in here…. It was an entirely new subject matter. [T]he Equity Rules or Federal statutes… have only in the very slightest degree provided for what I tried to do.").

129 *final draft even dispensed with:* Subrin, 39 *Boston College Law Review* at 729 ("except for the demand on the opponent to list documents and things, every major discovery device previously known anywhere in the United States, and all of those drafted by Sunderland, ended up in the final draft, and in many ways, with fewer constraining devices than he had originally drafted or than were contemplated by the Advisory Committee during its deliberations").

129 *"be inadmissible at trial"*: Fed. R. Civ. P. 26, 329 U.S. 854 (1946).

129 *"fishing expeditions"*: Mr. Wickersham's Memorandum Regarding Professor Sunderland's Draft of Rules 28 to 42, Regarding Depositions, Discovery and Summary Judgments (Dec. 18, 1935), in Records of the U.S. Judicial Conference, at CI-1921-25—CI-1921-27; Proceedings of the Meeting of the Advisor, Committee on Rules For Civil Procedure of the Supreme Court of the United States (Feb. 22, 1936), in Records of the U.S. Judicial Conference, at CI-209-59-61.

129 *"notice"…"plain statement":* Fed. R. Civ. P. 8.

130 *"notice pleading":* Swierkiewicz v. Sorema, 534 U.S. 506 (2002) ("The liberal notice pleading of Rule 8(a) is the starting point of a simplified pleading system, which was adopted to focus litigation on the merits of a claim."); Charles E. Clark, "The New Federal Rules of Civil Procedure: The Last Phase— Underlying Philosophy Embodied in Some of the Basic Provisions of the New Procedure," 23 *A. B. A. Journal* 976 (1937) ("Experience has shown…that we cannot expect the proof of the case to be made through the pleadings, and that such proof is really not their function. We can expect a general statement distinguishing the case from all others, so that the manner and form of trial and remedy expected are clear, and so that a permanent judgment will result.").

130 *constitutes as much as 90 percent of all litigation expenses:* Judicial Conference Adopts Rules Changes, Confronts Projected Budget Shortfalls, *Third Branch*, Sept. 1999 ("Discovery represents 50 percent of the litigation costs in the average case and up to 90 percent of the litigation costs in cases in which it is actively used.").

130 *essentially every study finds:* See, e.g., H.R. Rep. No. 104-369, at 37 (1995) (Conf. Rep.) (finding that "discovery cost accounts for roughly 80 percent of total litigation costs in securities fraud cases"); John H. Beisner, "Discovering a Better Way: The Need for Effective Civil Litigation Reform," 60 *Duke Law Journal* 547 (2010) (collecting evidence that "discovery costs now comprise between 50 and 90 percent of the total litigation costs in a case").

130 *a pile 137 miles high:* In re Intel Corp. Microprocessor Antitrust Litigation, 496 F. Supp. 2d 404 (D. Del. 2007).

130 *Bell Atlantic Corp. v. Twombly*, 550 U.S. 544 (2007).

131 *"bill of peace":* See Thomas D. Rowe, Jr., "A Distant Mirror: The Bill of Peace in Early American Mass Torts and Its Implications for Modern Class Actions," 39 *Arizona Law Review* 711 (1997).

131 *"so numerous as to make it impracticable…":* See James Love Hopkins, *The New Federal Equity Rules* 231 (1930); John G Harkins, Jr., "Federal Rule 23—The Early Years," 39 *Arizona Law Review* 705 (1997).

132 *three categories of class action lawsuit:* See James William Moore & Marcus Cohn, "Federal Class Actions-Jurisdiction and Effect of Judgment," 32 *Illinois Law Review* 555 (1938).

132 *Union Carbide & Carbon Corp. v. Nisley*, 300 F.2d 561 (10th Cir. 1962), *cert. dismissed*, 371 U.S. 801 (1963).

132 *as they took a ferry to Kaplan's summer home in Martha's Vineyard:* Arthur R. Miller, "Some Very Personal Reflections on the Rules, Rulemaking, and Reporters," 46 *University of Michigan Journal of Law Reform* 651, 652 (2013).

132 *Bill Lerach:* Neil Weinberg, "Shakedown Street," *Forbes*, Feb. 11, 2008.

133 *"to get at the cases where a class action promises important advantages…":* Benjamin Kaplan, "Continuing Work of the Civil Committee: 1966 Amendments of the Federal Rules of Civil Procedure (I)," 81 *Harvard Law Review* 356 (1967).

133 *Guaranty Trust Co. v. York*, 326 U.S. 99 (1945).

134 *Among the thirty-eight states: See* Joanna M. Shepherd-Bailey, Consumer Protection Acts or Consumer Litigation Acts? A Historical and Empirical Examination of State CPAs (ATR Foundation 2014), at 18.

134 *increased 119 percent from 2000 to 2007:* Searle Civil Justice Institute, State Consumer Protection Acts: An Empirical Investigation of Private Litigation (2009), at 20.

134 *a dissatisfied customer sued a dry cleaner: Pearson v. Chung,* No. 07-CV-872 (D.C. App. Dec. 18, 2008).

134 *Pop-Tarts, Froot Loops, and Fruit Roll-Ups:* ATR Foundation, State Consumer Protection Laws: Unhinged—It Is Time to Restore Sanity to the Litigation (2013).

134 *On a single day in October 2016: Trentham v. Continental Mills, Inc.,* No. 16PH-CV01563 (Mo. Cir. Ct., Phelps County, filed Oct. 25, 2016); *Skornia v. General Mills, Inc.,* No. 16AC-CC00452 (Mo. Cir. Ct., Cole County, filed Oct. 25, 2016); *Bratton v. The Hershey Co.,* No. 16AC-CC00451 (Mo. Cir. Ct., Cole County, filed Oct. 25, 2016); *Melton v. Kellogg Co.,* No. 16PH-CV01564 (Mo. Cir. Ct., Phelps County, filed Oct. 25, 2016); *Grisham v. The Kroger Co.,* No. 16PH-CV01562 (Mo. Cir. Ct., Phelps County, filed Oct. 25, 2016); *Skornia v. Mars, Inc.,* No. 16AC-CC00453 (Mo. Cir. Ct., Cole County, filed Oct. 25, 2016); *White v. Mott's LLP,* No. 16PH-CV01566 (Mo. Cir. Ct., Phelps County, filed Oct. 25, 2016); *Hawkins v. Pearson Candy Co.,* No. 16PH-CV01565 (Mo. Cir. Ct., Phelps County, filed Oct. 25, 2016); *Bratton v. Tootsie Roll Indus., Inc.,* No. 16AC-CC00454 (Mo. Cir. Ct., Cole County, filed Oct. 25, 2016).

134 *a consumer-fraud action is not precluded by accurate package labeling: Murphy v. Stonewall Kitchen, LLC,* 503 S.W.3d 308, 312 (Mo. Ct. App. 2016).

135 *More than a quarter of class action lawsuits today:* 2019 Carlton Fields Class Action Survey Best Practices in Reducing Cost and Managing Risk in Class Action Litigation, at 4 ("Labor and employment cases remain the most common type of action, accounting for 28.7 percent of matters and 26.1 percent of spending.")

135 *Pension-related lawsuits:* Nick Thornton, "ERISA Settlements Top $1 Billion," *BenefitsPro,* Jan. 6, 2015.

135 *typically pay out more than $1 billion annually: See, e.g.,* Andrew J. Pincus, Securities and M&A Litigation, in Lawsuit Ecosystem II: New Trends, Targets and Players (U.S. Chamber Institute for Legal Reform, Dec. 2014), at 39.

135 Securities Act of 1933, Pub. L. 73–22, 48 Stat. 74.

135 Securities Exchange Act of 1934, Pub. L. 73–291, 48 Stat. 881.

135 *it said nothing about private lawsuits:* Matthew J. Barrett, "Does SEC Rule 10-b5 Provide an Implied Private Right of Action for Aiding and Abetting Securities Fraud?," ?, 1993-1994 *Preview U.S. Supreme Court Cases* 109 (1993-1994) ("Neither Section 10(b) nor Rule 10b-5 . . . create an express private right of action for violations.").

135 *federal courts saw "implied" rights to sue in the statutes: Kardon v. National Gypsum Co.,* 69 F. Supp. 512 (E.D. Pa. 1946); *Superintendent of Ins. v. Bankers Life & Casualty Co.,* 404 U.S. 6, 13 n.9 (1971).

135 *courts deemed it possible to bring a class action lawsuit: See, e.g., Peil v. Speiser,* 806 F.2d 1154 (3rd Cir. 1986).

135 *In 1988, the U.S. Supreme Court agreed.*: Basic Inc. v. Levinson, 485 U.S. 224 (1988).

135 *roots going back to the legal code of the sixth-century Byzantine emperor Justinian:* Martin H. Redish et al., "Cy Pres Relief and the Pathologies of the Modern Class Action: A Normative and Empirical Analysis," 62 *Florida Law Review* 617 (2010).

136 *the Massachusetts Supreme Judicial Court permitted trustees:* See Jackson v. *Phillips*, 96 Mass. (14 Allen) 539 (1867).

136 *a law student at the University of Chicago:* Stewart R. Shepherd, "Damage Distribution in Class Actions: The *Cy Pres* Remedy," 39 *University of Chicago Law Review* 448 (1971).

136 *judges began rubber-stamping:* See, e.g., Miller v. Steinbach, 268 F. Supp. 255 (S.D.N.Y. 1974).

136 *The average* cy pres *award has totaled more than $5.8 million:* See Redish et al., 62 *Florida Law Review* at 658.

136 Ohio Lawyers Give Back, Dworken & Bernstein, LPA (website screenshot on file with author).

136 *"fair, reasonable, and adequate":* Fed. R. Civ. Pro. 23(e)(B)(2).

137 *"bet the company":* Carlton Fields & Jorden Burt, The 2015 Carlton Fields Jorden Burt Class Action Survey: Best Practices in Reducing Cost and Managing Risk in Class Action Litigation, at 15.

137 *Wal-Mart Stores, Inc. v. Dukes*, 564 U.S. 338 (2011).

137 *AT&T Mobility v. Concepcion*, 563 U.S. 333 (2011).

137 Federal Arbitration Act, Pub. L. 68–401, 43 Stat. 883 (1925).

137 *There's some evidence that the savings:* Ted Frank, Class Actions, Arbitration, and Consumer Rights: Why Concepcion is a Pro-Consumer Decision (Manhattan Institute Legal Policy Report, Feb. 2013).

137 *Sympathetic news outlets presented horror stories:* See, e.g., Jessica Silver-Greenberg & Robert Gebeloff, "Arbitration Everywhere, Stacking the Deck of Justice," *N.Y. Times*, Oct. 31, 2015.

138 *A 1995 bill:* Private Securities Litigation Reform Act of 1995, Pub. L. 104–67, 109 Stat. 737.

138 *A 2005 bill:* Class Action Fairness Act of 2005, Pub. L. 109–2, 119 Stat. 4.

CHAPTER 9. BOTTOM-UP REGULATORS

139 *Stella Liebeck v. McDonald's Restaurants*, No. D-202 CV-93-02419, 1995 WL 360309 (Bernalillo County, N.M. Dist. Ct. 1994).

139 *The verdict quickly circulated on the press wires:* See, e.g., Andrea Gerlin, "A Matter of Degree: How a Jury Decided that a Coffee Spill Is Worth $2.9 Million," *Wall Street Journal*, Sept. 1, 1994. See also Mark B. Greenlee, "*Kramer v. Java World*: Images, Issues, and Idols in the Debate Over Tort Reform," 26 *Capital University Law Review* 701 (1997).

139 *"the poster child of excessive lawsuits":* Lauren Pearle, "I'm Being Sued for WHAT?," *ABC News*, May 2, 2007.

139 *Seinfeld* (West-Shapiro Productions & Castle Rock Entertainment, episodes 112, 113 (1995)).

140 *But Morgan had spun a fable: See* James M. Dedman IV, *"Liebeck v. McDonalds Restaurants*: The Original Coffee Product Liability Case," *DRI Today*, Apr. 15, 2014. Ted Frank, "Questions for Susan Saladoff about 'Hot Coffee,'" http://www.pointoflaw.com/archives/2011/10/questions-for-s.php (Oct. 31, 2011); U.S. Chamber of Commerce Institute for Legal Reform, http://www.hotcoffeetruth.com/.

140 *consistent with guidelines from the National Coffee Association:* National Coffee Association, How to Brew Coffee: The NCA Guide to Brewing Essentials.

140 *the* Los Angeles Times *did its own investigation: See* Denise Gellene, "A Hot Tip for Coffee Lovers: Most Retailers Prefer to Make It Scalding," *L.A. Times*, Sept. 16, 1994.

140 *involving a "public duty": See, e.g., Trout v. Watkins Livery & Undertaking Co.*, 130 S.W. 136 (Mo. App. 1910).

141 *A horse-drawn mail coach in Chester County: Winterbottom w. Wright*, 152 Eng. Rep. 402 (Exch. 1842).

141 *MacPherson v. Buick Motor Co.*, 111 N.E. 1050 (N.Y. 1916).

142 *Professor George Priest...studied accident rates: See* George Priest, "Products Liability Law and the Accident Rate," *in Liability: Perspectives and Policy* (Robert Litan & Clifford Winston, eds., 1988).

142 *Escola v. Coca-Cola Bottling Co.*, 150 P.2d 436 (Cal. 1944).

142 *doctrine of* res ipsa loquitur: *Byrne v. Boadle*, 159 Eng. Rep. 299 (Exch. 1863).

143 *"If there is one legal decision upon which Ralph Nader built...":* Paul A. Offit, *The Cutter Incident: How America's First Polio Vaccine Led to the Growing Vaccine Crisis* (2005).

143 *According to a poll of the membership:* Jeffrey Robert White, "Top 10 in Torts: Evolution in the Common Law," *Trial*, July 1996.

143 *Greenman v. Yuba Power Products*, 377 P.2d 897 (Cal. 1963).

143 *argued for strict product liability in his 1941 torts treatise: See* William L. Prosser, *Prosser on Torts*, 688-89 (1941).

143 Restatement (Second) of Torts § 402A (1965).

143 *"the cream of the American legal establishment":* N. E. H. Hull, "Restatement and Reform: A New Perspective on the Origins of the American Law Institute," 8 *Law and History Review* 55 (1990).

143 *"unmanageable"..."minimize, if not dispense with":* John Fleming, "The Restatements and Codification," 2 *Jewish Law Annual* 108, 111–12 (1979).

144 *Among those taking this view was Professor Clark:* G. Edward White, "The American Law Institute and the Triumph of Modernist Jurisprudence," 15 *Law & History Review* 1 (1997).

144 *"Good butter is not unreasonably dangerous...":* Restatement (Second) of Torts § 402A (comment (i)).

145 *Ted Frank, a lawyer who is critical of the Liebeck verdict:* Ted Frank, "Zippers, Penis Injuries, and McDonald's Hot Coffee Redux," *PointofLaw.com*, April 24, 2013.

145 *There's Something About Mary* (Michael Steinberg et al. 1998).

146 *"…Good thing this is Canada!"*: Walter Olson, "Good Thing This Is Canada!," *Cato at Liberty Blog*, Apr. 22, 2013.

146 *"wacky warning labels"*: Bob Dorigo Jones, *Remove Child Before Folding: The 101 Stupidest, Silliest and Wackiest Warning Labels Ever* (2007).

147 *"a man of scarlet silk-lined suits…"*: John Fabian Witt, "The Political Economy of Pain," in *Making Legal History: Essays in Honor of William E. Nelson* (2013).

147 *"King of Torts"*: Robert Wallace, "The King of Torts," *Life*, Oct. 18, 1954.

147 Melvin M. Belli, *Modern Trials* (1954).

148 *"demonstrative evidence"*: John Fabian Witt, "The Political Economy of Pain."

148 *"by having a client bare her chest…"*: Jim Herron Zamora, "'King of Torts' Belli Dead at 88," *S.F. Chronicle*, July 10, 1996.

149 *"rather be governed by the first two thousand people…"*: William F. Buckley, *Meet the Press*, Oct. 17, 1965.

150 *BMW of North America, Inc. v. Gore*, 517 U.S. 559 (1996).

150 *State Farm Mutual Automobile Insurance Co. v. Campbell*, 538 U.S. 408 (2003).

150 *Hot Coffee* (Susan Saladoff, 2011).

CHAPTER 10. THE LAWSUIT INDUSTRY

151 *In re Silica Products Liability Litigation*, MDL No. 1553 (S.D. Tex. 2005).

151 For more on Judge Jack and silica litigation, see *Trial Lawyers, Inc.: Asbestos* (Manhattan Institute for Policy Research, 2008).

151 *"double-dip"*: See Daniel Fisher, "Double-Dippers," *Forbes*, Sept. 4, 2006.

152 *For years, rumors abounded*: Lester Brickman, "The Asbestos Litigation Crisis: Is There a Need for an Administrative Alternative?," 13 *Cardozo Law Review* 1819 (1992); Jonathan D. Glater, "Suits on Silica Being Compared to Asbestos Cases," *N.Y. Times*, Sept. 6, 2003.

152 *junior college dropout*: Transcript of Direct Testimony of Heath Mason, Daubert Hearing, *In re Silica Products Liability Litigation*, MDL No. 1553.

152 *"diagnosed more than 800 patients"*: *In re Silica Products Liability Litigation*, MDL No. 1553.

153 *"B readers"*: Lester Brickman, "Disparities between Asbestosis and Silicosis Claims Generated by Litigation Screenings and Clinical Studies," 29 *Cardozo Law Review* 513 (2007).

153 *Johns Hopkins radiologists*: Joseph N. Gitlin et al., "Comparison of 'B' Readers' Interpretations of Chest Radiographs for Asbestos Related Changes," 11 *Academic Radiology* 843 (2004).

153 *Baron & Budd prepared a memorandum*: Walter Olson, Creative Deposition (Manhattan Institute for Policy Research, May 1998); Walter Olson, "Thanks for the Memories," *Reason*, June 1998.

154 *protected millions of American schoolchildren*: The ABCs of Asbestos in Schools (EPA 2003).

154 *Millions of Americans would be employed*: Jock McCulloch, "Beyond the Factory Gates: Asbestos and Health in Twentieth Century America," 32 *Journal of Health Politics, Policy & Law* 543 (2007).

154 *"urgent need for more qualified extensive investigation"*: "Earliest Known Facts About Asbestos," The National Rural Bioethics Project, http://www.umt. edu/bioethics/libbyhealth/introduction/background/asbestos_timeline.aspx (accessed June 14, 2020).

154 W. E. Cooke, "Fibrosis of the Lungs Due to the Inhalation of Asbestos Dust," 2 *British Medical Journal* 140 (1924).

154 *"until better data are available"*: Barry L. Castleman, *Asbestos: Medical and Legal Aspects* (5th ed. 2005).

154 *Dr. Irving Selikoff: See* Peter Huber, "The Risk Race," *The New Republic*, Feb. 3, 1986.

154 *Borel v. Fibreboard Paper Products Corp.*, 493 F.2d 1076 (5th Cir. 1973).

154 *25,000 asbestos cases*: Michelle J. White, Asbestos Litigation: The Problem of Forum Shopping and Procedural Innovations and Potential Solutions, Transcript, Manhattan Institute Lecture, Sept. 14, 2005.

154 *By 1981…By 1982…*: Barry L. Castleman, *Asbestos: Medical and Legal Aspects* (5th ed. 2005).

155 *the lawsuits kept piling on*: Stephen J. Carroll et al., *Asbestos Litigation* (Rand Institute for Civil Justice 2005).

155 *"two to three new claims"*: Lester Brickman, "The Asbestos Litigation Crisis: Is There a Need for an Administrative Alternative?," 13 *Cardozo Law Review* 1819 (1992).

155 *an estimated 322,000 claims*: American Academy of Actuaries' Mass Torts Subcommittee, Overview of Asbestos Claims Issues and Trends (Aug. 2007), at 32.

155 *may hit $265 billion: Ibid.*, at Executive Summary.

155 *"mesothelioma treatment options": Trial Lawyers, Inc.: Asbestos* (Manhattan Institute for Policy Research, 2008), at 9 (citing Google ad-search data).

155 *"the most expensive recruitment process…"*: Recorded telephone interview with Lester Brickman, Oct. 10, 2006.

155 *Bates v. State Bar of Arizona*, 433 U.S. 350 (1977).

155 *"Never stir up litigation…."*: Abraham Lincoln, Notes for a Law Lecture, July 1, 1850.

156 *mass tort law firms were five of the top six legal advertisers*: Ken Goldstein & Dhavan V. Shah, Trial Lawyer Marketing: Broadcast, Search and Social Strategies, U.S. Chamber Institute for Legal Reform (Oct. 2015).

156 *Nine of the top ten: Ibid.*

156 *"junk science": See, e.g.*, Peter W. Huber & Kenneth R. Foster, eds., *Phantom Risk: Scientific Inference and the Law* (1993).

156 *400,000 women registered*: Barry Meier, "3 Implant Companies Offer New Settlement," *N.Y. Times*, Oct. 3, 1995.

156 *lost a $7 million verdict*: David E. Bernstein, Breast Implants: A Study in Phantom Risks (Manhattan Institute for Policy Research (Apr. 1995)).

156 *20,000 women sued Dow*: Marcia Angell, Science on Trial: Medical Evidence and the Law in the Breast Implant Case (Manhattan Institute for Policy Research, Aug. 1996).

156 *no scientific basis:* David E. Bernstein, Breast Implants: A Study in Phantom Risks (Manhattan Institute for Policy Research, Apr. 1995).

156 *"breast implants were associated…":* Ibid.; *see, e.g.,* Hans Berkel, "Breast Augmentation: A Risk Factor for Breast Cancer?," 326 *New England Journal of Medicine* 1649 (1992).

157 *"no association between implants…":* Sherine E. Gabriel et al., "Risk of Connective-Tissue Diseases and Other Disorders after Breast Implantation," 330 *New England Journal of Medicine* 1697 (1994).

157 *one in four of all expectant mothers:* L. B. Holmes, "Teratogen Update: Bendectin," 27 *Teratology* 277 (Apr. 1983).

157 *aborted their unborn children:* David E. Bernstein, "Learning the Wrong Lessons from 'An American Tragedy': A Critique of the Berger-Twerski Informed Choice Proposal, George Mason Law & Economics Research Paper No. 05-15 31 (Aug. 2005).

157 *By 1983, the drug's manufacturer:* Michael D. Stovsky, Comment, "Product Liability Barriers to the Commercialization of Biotechnology: Improving the Competitiveness of the U.S. Biotechnology Industry," 6 *High Technology Law Journal* 363, 372 (Fall 1991).

157 *studies examining over 130,000 patients: See Daubert v. Merrell Dow Pharmaceuticals, Inc.,* 509 U.S. 579 (1993).

157 *The percentage of pregnant women hospitalized… The incidence of birth defects:* See Paolo Mazzotta et al., "Attitudes, Management and Consequences of Nausea and Vomiting of Pregnancy in the United States and Canada," 70 *International Journal of Gynecology & Obstetrics* 359 (2000).

157 *The drug had remained on the European market:* Melanie Ornstein et al., "Bendectin/Diclectin for Morning Sickness: A Canadian Follow-Up of an American Tragedy," 9 *Reproductive Toxicology* 1 (1995).

158 *courts loosened these restrictions: See, e.g., Givens v. Lederle,* 556 F.2d 1341 (5th Cir. 1977); *Reyes v. Wyeth Laboratories,* 498 F.2d 1264 (5th Cir. 1974); *Davis v. Wyeth Laboratories,* 399 F.2d 121 (9th Cir. 1968).

158 *The manufacturer of the diphtheria, pertussis, and tetanus (DPT) vaccine:* Thomas F. Burke, *Lawyers, Lawsuits, and Legal Rights: The Battle over Litigation in American Society* (2002).

158 *The first, against a manufacturer of the DPT vaccine: Toner v. Lederle,* 828 F.2d 510 (1987).

158 *The second, against a manufacturer of the Sabin polio vaccine: Johnson v. American Cyanamid Co.,* 718 P.2d 1318 (Kan. 1986).

158 *Claims multiplied:* Statement of Robert B. Johnson, president, Lederle Laboratories Division, American Cyanamid, House Subcommittee on Health and the Environment, Vaccine Injury Compensation, Sept. 10, 1984.

158 *they exited the market:* U.S. General Accounting Office, Childhood Vaccines: Ensuring an Adequate Supply Poses Continuing Challenges (Sept. 2002).

158 *remaining manufacturers raised prices:* Thomas F. Burke, *Lawyers, Lawsuits, and Legal Rights,* at 150.

159 *the Centers for Disease Control, fearing a shortage:* Testimony of James Mason,

director, Division of Immunization of the Center for Prevention Services, Centers for Disease Control, Public Health Service, House Subcommittee on Health and the Environment, Vaccine Injury Compensation, Dec. 19, 1984.

159 *Vaccine Injury Compensation Program: See* National Childhood Vaccine Injury Act of 1986, Pub. L. 99–2660, 100 Stat. 3755.

159 *research into new vaccines began to proliferate:* Thomas F. Burke, *Lawyers, Lawsuits, and Legal Rights,* at 161–63.

159 *two attorneys...formed the National Association of Claimants' Compensation Attorneys:* American Association for Justice, "An Expanded History of ATLA/ AAJ," https://www.justice.org/who-we-are/mission-history/expanded-history-association-trial-lawyers-america-atla%C2%AEamerican (July 1980) (accessed June 14, 2020).

160 *"took his family on a three-month, 10,800-mile tour...":* John Fabian Witt, *Patriots and Cosmopolitans: Hidden Histories of American Law* (2007), at 241.

160 *renamed itself the American Trial Lawyers Association:* John Fabian Witt, "First, Rename All the Lawyers," *N.Y. Times,* Oct. 24, 2006.

160 The Justice League of America first appeared in DC Comics in 1960. *See The Brave and the Bold* No. 28 (March 1960).

160 *Senator Dick Durbin: See* "Dick Durbin," OpenSecrets.org Database.

160 *trial lawyers heavily fund the campaigns: See generally Trial Lawyers, Inc. K Street: A Report on the Litigation Lobby 2010* (Manhattan Institute for Policy Research).

161 *befriended Roscoe Pound:* John Fabian Witt, *Patriots and Cosmopolitans: Hidden Histories of American Law,* at 246–52.

161 *penned a glowing introduction to Belli's book* Modern Trials: Melvin M. Belli, *Modern Trials* (1954).

161 *"the 1960–63 Corvair compares favorably...":* "U. S. Car Study Disputes Nader On Corvair Safety Charge in '65," *N.Y. Times,* July 21, 1972.

162 *"overtly, covertly..."/ "a huge percentage of what he raises":* Peter Brimelow & Leslie Spencer, "The Plaintiff Attorneys' Great Honey Rush," *Forbes,* Oct 16, 1989.

162 *"perfect source":* John Stossel, *Give Me a Break: How I Exposed Hucksters, Cheats, and Scam Artists and Became the Scourge of the Liberal Media* (2004), at 158.

163 *"If the Bar is to become merely a method of making money...":* Samuel J. Tilden, Speech to the Bar Association of the City of New York, Feb. 1, 1870), *in* Letters and Literary Memorials of Samuel J. Tilden (2014).

163 *kill off other contraceptives:* Marc Arkin, "Products Liability and the Threat to Contraception," (Manhattan Institute for Policy Research, Feb. 1999).

CHAPTER 11. MAGIC JURISDICTIONS

165 *on May 19, 2020:* Johnson & Johnson, Press Release, Johnson & Johnson Consumer Health Announces Discontinuation of Talc-based Johnson's Baby Powder in U.S. and Canada (May 19, 2020); Tiffany Hsu & Roni Caryn Rabin, "Johnson & Johnson to End Talc-Based Baby Powder Sales in North America," *N.Y. Times,* May 19, 2020.

165 *"case cohort" studies:* American Cancer Society Medical and Editorial Content Team, "Talcum Powder and Cancer," American Cancer Society (Nov. 13, 2017).

165 *doctors…published a prospective-cohort study:* Katie M. O'Brien et al., "Association of Powder Use in the Genital Area with Risk of Ovarian Cancer," 323 *JAMA* 49 (2020).

166 *Centers for Disease Control do not list talc:* CDC, What Are the Risk Factors for Ovarian Cancer?, Aug. 15, 2019.

166 *FDA has consistently found insufficient evidence: See Carl v. Johnson & Johnson,* ATL-L-6546-14 & ALT-L-6540-14 (N.J. Super. Ct. Law Div., Sep. 2, 2016), at 23–26.

166 *most juries…have not found that the product was carcinogenic:* Nate Robson and Alaina Lancaster, "Johnson & Johnson Gets Second Talc Defense Win in a Week," *Law.com*, Dec. 21, 2019.

166 *In 2016 and 2017, four different juries:* Reuters, "After $195 Million in Talc Verdicts in St. Louis, J&J Looks for a New Court," *St. Louis Post-Dispatch* (Nov. 7, 2016); Joel Currier, "$110 Million Verdict for Plaintiff in Fifth Talcum Powder Cancer Trial in St. Louis," St. Louis Post-Dispatch (May 5, 2017).

166 *the average person in the St. Louis area remembered:* Cary Silverman, Bad for Your Health Lawsuit Advertising Implications and Solutions (U.S. Chamber Institute for Legal Reform, Oct. 2017), at 42; *see Hogans v. Johnson & Johnson,* Case No. 1422-CC09012-01, Motion for Change in Venue, July 28, 2016.

166 *among the 2,100 lawsuits nationwide: See* American Tort Reform Foundation, City of St. Louis, Missouri, *Judicial Hellholes 2016–2017.*

167 *Missouri appellate courts knocked out the four big St. Louis verdicts: See* Amanda Bronstad, "Missouri Appeals Court Weighs J&J's Bid to Reverse $4.7B Talc Verdict," *Law.com*, Apr. 24, 2020; Carl O'Donnell, "Missouri Appeals Court Overturns $110 Million Johnson & Johnson Talc Verdict," *St. Louis Post-Dispatch*, Oct. 15, 2019.

167 *small number of tests…have detected some asbestos: See* Chad Terhune & Lisa Girion, "U.S. Government Experts, Industry Spar Over Asbestos Testing in Talc," *Reuters*, Feb. 4, 2020.

167 *may have been false positives: See* Berkeley Lovelace Jr., "Johnson & Johnson Shares Rise after It Says No Signs of Asbestos Found in Baby Powder after Testing," *CNBC*, Oct. 29, 2019.

167 Judiciary Act of 1789, Pub. L. 1–20, 1 Stat. 73.

168 *Swift v. Tyson*, 41 U.S. 1 (1842).

168 *"a transcendental body of law…": Black & White Taxicab & Transfer Co. v. Brown & Yellow Taxicab & Transfer Co.,* 276 U.S. 518 (1928) (Holmes, J., dissenting).

169 *Erie Railroad Co. v. Tompkins,* 304 U.S. 64 (1938).

170 *Pennoyer v. Neff,* 95 U.S. 714 (1878).

170 *International Shoe Co. v. State of Washington,* 326 U.S. 310 (1945).

171 *"[W]hat I call the 'magic jurisdiction'…'":* Richard Scruggs, Asbestos for Lunch, Prudential Securities Financial Research and Regulatory Conference (May 9, 2002), *in Industry Commentary* (Prudential Securities, Inc., New York, June 11, 2002).

171 *"As long as I am allowed to redistribute wealth…":* Richard Neely, *The Product Liability Mess: How Business Can Be Rescued from the Politics of State Courts* (1988), at 4.

172 Eric Helland & Alex Tabarrok, "The Effect of Electoral Institutions on Tort Awards," 4 *American Law and Economics Review* 341 (2002).

172 *"fraudulent joinder":* Matthew C. Monahan, "De-Frauding the System: Sham Plaintiffs and the Fraudulent Joinder Doctrine," 110 *Michigan Law Review* 1341 (2012).

172 *"complete" diversity: See* 28 U.S.C. § 1332.

172 *Jefferson County, Mississippi:* John H. Beisner et al., One Small Step for a County Court... One Giant Calamity for the National Legal System (Manhattan Institute for Policy Research, Apr. 2003).

172 *"ground zero for the largest legal attack...":* Mark Ballard, "Mississippi Becomes a Mecca for Tort Suits," *National Law Journal,* Apr. 30, 2001.

172 *"No small business should have to endure...":* Testimony by Hilda Bankston, Senate Committee on the Judiciary, July 31, 2002.

173 *"vote with their feet": See* Ilya Somin, *Free to Move: Foot Voting, Migration, and Political Freedom* (2020).

173 *a state that permits excessive recoveries: See, e.g.,* Alastair MacLennan et al., "Who Will Deliver Our Grandchildren?," 294 *JAMA* 1688 (Oct. 5, 2005); Randall R. Bovbjerg & Anna Bartow, Project on Medical Liability in Pennsylvania, Understanding Pennsylvania's Medical Malpractice Crisis (2003); Marie McCullough, "No Deliveries Due at Mercy Fitzgerald," *Philadelphia Inquirer,* June 3, 2003; Dan Mangan, "Contractions – 2nd Midwife Birth Center to Close," *N.Y. Post,* Aug. 12, 2003; Joseph B. Treater, "Rise in Insurance Forces Hospitals to Shutter Wards," *N.Y. Times,* Aug. 25, 2002; Steven Malanga, "Tort Turns Toxic," *City Journal,* Autumn 2002.

173 *"race to the bottom":* William L. Cary, "Federalism and Corporate Law: Reflections upon Delaware," 83 *Yale Law Journal* 663 (1974) (calling Delaware "both the sponsor and the victim of a system contributing to the deterioration of corporation standards" and decrying corporate law's "race for the bottom, with Delaware in the lead"). Cary's article is a classic exponent of a "race to the bottom" in federalism; but it was probably wrong. *See* Ralph K. Winter, "State Law, Shareholder Protection, and the Theory of the Corporation," 6 *Journal of Legal Studies* 251 (1977); Winter, "The 'Race for the Top' Revisited: A Comment on Eisenberg," 89 *Columbia Law Review* 1526 (1989). *See also* Roberta Romano, "Law as a Product: Some Pieces of the Incorporation Puzzle," 1 *Journal of Law, Economics, and Organization* 225 (1985) (finding the "race to the top" hypothesis more supported than the "race to the bottom" hypothesis, in the corporate-law context, in empirical testing).

174 *"misbranding":* Price v. Philip Morris, Inc., 848 N.E.2d 1 (Ill. 2005).

174 *a federal regulatory scheme: See* Cipollone v. Liggett Group, Inc., 505 U.S. 504 (1992).

174 *a 1990s-era settlement: See* Robert A. Levy, "The Great Tobacco Robbery," *Legal Times,* Feb. 1, 1999.

174 *lawsuits in East St. Louis exploded:* John H. Beisner & Jessica Davidson Miller, "They're Making a Federal Case out of It... in State Court," 25 *Harvard Journal of Law & Public Policy* 1 (2001).

174 *Four in five involved:* John H. Beisner & Jessica Davidson Miller, Class Action Magnet Courts: The Allure Intensifies (Manhattan Institute for Policy

Research, July 2002), at 1 ("Of the 43 [class action] cases brought [in Madison County] in 2001, 33 (77 percent) sought to certify multistate or nationwide classes, and all of the 13 cases filed in the first two months of 2002 (100 percent) sought approval of classes that crossed state boundaries.").

174 *the State Farm insurance company: Avery v. State Farm Mutual Auto Insurance Co.*, 835 N.E.2d 801 (Ill. 2005); *Gridley v. State Farm Mutual Auto Insurance Co.*, 840 N.E.2d 269 (Ill. 2005).

174 Class Action Fairness Act of 2005, Pub. L. 109–2, 119 Stat. 4.

175 *Wyeth v. Levine*, 555 U.S. 555 (2009).

175 *fills in the "gaps"*: Robert E. Keeton, "Statutes, Gaps, and Values in Tort Law," 44 *Journal of Air Law & Commerce* 1 (1978); Aaron S. Kesselheim & Jerry Avorn, "The Role of Litigation in Defining Drug Risks," 297 *JAMA* 308 (2007).

175 *safety isn't unidirectional: See* Paul Howard & James R. Copland, In the Wake of *Wyeth v. Levine*: Making the Case for FDA Preemption and Administrative Compensation (Manhattan Institute for Policy Research, March 2009) (discussing two types of error: "'Type I' error, or approving a drug as reasonably safe that later turns out to be unsafe or ineffective; and "Type II" error, or withholding from the public a drug that is reasonably safe and effective."); John E. Calfee et al., "Supreme Court Amicus Brief Regarding Wyeth v. Levine" (June 3, 2008) ("Because the harmful side-effects of the drug may be highly visible, a Type I error can and often does lead to impassioned criticism of the agency. On the other hand, a Type II error—the failure to permit marketing of a drug that would in fact provide benefits in excess of harms—is typically known only to the relatively few persons who are intimately involved in developing the drug and are largely hidden from patients and the larger medical community.").

175 *risk of overwarning:* Howard & Copland, In the Wake of *Wyeth v. Levine* ("strong doctor and patient reactions to litigation highlight the risks of overwarning, one reason that the FDA maintains tight control over drug labeling decisions"). *See also* Washington Legal Foundation & American College of Emergency Physicians (2008), *amicus curiae* supporting petitioner in *Wyeth v. Levine*.

CHAPTER 12. ACT LOCALLY, SUE GLOBALLY

177 *"We are fighting for our lives…"*: Mayor Bill de Blasio (@NYCMayor), Tweet, Jan 10, 2018.

177 *"We never make the mistake…"*: Transcript: Mayor de Blasio Announces First-in-the-Nation Goal to Divest from Fossil Fuels, Jan. 10, 2018.

177 *similar litigation initiated:* Press Release, City Attorney of San Francisco, San Francisco and Oakland Sue Top Five Oil and Gas Companies Over Costs of Climate Change, Sept. 19, 2017.

177 *as far back as 2004: American Electric Power Co. v. Connecticut*, 564 U.S. 410 (2011).

178 *the 1990s-era suits by state governments: See* Michael I. Krauss, *Fire & Smoke: Government, Lawsuits, and the Rule of Law* (2000).

179 *"Sheriff of Wall Street"*: Rebecca Leung, "The Sheriff of Wall Street," *CBS News*, May 23, 2003.

179 Martin Act, N.Y. General Business Law, article 23-A, §§ 352–353. For a discussion of the Martin Act and its evolution, see James R. Copland, "What's Wrong—and Right—with New York Criminal Law," *in One Nation Under Arrest* (Paul Rosenzweig & Brian W. Walsh eds., 2010).

179 *against Marsh & McLennan:* See *People of the State of New York v. Marsh & McLennan Companies, Inc., and Marsh, Inc.,* No. 04403342 (Sup. Ct., New York County, Oct. 14, 2004). *See also* James R. Copland, Regulation by Prosecution: The Problems with Treating Corporations as Criminals (Manhattan Institute for Policy Research, Dec. 2010), at 19 & n.94.

180 *with Greenberg out the door:* Andrew G. Simpson, "Greenberg: AIG's Risky Subprime Activity 'Exploded' After He Left," *Insurance Journal* (Oct. 10, 2008).

180 *AIG issued as many credit-default swaps:* Lynnley Browning, "AIG's House of Cards," *Portfolio.com* (Sept. 28, 2008).

180 *the federal government pumped $185 billion:* See William K. Sjostrom, Jr., "The AIG Bailout," 66 *Washington & Lee Law Review* 943 (2009).

180 *Mike Moore:* See Walter K. Olson, *The Rule of Lawyers* (2003), at 30–45.

180 *U.S. Supreme Court held:* See *Cipollone v. Liggett Group, Inc.,* 505 U.S. 504 (1992).

180 Public Health Cigarette Smoking Act of 1969, Pub. L. 91–222, 84 Stat. 87.

181 *State excise taxes on cigarettes exceeded the cost:* Congressional Budget Office, Federal Taxation of Tobacco, Alcoholic Beverages, and Fuels (Washington: U.S. Government Printing Office, 1990). *See also* William Manning et al., "The Taxes of Sin: Do Smokers and Drinkers Pay Their Way?," 261 *JAMA* 1604 (1989); W. Kip Viscusi, "Cigarette Taxation and the Social Consequences of Smoking," *in Tax Policy and the Economy,* (J. Poterba, ed., 1995).

182 *$233 million each:* See Robert A. Levy, "The Great Tobacco Robbery," *Legal Times,* Feb. 1, 1999.

182 *states that joined the action late:* Walter Olson, "Puff, the Magic Settlement," *Reason,* Jan. 2000; Susan Beck, "Trophy Fees," *American Lawyer,* Dec. 2, 2002.

182 *Carla Stovall:* Olson, *The Rule of Lawyers,* at 40–44.

182 *Dan Morales:* Pete Slover, "Morales' Plea May Help Friend's Fraud Case, Attorney Says," *Dallas Morning News,* July 19, 2003; John Moritz, "Dan Morales Indicted in Tobacco Case," *Star-Telegram,* Mar. 6, 2003; Associated Press, "Former Attorney General Dan Morales Indicted on Fraud Charges," *AP Wires,* Mar. 7, 2003.

182 *Scruggs himself:* Richard Fausset, "Bribery Case Brings Down Legal Legend," *L.A. Times,* Mar. 15, 2008.

182 *"unique" affair:* Richard Scruggs, Comments, Regulation by Litigation: The New Wave of Government-Sponsored Litigation (Manhattan Institute for Policy Research, June 22, 1999), at 33 ("Tobacco is unique.").

183 *City of New Orleans:* Brian J. Siebel, "City Lawsuits Against the Gun Industry: A Roadmap for Reforming Gun Industry Misconduct," 18 *Saint Louis University Public Law Review* 247 (1999).

183 *Chicago filed its own gun lawsuit: Ibid.*

183 *David Kairys:* Timothy D. Lytton, *Suing the Gun Industry: A Battle at the Crossroads of Gun Control and Mass Torts* (2005), at 132; Temple University Beasley School of Law: David Kairys: Professor Emeritus (last accessed

June 18, 2020) ("In 1996, he conceived the city lawsuits against handgun manufacturers, and his public-nuisance theory has become the major basis for a range of challenges to corporate practices that endanger public health or safety.").

183 *"houses of ill repute"*: Larry Howard Whiteaker, *Seduction, Prostitution, and Moral Reform in New York, 1830–1860* (1997).

184 *"footnote" in the law of tort*: Louise A. Halper, "Untangling the Nuisance Knot," 26 *B.C. Environmental Affairs Law Review* 89 (1998).

184 Restatement (First) of Torts (1939).

184 *"death by a thousand cuts"*: Walter K. Olson, *The Rule of Lawyers* (2003), at 127.

184 *"firearms that by their design are unreasonably attractive to criminals"*: Michael I. Krauss & Robert A. Levy, "So Sue Them, Sue Them," *Weekly Standard*, May 24, 1999.

184 Protection of Lawful Commerce in Arms Act, Pub. L. 109–92, 119 Stat. 2095 (2005).

184 *the Connecticut state judge handling the case*: Dave Altimari, "State Supreme Court overturns lower court ruling, says Sandy Hook families can sue gun manufacturer Remington," *Hartford Courant*, May 14, 2019.

184 *the Connecticut Supreme Court disagreed*: Soto v. Bushmaster Firearms International, LLC, 202 A.3d 262 (Conn. 2019).

184 *filed for bankruptcy*: "Remington Files for Bankruptcy Amid a 'Trump Slump' in Gun Sales," *Bloomberg*, Mar. 26, 2018.

185 *Troy King*: ATRA, Beyond Reproach? Fostering Integrity and Public Trust in the Offices of State Attorneys Generals (2010).

185 *took in more than $20 million*: Ibid.

185 *Alabama Supreme Court*: John O'Brien, "Alabama SC Consolidates Two of King's AWP Lawsuits," *Legal Newsline.com*, Oct. 4 2010.

185 *24,000 American municipalities*: Eric Heisig, "Cities, Counties Across U.S. Should Unite to Negotiate Opioid Lawsuits Against Drug Companies, Attorneys Say," *Cleveland Plain-Dealer*, June 14, 2019; *In Re: National Prescription Opiate Litigation*, MDL 2804 Case No.: 1:17-md-2804, Plaintiffs' Renewed and Amended Notice of Motion and Motion for Certification of Rule 23(B)(3) Cities/Counties Negotiation Class (July 9, 2019).

185 *Purdue Pharma, the maker of Oxycontin*: Martha Bebinger, "Purdue Pharma Agrees To $270 Million Opioid Settlement with Oklahoma," *NPR*, Mar. 26, 2019.

185 *opioid drugs…have real social costs*: CDC, Understanding the Epidemic, Mar. 19, 2019 (citing Atlanta, GA: CDC, Wide-ranging online data for epidemiologic research (WONDER), National Center for Health Statistics (2020).).

186 *as high as $1 trillion*: Altarum, Economic Toll of Opioid Crisis in U.S. Exceeded $1 Trillion Since 2001 (Feb. 13, 2018).

186 *filed in 2001 by West Virginia against Purdue Pharma*: Chris Dickerson, "AG's Practices Questioned by House Committee," *West Virginia Record*, Feb. 2, 2007; West Virginia Citizens Against Lawsuit Abuse, Special Report: Flaunting [sic] Laws You Are Charged to Protect—A Critical Look at Fourteen Years in the Office of Attorney General Darrell McGraw (June 2007).

186 *hold more than $3 trillion:* Pew Charitable Trusts and Laura and John Arnold Foundation, State Public Pension Investments Shift over Last 30 Years (June 2014).

186 *brought in more than $100 billion in settlements:* Cornerstone Research, Securities Class Action Settlements: 2019 Review and Analysis, at 1 & fig. 1.

186 *nearly half of all such lawsuits: Ibid.*

186 *a pair of federal laws:* Securities Act of 1933, Pub. L. 73–22, 48 Stat. 74; Securities Exchange Act of 1934, Pub. L. 73–291, 48 Stat. 881.

186 *Rule 10b-5:* 17 CFR § 240.10b-5.

186 *a "private" enforcement mechanism enabling plaintiffs:* Matthew J. Barrett, "Does SEC Rule 10-b5 Provide an Implied Private Right of Action for Aiding and Abetting Securities Fraud?," 1993–1994 *Preview U.S. Supreme Court Cases* 109 (1993–1994) ("Neither Section 10(b) nor Rule 10b-5…create an express private right of action for violations.").

186 *a federal district court in Pennsylvania "found" an "implied" right to sue: Kardon v. National Gypsum Co.,* 69 F. Supp. 512 (E.D. Pa. 1946).

187 *"now established": Superintendent of Ins. v. Bankers Life & Casualty Co.,* 404 U.S. 6, 13 n.9 (1971).

187 *Basic Inc. v. Levinson,* 485 U.S. 224 (1988).

187 *"legal extortion":* H. Rep. 104-50, Part I (1995).

187 *"'squeegee boys' who…":* "Judge Compares Milberg Weiss Case to the Squeegee Man," *N.Y. Lawyer,* Apr. 18, 2002.

187 Private Securities Litigation Reform Act of 1995, Pub. L. 104–67, 109 Stat. 737.

188 *"race to the courthouse door":* "New York Attorney Sentenced in Kickback Scheme," *N.Y. Times,* Nov. 1, 2008 ("Before the Private Securities Litigation Reform Act of 1995, shareholder lawyers seeking to lead class action lawsuits against companies whose stock dropped needed simply to be the first to file. Law firms had stables of clients who owned shares in huge companies considered susceptible to such litigation.").

188 *Securities cases with public pension funds as lead plaintiffs:* Steven Skalak & Daniel Dooley, PricewaterhouseCoopers, Securities Litigation Update: The Pension Fund Factor (2003).

188 *Teachers' Retirement System of Louisiana: Cf.* Daniel Fisher & Neil Weinberg, "The Class Action Industrial Complex," *Forbes,* Sept. 20, 2004 ("Even some pension fund officials admit the lawyers, not the funds, guide this class action assault. 'We don't go to them, they come to us. They're simply looking for lead plaintiffs,' says William Reeves, general counsel to Teachers' Retirement System of Louisiana, a Bernstein Litowitz client in eight recent suits.").

188 *"professional plaintiff":* Editorial, "Pension Fund Shenanigans," *Wall Street Journal,* Aug. 20, 2004. The Private Securities Litigation Reform Act bars "professional plaintiffs" from serving as lead counsels in federal securities class action litigation. *See* 15 U.S.C. § 78u-4(a)(3)(B)(vi).

188 *Alan Hevesi: See* Editorial, "Milberg, Weiss, Hevesi, & Spitzer," *N.Y. Sun,* June 30, 2005; Editorial, "Hevesi vs. the Holdouts," *N.Y. Sun,* July 26, 2004; Editorial, "Hevesi's Haul," *N.Y. Sun,* May 14, 2004.

188 *Jim Hood:* Staff Report, "Hopkins Accuses Hood of Pay for Play—And Provides

His Evidence," *Y'all Politics*, Sept. 26, 2007; FollowTheMoney, Mississippi Attorney General Jim Hood.

189 *Ohio Democratic Party: See* Mark Maremont et al., "Trial Lawyers Contribute, Shareholder Suits Follow," *Wall Street Journal*, Feb 3, 2010; FollowTheMoney, Kaplan, Fox & Kilsheimer; FollowTheMoney, Bernstein, Litowitz, Berger & Grossmann.

CHAPTER 13. STOCK MARKET POLITICS

191 *more than $200 billion in assets: See* New York City Comptroller Scott M. Stringer, Pension / Investment Management: Asset Allocation, https://comptroller.nyc.gov/services/financial-matters/pension/asset-allocation/ (showing collective funds of $205.83 billion (as of Apr 2020)).

191 *a majority of shareholders at most of the targeted companies supported his shareholder proposal: See* James R. Copland, Proxy Monitor 2015: Finding 2— Mid-Season Report (Manhattan Institute for Policy Research).

192 *"ratchet up the pressure…":* Press Release, Comptroller Stringer, NYC Pension Funds Launch National Boardroom Accountability Project Campaign— Version 2.0, Sept. 8, 2017.

192 *suggests that diversity matters: See, e.g.,* Byron J. Hollowell, "Examining the Relationship Between Diversity and Firm Performance," 2 *Journal of Diversity Management* 51 (2007).

192 *empirical scholarship suggests: See, e.g.,* Daniel T. Greene et al., "Do Board Gender Quotas Affect Firm Value? Evidence from California Senate Bill No. 826," 60 *Journal of Corporate Finance* (Feb. 2020).

192 *"green" investing portfolios tend to underperform: See, e.g.,* Daniel R. Fischel, Fossil Fuel Divestment: A Costly and Ineffective Investment Strategy (2015) ("As of December 31, 2014, the $100 invested in the optimal risk-adjusted portfolio would have grown to about $14,600, whereas the $100 invested in the divested portfolio would have grown to only about $11,200, indicating a loss of 23 percent due to divestment.").

192 *a report by an outside consultant calculated:* Wilshire Associates, Comprehensive Divestment Analysis (Sept. 25, 2015), Presented to the CalPERS Investment Committee Meeting, Oct. 19, 2015.

194 *"tulip mania": See* Charles Mackay, *Extraordinary Popular Delusions and the Madness of Crowds* (1841).

194 *South Sea bubble:* Helen J. Paul, *The South Sea Bubble: An Economic History of Its Origins and Consequences* (2011).

194 Adam Smith, *An Inquiry into the Nature and Causes of the Wealth of Nations* (1776) (arguing that for the directors of a joint-stock company, "being the managers rather of other people's money than of their own, it cannot well be expected, that they should watch over it with the same anxious vigilance with which the partners in a private copartnery frequently watch over their own").

194 *only a handful of corporate charters had been granted: See* Richard Sylla, "How the American Corporation Evolved Over Two Centuries," 158 *Proceedings of the American Philosophical Society* 354 (2014) (finding that there were only seven incorporated businesses in the thirteen colonies and only 28 as of 1790);

Samuel Williston, "History of the Law of Business Corporations Before 1800," 2 *Harvard Law Review* 149 (1888) (discovering only one joint-stock business corporation before 1776 and five more by 1787; but almost 350 by 1801). *See generally* Ronald E. Seavoy, *The Origins of the American Business Corporation, 1784–1855: Broadening the Concept of Public Service During Industrialization* (1982); James W. Hurst, *The Legitimacy of the Business Corporation in the Law of the United States, 1780–1970* (1970).

194 *statutes allowing incorporation without special legislation: See* Susan Pace Hamill, "From Special Privilege to General Utility: A Continuation of Willard Hurst's Study of Corporations," 49 *American University Law Review* 81 (1999).

194 *Supreme Court ruled that a state could not prevent companies: See Paul v. Virginia,* 75 U.S. (8 Wall.) 168 (1869). *See also* Henry N. Butler, "Nineteenth Century Jurisdictional Competition in the Granting of Corporate Privileges," 14 *Journal of Legal Studies* 129 (1985).

194 *New Jersey liberalized its corporation laws: See* Christopher Grandy, "New Jersey Corporate Chartermongering, 1875–1929," 49 *Journal of Economic History* 677 (1989).

194 *Delaware followed suit: See* Maurice A. Hartnett, III, "Delaware's Charters and Prior Constitutions," *in The Delaware Constitution of 1897* (Randy J. Holland et al. eds., 1997), at 21; Mark J. Roe, "Delaware's Competition," 117 *Harvard Law Review* 588, 609 (2003). *See also* William Ripley, *Wall Street and Main Street* (1927).

195 *Two-thirds of large corporations:* Delaware Division of Corporations, About the Division of Corporations, https://corp.delaware.gov/aboutagency/ ("More than 66% of the Fortune 500 have chosen Delaware as their legal home.").

195 *Daniel Drew:* Bouck White, *The Book of Daniel Drew: A Glimpse of the Fisk-Gould-Tweed Regime from the Inside* (1996).

195 *"blue sky" law:* Jonathan R. Macey & Geoffrey P. Miller, "Origin of the Blue Sky Laws," 70 *Texas Law Review* 347 (1991); "Joe Dolley Is After the Blue Sky Merchants," *Topeka Capital-Journal,* Dec. 22, 1910.

195 *"to stop the sale of stock in fly-by-night concerns…": Hall v. Geiger-Jones Co.,* 242 U.S. 539 (1917).

195 *every state but Nevada:* Carol J. Simon, "The Effect of the 1933 Securities Act on Investor Information and the Performance of New Issues," 79 *American Economic Review* 295 (1989).

196 *"new deal for the American people":* Franklin Delano Roosevelt, Acceptance Speech to the 1932 Democratic Convention.

196 Securities Act of 1933, Pub. L. 73–22, 48 Stat. 74.

196 Securities Exchange Act of 1934, Pub. L. 73–291, 48 Stat. 881.

196 *central premise of the new federal regulatory regime: See, e.g., J.I. Case Co. v. Borak,* 377 U.S. 426, 431 (1964).

196 *"genius" of American corporate law:* Roberta Romano, *The Genius of American Corporate Law* (1993).

196 *the* substantive *allocation of power between shareholders and directors: See, e.g., CTS Corp. v. Dynamics Corp.,* 481 U.S. 69, 89 (1987) ("No principle of corporation law and practice is more firmly established than a State's authority

to regulate domestic corporations, including the authority to define the voting rights of shareholders."); *Santa Fe Industries, Inc. v. Green*, 430 U.S. 462, 479 (1977) ("Corporations are creatures of state law, and investors commit their funds to corporate directors on the understanding that, except where federal law expressly requires certain responsibilities of directors with respect to stockholders, state law will govern the internal affairs of the corporation.").

196 *43 percent of world stock market valuation:* Ron Surz, "U.S. Stock Market Is Biggest & Most Expensive In World, But U.S. Economy Is Not The Most Productive," *Nasdaq*, Apr. 2, 2018.

197 *"shareholder proposal rule":* See Securities Exchange Act of 1934 Release No. 3347 (Dec. 18,1942), 7 Fed. Reg. 10,653 (1942).

197 *"proxy statements": See* 17 C.F.R. § 240.14a-101.

197 *"at the time when he considers…":* Hearings on H.R. 1498, H.R. 1821, and H.R. 2019, Before the House Committee on Interstate and Foreign Commerce, 78th Cong., 1st Sess., pt. 2, at 174–75 (1943).

197 *"the proxy a real instrument…": Ibid.*

197 *appears nowhere in the statutory text: See* Pub. L. No. 73–291, Ch. 404, 48 Stat. 881 (1934).

197 *only mentioned briefly by a single House representative:* H.R. Rep. No. 1383, 73d Cong., 2d Sess. 14 (1934).

197 *was meant to ensure corporate disclosures: See Borak*, 377 U.S. at 431 ("The purpose of § 14(a) is to prevent management or others from obtaining authorization for corporate action by means of deceptive or inadequate disclosure in proxy solicitation.").

198 *"proper subjects of stockholders' action…":* Securities Exchange Act Release No. 3638 (Jan. 3, 1945), 11 Fed. Reg. 10,995 (1946).

198 *"permit stockholders to obtain the consensus…": Ibid.*

198 *the D.C. Circuit Court of Appeals sent the case back to the agency: See Medical Committee for Human Rights v. Securities and Exchange Commission*, 432 F.2d 659, 663 (D.C. Cir. 1970), *vacated as moot*, 404 U.S. 403 (1972).

198 *"interpretive release":* Adoption of Amendments Relating to Proposals by Security Holders, Exchange Act Release No. 12,999, 41 Fed. Reg. 52,994, 52,997–98 (1976).

199 *PETA:* Tonya Garcia, "PETA Takes a Stake in Levi's to Press for Vegan Leather Patches," *MarketWatch*, Mar. 22, 2019.

199 *recently proposed a modified rule:* Procedural Requirements and Resubmission Thresholds under Exchange Act Rule 14a-8, File No. S7-23-19.

199 *between 43 percent and 56 percent:* Data for *Fortune* 250 companies, from the Manhattan Institute's *ProxyMonitor.org* database.

200 *"plan assets to support…":* Department of Labor, Office of the Inspector General, Proxy-Voting May Not Be Solely for the Economic Benefit of Retirement Plans (2011).

200 *targets of union-organizing campaigns: See* James R. Copland & Margaret M. O'Keefe, Proxy Monitor: A Report on Corporate Governance and Shareholder Activism 2015 (Manhattan Institute for Policy Research), at 19.

200 *give disproportionately to Republican political candidates: See* James R. Copland & Margaret M. O'Keefe, Proxy Monitor: A Report on Corporate Governance and Shareholder Activism 2014 (Manhattan Institute for Policy Research), at 2.

200 *Evelyn Davis: See* James R. Copland et al., Proxy Monitor: A Report on Corporate Governance and Shareholder Activism 2012 (Manhattan Institute for Policy Research), at 9.

200 *"cajoled the nation's business titans…":* Amy Feldman, "Fighting the Fat Cats for Decades, Evelyn Davis Has Grilled Biz Bigwigs in Outrageous Fashion," *N.Y. Daily News*, May 24, 1998.

201 *in 1878, three years after: See* John Iekel, "Retirement: An Historical Perspective," *ASPPA*, Sept. 21, 2018.

201 *In 1894…in 1911:* National Conference on Public Employee Retirement Systems, The Evolution of Public Pension Plans: Past, Present and Future (2008).

201 Civil Service Retirement Act, Pub. L. 66–215, 41 Stat. 614 (1920).

201 *fallen woefully short in recent years: See, e.g.,* James R. Copland & Steven Malanga, Safeguarding Public-Pension Systems: A Governance-Based Approach (Manhattan Institute for Policy Research, March 2016).

202 *evidence suggests anything but:* Tracie Woidtke, Public Pension Fund Activism and Firm Value (Manhattan Institute for Policy Research, Sept. 2015).

CHAPTER 14. RESTORING THE REPUBLIC

203 *appropriations allocated by the First Congress: See* House Committee on Appropriations: History, https://appropriations.house.gov/about/history ("In 1789, a single appropriations bill, totaling $639,000, supported all of our young nation's needs.").

203 *the federal budget for 2019:* Congressional Budget Office, The Federal Budget in 2019: An Infographic, Apr. 15, 2020.

204 *looking to the original understanding of the American constitutional design: See, e.g.,* Keith E. Whittington, *Constitutional Interpretation: Textual Meaning, Original Intent, and Judicial Review* (1999); Jack N. Rakove, *Original Meanings: Politics and Ideas in the Making of the Constitution* (1997); Alexander Bickel, *The Morality of Consent* (1975).

206 *contract-law doctrine* caveat emptor: The Latin maxim *caveat emptor* means, "Let the buyer take care." Bryan A. Garner, *Black's Law Dictionary* (11th ed., 2019) ("This maxim summarizes the rule that the purchaser of an article must examine, judge, and test it for himself, being bound to discover any obvious defects or imperfections.").

207 Federal Food, Drug, and Cosmetic Act, Pub. L. 75–717, 52 Stat. 1040 (1938).

207 Drug Amendments Act of 1962, Pub. L. 87–781, 76 Stat. 780.

207 Medical Device Amendments of 1976, Pub. L. 94–295, 90 Stat. 539.

208 *Professor Richard Epstein, my colleague: See* Richard A. Epstein, *The Dubious Morality of Administrative Law* (2019).

208 *Gundy v. United States,* 588 U.S. ____, 139 S. Ct. 2116 (2019).

208 *Wayman v. Southard,* 23 U.S. (10 Wheat.) 1 (1825).

208 Regulations from the Executive In Need of Scrutiny (REINS) Act, S. 92, 119th Cong. (2019).

209 *"trade negotiating authority": See generally* J. F. Hornbeck & William H. Cooper, Trade Promotion Authority (TPA) and the Role of Congress in Trade Policy, Congressional Research Service, Jan. 14, 2013.

209 Congressional Review Act, Pub. L. 104–121, 110 Stat. 874 (1996).

209 *undid a spate of rulemaking from late in the Obama administration: See* Kellie Mejdrich, "GOP Leaps on Congressional Review Act to Kill Obama Rules," *Roll Call*, Feb. 23, 2017.

209 *The "sunset" idea: Cf.* Frank H. Easterbrook et al., "Showcase Panel IV: A Federal Sunset Law," 16 *Texas Review of Law & Politics* 339 (2012). For an excellent discussion of the pros and cons of a sunset provision, as well as the REINS Act and cost-benefit analysis in judicial review, see Christopher DeMuth, "Can the Administrative State Be Tamed?," 8 *Journal of Legal Analysis* 121 (2016).

210 *nullify a statutory grant of power:* For a clear explication of the *presumption* of liberty in the U.S. Constitution as adopted, see Randy E. Barnett, *Restoring the Lost Constitution: The Presumption of Liberty* (2013).

212 *Office of Information and Regulatory Affairs: See* Paperwork Reduction Act of 1980, Pub. L. 96–511, 94 Stat. 2812. *See also* Executive Order 12291, 46 Fed. Reg. 13193 (1981).

214 *bright-line* ex ante *administrative rule: Cf.* Barbara H. Fried, "The Limits of a Nonconsequentialist Approach to Torts," 18 *Legal Theory* 231 (2012).

214 *Some libertarian defenders of the modern tort regime:* For a discussion of competing views of common-law liability regimes—Hayek's broadly sympathetic view (from a distance, in terms of modern liability procedures) and Gordon Tullock's critical view (comparing common- and civil-law approaches through the lens of public-choice theory)—see Todd J. Zywicki, "Spontaneous Order and the Common Law: Gordon Tullock's Critique," 135 *Public Choice* 35 (2008).

215 *Congress acted to protect vaccine manufacturers: See* National Childhood Vaccine Injury Act of 1986, Pub. L. 99–2660, 100 Stat. 3755.

215 *in the wake of the September 11 terror attacks:* The September 11th Victim Compensation Fund was created through the Transportation Safety and System Stabilization Act of 2001, Pub. L. 107–42, 115 Stat. 230.

215 *in 1995:* Private Securities Litigation Reform Act of 1995, Pub. L. 104–67, 109 Stat. 737.

215 *2005:* Class Action Fairness Act of 2005, Pub. L. 109–2, 119 Stat. 4.

215 Public Readiness and Emergency Preparedness (PREP) Act, Pub. L. 109–148, 119 Stat. 2818 (2005).

215 *Alex Tabarrok of George Mason University: See, e.g.,* Daniel B. Klein & Alexander Tabarrok, "Do Off-Label Drug Practices Argue Against FDA Efficacy Requirements? A Critical Analysis of Physicians' Argumentation for Initial Efficacy Requirements," 67 *American Journal of Economics & Sociology* 743 (2008).

218 *"complete diversity" limits: See* 28 U.S.C. § 1332.

218 *"choice of law": See* Michael I. Krauss, "Product Liability and Game Theory: One More Trip to the Choice-of-Law Well," 2002 *B.Y.U. Law Review* 759 (2002).

218 *require states that contract out the work of federal law enforcement to use transparent hiring principles: See, e.g.,* James R. Copland, Statement Before the House Committee on the Judiciary Subcommittee on the Constitution, Hearing on Contingent Fees and Conflicts of Interest in State AG Enforcement of Federal Law Abuses in State AG Contingent-Fee Litigation and Dangers for Federal Delegation of Enforcement Authority, Feb. 2, 2012.

219 *Reforming the SEC's power grab over corporate annual meetings: See, e.g.,* James R. Copland, Comment, Re: File Number S7-22-19: Procedural Requirements and Resubmission Thresholds under Exchange Act Rule 14a-8, Feb. 3, 2020.

EPILOGUE: THE UNELECTED IN A PANDEMIC

221 *America "is at a severe disadvantage…":* Katie Glueck & Sydney Ember, "Joe Biden and Bernie Sanders Rebuke Trump Over Virus: 'The Clock Is Ticking,'" *N.Y. Times*, Mar. 12, 2020.

221 *one of the classic government functions: See* Richard A. Epstein, "In Defense of the 'Old' Public Health: The Legal Framework for the Regulation of Public Health," 69 *Brooklyn Law Review* 1421 (2004) ("The traditional position by and large reserved the strong powers of the state to containing epidemics, contagion, and nuisances, which, for reasons that I shall presently discuss, do not lend themselves effectively to either market solutions or to private actions in tort."). *See also* Elizabeth C. Tandy, "Local Quarantine and Inoculation for Smallpox in the American Colonies, 1620–1775," 13 *American Journal of Public Health* 203 (1923).

222 *association between government spending and Covid-19 mortality has run in the opposite direction: See* John Hood, "Radical Takes on Pandemic Are Faulty," *Carolina Journal*, Apr. 29, 2020.

222 *a yellow fever epidemic hit Philadelphia: See generally* Jim Murphy, *An American Plague: The True and Terrifying Story of the Yellow Fever Epidemic of 1793* (2003).

223 *Compagnie Francaise de Navigation a Vapeur v. Louisiana Board of Health,* 186 U.S. 380 (1902).

223 *Spanish influenza outbreak of 1918–19:* John M. Barry, *The Great Influenza: The Story of the Deadliest Pandemic in History* (2004).

223 *smallpox vaccine: See* Stefan Riedel, "Edward Jenner and the History of Smallpox and Vaccination," 18 *Baylor University Medical Center Proceedings* 21 (2005).

223 *cholera spread through London's water supply: See* Kathleen Tuthill, "John Snow and the Broad Street Pimp: On the Trail of an Epidemic," 31 *Cricket* 23 (2003).

223 *polio vaccine: See* Siang Yong Tan & Nate Ponstein, "Jonas Salk (1914–1995): A Vaccine Against Polio," 60 *Singapore Medical Journal* 9 (2019).

223 *"The time has come to close the book…":* Obituary: William H. Stewart, 372 *Lancet* 110 (2008). The quote may be apocryphal, notwithstanding its appearance in Stewart's obituary, in a leading medical journal. *See* Brad Spellberg & Bonnie Taylor-Blake, "On the Exoneration of Dr. William H. Stewart: Debunking an Urban Legend," 2 *Infectious Diseases of Poverty* 3 (2013). Stewart *did* make the following public statement in 1968: "This success story brings us to the here and now. And largely as a result of this success

story, times have changed. The purpose of our efforts—the preservation and improvement of health—can no longer be measured on the scale of microbiology. Our exploitation of that science has just about caught up with the frontiers of public need." William H. Stewart, "Areas of challenge for the future," Symposium, Schools of Public Health: Changing Institutions in a Changing World, The Johns Hopkins University School of Hygiene and Public Health (1968). But he qualified that: "Clearly we cannot turn our backs on microbiology—certain notable gaps remain in our knowledge and capability, and maintenance of a vigilant effort will always be required." *Ibid.* Spellberg and Taylor-Blake, while hoping to rehabilitate Stewart, emphasize that one reason the statement attributed to him went unquestioned was widespread belief along similar lines among many public-health thought leaders: "[T]he belief that infectious diseases had been successfully overcome was pervasive in biomedical circles—including among a Nobel Laureate, medical Dean, and other thought leaders—from as early as 1948, and extending all the way into the mid-1980s."

224 *"Germs no longer need to be smarter than our scientists…":* Peter Huber, "The Coming Plague," *Wall Street Journal*, Apr. 10, 2007.

224 *It was March 25:* Enforcement Policy for Face Masks and Respirators During the Coronavirus Disease (COVID-19) Public Health Emergency, issued Mar. 25, 2020.

224 *On March 28, the FDA:* Nevin Smith, "FDA Limits Ohio Company's Mask Sterilization Plan," *Dayton247Now*, Mar. 29, 2020.

224 *ethyl-alcohol hand sanitizer:* Temporary Policy for Manufacture of Alcohol for Incorporation into Alcohol-Based Hand Sanitizer Products During the Public Health Emergency (COVID-19) Guidance for Industry, FDA-2020-D-1106-0038, Mar. 24, 2020.

224 *Democratic partisans hoping to score points:* Katie Glueck & Sydney Ember, "Joe Biden and Bernie Sanders Rebuke Trump Over Virus: 'The Clock Is Ticking,'" *N.Y. Times*, Mar. 12, 2020.

225 *"an implied guarantee of safety and sound design":* Peter Huber, "The Coming Plague," *Wall Street Journal*, Apr. 10, 2007.

225 *complaint-tracking website:* Hunton Andrews Kurth LLP, "COVID-19 Complaint Tracker," https://www.huntonak.com/en/covid-19-tracker.html (accessed June 14, 2020).

226 *On April 6, the family of a Walmart employee:* David McAfee, "Walmart Hit with Employee Wrongful Death Suit Over Covid-19," *Bloomberg Law*, Apr. 6, 2020.

226 *wrongful-death lawsuit on April 14:* Brian Day & Rick Chambers, "Woman Files Lawsuit Against Princess Cruise Lines Over Husband's COVID-19 Death," *KTLA5*, Apr. 15, 2020.

226 *against nursing homes:* See, e.g., Ryan Tarinelli, "'Trapped in Litigation': Lawsuit Warned of Staffing Shortfalls at Bronx Nursing Home Before COVID-19 Wave," *N.Y. Law Journal*, Apr. 23, 2020.

226 *against hospitals:* See, e.g., Lauren del Valle & Sonia Moghe, "New York State Nurses Union Files Three Lawsuits Alleging Poor Covid-19 Working Conditions," *CNN*, Apr. 20, 2020.

226 *workers sued Smithfield Foods:* Sebastian Martinez Valdivia & Dan Margolies, "Workers Sue Smithfield Foods, Allege Conditions Put Them at Risk for COVID-19," *NPR*, Apr. 24, 2020.

226 *invoked the Defense Production Act:* Executive Order on Delegating Authority Under the DPA with Respect to Food Supply Chain Resources During the National Emergency Caused by the Outbreak of COVID-19, Apr. 28, 2020; *see* Defense Production Act of 1950, Pub. L. 81–774, 123 Stat. 2006.

226 *subscription fees from gyms: See* Amanda Bronstad, "Prominent Plaintiffs Firms Preparing COVID-19 Lawsuits," *Law.com*, Mar. 30, 2020.

226 *Universities going online-only: See ibid.*

226 *lawyers hit manufacturers of sanitizer with class action lawsuits: Taslakian v. Target Corp.*, No. 20-CV-02667 (C.D. Cal. Mar. 20, 2020).

227 *Bill Gates argued for a large-scale government effort:* Jane Wakefield, "TED 2015: Bill Gates warns on future disease epidemic," *BBC News*, Mar. 19, 2015.

INDEX